THE ENCYCLOPEDIA *of*

HOME FURNISHING

TECHNIQUES

THE ENCYCLOPEDIA *of*
HOME FURNISHING
TECHNIQUES

A step-by-step visual directory to soft furnishing techniques for the home

ALISON WORMLEIGHTON

HEADLINE

A QUARTO BOOK

Copyright © 1997 Quarto Publishing plc

First published in Great Britain in 1997 by
HEADLINE BOOK PUBLISHING LTD.

HEADLINE BOOK PUBLISHING LTD
A division of Hodder Headline PLC
338 Euston Road , London NW1 3BH

BRITISH LIBRARY CATALOGUING IN DATA
Wormleighton, Alison
The encyclopedia of home furnishing techniques
1. Interior decoration
1. Title
747
ISBN 0-7472-1998-2

This book was designed and produced by
Quarto Publishing plc, The Old Brewery
6 Blundell Street, London N7 9BH
Senior art editor • Penny Cobb
Designer • Debbie Mole
Illustrator • Kate Simunek
Picture researcher • Zoe Holtermann
Senior editor • Sally MacEachern
Copy editors • Suzanne Kendall, Hilary More
Indexer • Alison Wormleighton
Picture research manager • Giulia Hetherington
Editorial director • Pippa Rubinstein
Art Director • Moira Clinch

Typeset by Central Southern Typesetters, Eastbourne
Manufactured in Hong Kong by Regent Publishing Services Ltd
Printed in China by Leefung-Asco Printers Ltd

PUBLISHER'S NOTE

CONTENTS

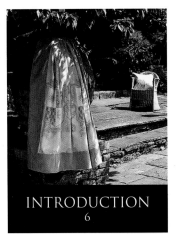

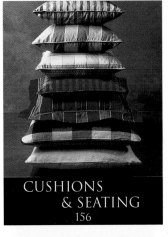
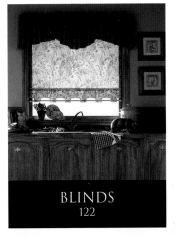

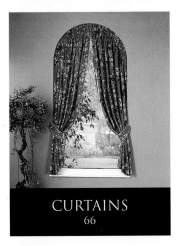
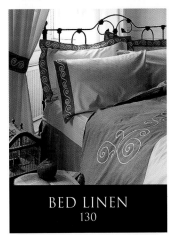
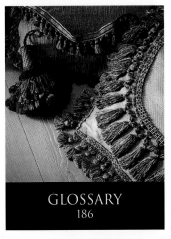
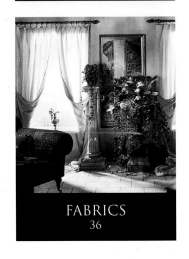

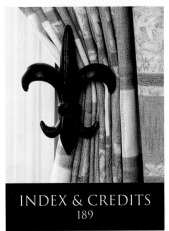

INTRODUCTION

Sewing for the home has become increasingly popular in recent years – and justifiably so, for it offers an unbeatable way to transform a room.

DECORATING WITH FABRICS that you love is the quickest and easiest way to brighten up a scheme or even to change it entirely. Whether you want simply to sew a few quick cushions or to completely redecorate a whole room, fabrics are the key to the process.

Making a project yourself allows you to give it the stamp of your own personality, and you can ensure that you get exactly the look you want. You have a much greater choice of fabrics and styles, since you are devising your own combinations rather than depending on someone else's choices. You don't have to wait weeks for someone to make it up for you, and you can experiment to find the effect that is just right for you – which a shop or other supplier is unlikely to spend much time on.

You'll also save a lot of money. Find out the cost of someone making a pair of curtains for you, and you'll realize just what an enormous advantage it is to be able to make them yourself. The same applies to other soft furnishings.

Just as important, however, is the enormous satisfaction it gives. The actual sewing is relaxing and enjoyable, and at the end you have something to show for your efforts. The next time you get the nest-building urge, there's no need to move house or build an extension – just think up a new soft furnishing idea.

Whereas at one time people would make their curtains and their table and bed linens last for decades, today these items are changed frequently – with fashion, the seasons, the tastes of growing children or simply your own whim. Sewing the items yourself makes this feasible.

LEFT ~ *Learning home-sewing techniques will enable you to make a wide variety of soft furnishings.*

USING THIS BOOK

MAGAZINES ARE FULL of stylish ideas, but, more often than not, they do not include instructions on how actually to carry out the project. That's where this book comes in. It offers practical instructions for the principal ways of making each type of soft furnishing – in other words, it sets out all the options for whatever project you are considering.

Each technique is explained in detail, with variations where relevant, copious illustrations and photographs of most of the finished items. Thus, you'll learn both the basics *and* the finer points of every technique.

What you won't find is much repetition. Procedures like piping, for example, are not explained every time something is piped – only at the beginning of the book along with other basic techniques. The same applies to the "pin, tack and stitch" procedure which is usually referred to in the projects simply as "join" or "stitch" – the methods of pressing a seam

LEFT ~ *Elaborate-looking soft furnishing projects can be broken down into manageable stages.*

So that the instructions for a particular technique like piping are easy to locate, the book makes much use of cross-referencing, and there is an exceptionally detailed index as well as a comprehensive glossary.

Although some of the techniques and projects in this book are easier than others, none is difficult – a person with only basic sewing skills will be able to manage them. Some projects look quite complicated, but these are all broken down into simple stages, making them easily achieved.

STRUCTURE OF THE BOOK

FOR NOVICES, and also experienced sewers who want to remind themselves of some of the finer points of particular techniques, an extensive section on basic techniques begins the book. This is followed by advice and information on working with various fabrics.

Another extremely useful section covers decorative techniques: needlecrafts like embroidery, appliqué, patchwork and so on that can be used to decorate soft furnishings. These needlecrafts offer enormous potential for soft furnishings, and so they are covered in considerable detail and specifically with regard to their use on soft furnishings.

The remainder of the book covers all the main areas of

and so forth. (If, however, a particular project calls for a different way of applying piping, joining, pressing or whatever, it is, of course, fully explained in the relevant place.)

As a result, you can find out quickly just what is involved in making a project you are considering tackling, without having to read laborious accounts of the same techniques over and over again. Avoiding repetition has also allowed many more techniques to be packed into the book, making it truly comprehensive.

MEASUREMENTS

When making a project, follow either the metric or the imperial measurements (shown in brackets), but do not interchange them, since the equivalents are only approximate. For example, sometimes a quarter of an inch is given as five millimetres, and at other times it is given as six, depending on other measurements used in the project.

RIGHT~ *Often it's the added decorative details that make a soft-furnishing project look stylish and interesting.*

LEFT ~ Even making a handsome pair of curtains requires very little equipment apart from a sewing machine.

soft furnishings – window treatments (curtains, tiebacks, "top treatments" like swags and tails, and blinds), bed linen (including fashionable bed hangings), table linen, loose covers and plenty of cushions.

Being able to make your own soft furnishings is just a matter of knowing what to do – the skills themselves are simple to acquire. The aim of this book is to demystify the whole subject and provide all the soft furnishings information you need in an accessible and concise but detailed form, for maximum ease of use.

THE SEWING MACHINE

IF YOU WANT to make anything more than a few small items, a sewing machine is essential. The most basic model is perfectly adequate. Buying a more expensive machine, which is semi-automatic, will enable you to do blind hemming, buttonholing and simple machine embroidery stitches automatically, instead of manually. Top-of-the-range machines, which are fully auto-

matic, will do many embroidery stitches automatically (and also a stretch stitch for knit fabrics, if you will be doing dressmaking). Speciality presser feet are available for all machines as optional extras.

An overlock machine, or serger, which will stitch, finish and trim seams in one step, is sometimes used along with a sewing machine by people who do a lot of sewing.

Once you have bought a sewing machine, read the instruction manual carefully before attempting to use it.

THE WORK SURFACE

THE SEWING MACHINE should be set on a table so that the project can be spread out flat to the left of the machine, rather than hanging down. Make sure that your sewing area is well lit.

For measuring, cutting out and marking large items like bed covers, curtains and tablecloths, a good-sized table – with a cloth on top to protect the surface – is best. Alternatively, improvise one with a sheet of plywood padded with wadding or a blanket and then covered with muslin which is stretched taut and stapled to the underside. (This is also useful for pressing.) You can also get laminated Kraft boards, which unfold to form a large cutting surface with a grid for easy measuring. If necessary, the floor can be used, provided it is really clean.

OTHER EQUIPMENT

DESPITE THE SCALE of some of the more ambitious projects, there is very little other equipment you will need apart from a sewing machine.

• PRESSING with a steam iron will remove creases better than a dry iron. Pressing as you go is essential for a professional look, so ideally keep your ironing board or table set up next to your machine while you are working. To protect fabrics when pressing on the right side or when applying fusible materials, use a piece of muslin (or a large handkerchief) as a pressing cloth.

• FOR CUTTING, you'll need two pairs of good sharp scissors which you use only for sewing. (Using scissors on paper will quickly make them blunt.) One pair should be large dressmaker's shears with angled handles – these will be used for cutting out fabrics. The other pair should be small and pointy – these are for trimming and clipping seam allowances and cutting threads. A rotary cutter is also useful for cutting out several layers of fabric at once when the edges are straight. A cutting mat and a straightedge or quilter's ruler (a see-through plastic ruler with calibrated lines) are handy to use with the rotary cutter.

• FOR MEASURING WINDOWS, table tops and other flat surfaces, you'll need a retractable steel tape measure. For marking out long, straight edges use a metre ruler, and for curved lines and soft or contoured surfaces use a flexible fibreglass or linen tape measure. A set square is useful for checking that corners are square and edges are on the straight grain (or improvise with a CD case or a book).

• FABRIC MARKERS for which the ink can be easily removed with water or which will fade away over time can be used for marking fabric. Alternatively, use tailor's chalk, which is available as wedges or pencils and is brushed off.

• VARIOUS NEEDLES are used on the sewing machine. For furnishing fabrics you will need sharp needles (as opposed to ballpoint and wedge-shaped ones, which are used for knits and leather respectively). The sizes are either in metric, ranging from 60 to 120, or in the so-called "15 x 1" system, ranging from 9 to 19. The lightest fabrics require the finest needles – about size 70 (9) – and the heaviest fabrics need the coarsest needles – about size 100 (16). A medium-sized needle is about size 80–90 (11–14).

You'll also need a range of hand-sewing needles so that you can suit the needle to the fabric as well as to the type of stitching. The eyes of the needles are either round or long, use the latter for thick thread or several strands. Needles known as *sharps*, which are long and sharp and have round eyes, are used for general hand sewing and most weights of fabric. *Betweens*, or *quilter's needles*, are shorter than sharps but otherwise similar and are used for making small stitches in heavy fabrics. *Milliner's needles*, which are larger than sharps but otherwise similar, are best for hand tacking and finishing. The sizes of these needles range from 3 (the coarsest) to 12 (the

finest), with 6–8 being versatile medium sizes. As for machine needles, the size you use depends on the fabric, with light fabrics needing the finest needles and heavy fabrics the coarsest.

The easiest pins to use are the long, glass-headed type. Make sure you have plenty. For loose covers, you will also need T-pins, which are extra-long and shaped like the letter "T".

• OPTIONAL ITEMS: A *needle threader* makes threading hand or machine needles easier. A *bodkin* (a thick, blunt needle with a long eye) is helpful for threading elastic, cord or ribbon through casings. A *thimble* is handy to protect your middle finger when hand sewing. A *seam ripper* will make unpicking seams (unavoidable even for experienced sewers!) quicker and less onerous.

Once you have assembled your equipment, choose a small project such as a cushion or some table linen and make a start. You'll soon discover, if you haven't done so already, the enormous rewards to be gained from home sewing.

RIGHT ~ *Projects like a tablecloth and coordinating napkins offer maximum impact for minimum effort.*

BASIC TECHNIQUES

PREPARATION

The care you take over preparing your fabric prior to stitching will make all the difference to the appearance of the finished item. Mistakes at this stage are difficult to put right.

PREPARING FABRIC

PRE-SHRINKING AND PRESSING

If you are using washable fabric that you will be laundering regularly, you may wish to pre-shrink it before cutting it out. If the label gives an indication of how much it will shrink, decide whether this amount will matter.

To check the likely shrinkage for yourself, cut a small piece – ideally about 30cm (12in) square – and measure this before and after pre-shrinking it.

Bear in mind that many of today's fabrics have been treated with special finishes, which could be affected by washing. It may therefore be better not to pre-shrink or launder the fabric at all.

1 To pre-shrink washable fabric, follow the manufacturer's washing instructions, or send it to a dry cleaner for steaming.

TIP

When buying fabric, always allow extra for testing for pre-shrinking (if washable), for squaring ends and for trimming off selvedges.

2 If you have pre-shrunk the fabric yourself, press it while still damp. Otherwise, press it with a steam iron to get rid of creases. If the fabric is delicate, place a pressing cloth between it and the iron. Press the fabric from the wrong side, particularly if it is glazed, highly textured or embossed.

SQUARING THE END

Before beginning to cut, you need to square one end of the fabric. First lay the fabric out on a large, flat, clean surface. Support any excess fabric so that it is at the same height or higher and does not hang over the end of the work surface, which could pull it out of shape. Check the fabric for flaws or inconsistencies of colour or weave.

1 If it is an unpatterned, tightly woven fabric, you may be able to square the end simply by tearing it along the *crosswise grain* (which is at right angles to the *selvedges*, or finished edges running the length of the fabric). Snip into the selvedge, tear across the grain then snip through the other selvedge.

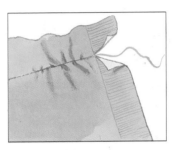

2 For an unpatterned, loosely woven or knitted fabric, straighten one end by pulling a thread. (To do this, snip into the selvedge, ease the snip open and pull one of the crosswise threads. The fabric will gather up at first, but the thread will finally come out.) Cut along the resulting line.

3 Virtually all prints and even some woven patterns are slightly off-grain. The allowed tolerance is 3cm (1¼in) but you may prefer to return the fabric to the shop even if it is off-grain by a bit less than that. Because cutting along the grain line could make the pattern noticeably slanted when widths are joined, the end of patterned fabric is cut along the line of the pattern. (The sides will eventually be squared off as you match the pattern when stitching seams.)

STRAIGHTENING FABRICS

Sometimes a fabric's *straight*, or *lengthwise*, *grain* (parallel to the selvedges) and crosswise grain are not exactly at right angles to each other. Check this with a set square.

Conventional wisdom is to try to straighten the fabric, as described on page 12. However, this will really only work for some cottons and wools, since most modern furnishing fabrics have a permanent, heat-set finish that locks the threads in position preventing you from straightening the fabric.

If you are using a small amount of fabric, try to straighten it prior to cutting lengths. Otherwise, you will have to do it afterwards.

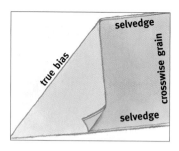

The fabric needs to be pulled along the *true bias*, where the fabric is most stretchy. (*Bias* is any diagonal direction on the fabric, but the true bias is the edge formed when you fold the fabric so that the lengthwise and crosswise grains match.)

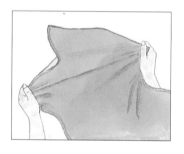

1 Hold corners that are diagonally opposite each other in your hands and pull firmly. (Be sure to choose the pair that are closer together, not the ones that are further apart.) You may need to dampen the fabric first.

2 If the pulling succeeds and if the fabric is washable, fold it in half lengthwise with right sides together, tack along all edges (see page 14) then wash the fabric. Press it while damp, ironing only along the lengthwise grain, then remove the tacking.

DEALING WITH SELVEDGES

Because selvedges do not fray and so do not need to be finished, it is tempting to incorporate them in the seam allowances of large items like curtains. However, they can make the seams pucker, so it is usually advisable to trim them off (unless the pattern repeat would be affected – see page 44). Be sure to allow for this when measuring the fabric width. If you don't remove them, you must at least clip into them at intervals of 3–4cm (1¼–1½in).

MARKING

If you need to draw on the fabric, for example to indicate a cutting line or a seamline, use tailor's chalk or fabric markers. (Choose either the vanishing type, the marks from which gradually disappear within about 24–48 hours, or the water-erasable type, the marks from which can be removed with clean water or with a damp cloth.) Pins can also be used for this (but not on napped or pile fabrics or delicately woven fabrics). Or you can make tailor tacks as shown above.

CUTTING OUT

When cutting out, treat the fabric as though it has a nap or direction (see page 43) unless you are absolutely certain it does not. Even if the right and wrong sides look the same, use the same side as the right side throughout.

If you are cutting out a piece on the fold, the fold should run along the grain exactly.

Whereas dressmaking generally involves using patterns, most soft furnishing projects involve measuring out simple rectangular pieces straight onto the fabric.

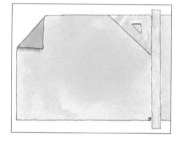

1 Measure from the squared end along both selvedges, mark the cutting line by making a 3mm (⅛in) clip on each edge and then check the new cutting line with a set square and metre stick. Check and recheck your calculations before cutting.

2 If you *are* using a pattern, such as one you've made for a loose chair cover, pin it on the fabric around all edges of the pattern.

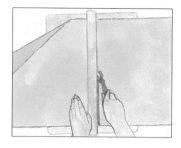

3 Cut out the fabric with sharp dressmaking shears or a rotary cutter, straightedge and cutting mat. If using shears, cut with long strokes, using the entire length of each blade. If using a rotary cutter, always cut in a vertical line away from yourself, and keep your other hand, which will be holding the fabric, away from the cutter.

4 Mark the lengthwise grain and top on the wrong side of each piece.

5 If you are cutting two or more layers of one piece, more than one layer can often be cut at once, depending on the fabric. Fold the fabric into as many layers as you can cut easily, trying to make as economical a use of the fabric as possible. Mark the top layer, and pin alongside the cutting lines through all layers. If there is a pattern, make sure it will be in the right place. A rotary cutter is useful for cutting more than one layer at once.

SEE ALSO

STITCHES

You can produce complicated-looking soft furnishings with even the simplest sewing machine. Some small projects can be sewn without a machine, but a large-scale project is only practicable with one.

MACHINE STITCHING

Study your machine manual carefully to learn how to adjust the tension, how to set stitch length and stitch width, whether it will stitch over pins placed at right angles to the stitching line, what special attachments come with the machine or are available, and so on.

Use good-quality thread: synthetic for synthetic fabrics (because a cotton thread may shrink and cause the seams to pucker), and cotton/linen/silk for cotton/linen/silk fabrics (because a synthetic thread can sometimes be too strong for a natural fabric).

Match the thread colour to the fabric as closely as possible, but if you can't get an exact match, choose a thread one shade darker. On patterned fabric, match the thread to the dominant colour.

STRAIGHT STITCH

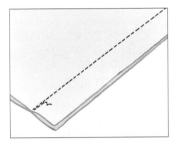

This is the principal machine stitch and is used for most seams, generally with a stitch length of about 2.5 (on a scale from 0 to 4) and a stitch width of 0. Stitching straight stitch in reverse for a few stitches at each end fastens off the thread so it won't unravel.

TOPSTITCHING

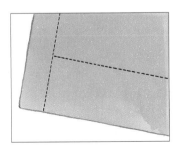

Topstitching is a straight stitch that is stitched from the right side and is visible when the item is completed. It can be worked in matching or contrasting thread. Because your usual stitching guide on the machine will be covered, use the presser foot, a line of hand tacking, a strip of tape or a quilting guide-bar attachment (see Quilting, page 56) to help ensure that the topstitching is straight and parallel to the seamline.

ZIGZAG STITCH

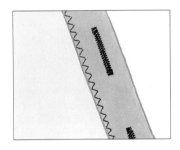

Zigzagging is possible on most modern sewing machines and is used for buttonholes, neatening raw edges and machine embroidery. A very slight zigzag is sometimes used when stitching seams on stretch fabrics (although most modern machines have a stretch stitch, made up of tight zigzags alternating with straight stitches).

STAYSTITCHING

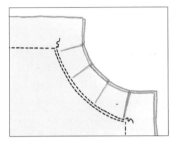

This is another straight stitch. It is done through a single thickness of fabric just inside the seamline, in order to prevent the fabric from stretching when the fabric is handled or the seam is stitched. It is also useful when clipping into a seam allowance to prevent the fabric from tearing.

TACKING

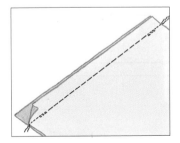

A long straight stitch is used for machine tacking.

HAND STITCHING

If you are left-handed, reverse the instructions.

RUNNING STITCH
This is a straight stitch used for seams and for gathering.

1 After fastening the thread with a couple of backstitches, work small, evenly spaced stitches by bringing the needle up through the fabric and back down again several times.

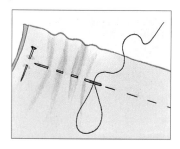

2 Pick up several stitches and pull the needle and thread through. Repeat, being careful to keep the stitches and spaces the same size.

TACKING

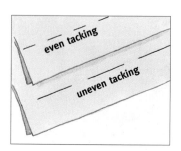

even tacking

uneven tacking

Tacking consists of long running stitches and is used to

hold fabric layers together while stitching. The stitches are about 6mm (¼in) long and either 6mm (¼in) apart (known as *even tacking*) or 2–3cm (¾–1¼in) apart (*uneven tacking*). The tacking is removed after the permanent stitching is completed. Special tacking thread is available, or you can use ordinary thread. It's a good idea to choose a colour that contrasts with the fabric so that it will be easier to see when you are removing it.

DIAGONAL TACKING
This is used to hold whole areas temporarily.

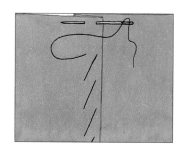

1 Working from bottom to top, with the needle held horizontally, take a series of horizontal stitches, one above the other. These will form slanting stitches on the right side of the fabric.

2 The stitches can be small or large, depending on how secure they need to be.

3 Repeat the process over the entire area.

BACKSTITCH
This is the strongest hand stitch and may be used for seams instead of machine stitching. It is also worked on the spot at the beginning and end of other hand stitches in order to secure the thread.

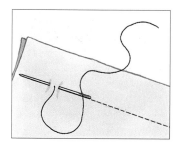

1 Working from right to left, bring the needle to the top of the fabric, insert it about 3mm (⅛in) behind this point on the seamline and then bring it up the same distance ahead of the thread.

2 Continue in the same way so that with each stitch you insert the needle at the end of the previous stitch.

TIP
A variety of tacking aids are also now available, including water-soluble tacking tapes, fusible webs and dressmaker's gluesticks. The gluesticks are washable, but you have to avoid stitching over them until they are dry or you will gum up your needle.

PRICKSTITCH

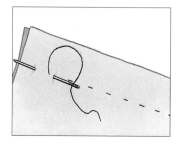

Prickstitch is a decorative backstitch. Work it in the same way as backstitch but insert the needle a few threads behind where the thread emerges, and 3–6mm (⅛–¼in) ahead of the thread.

SLIPSTITCH
Slipstitch is used to sew a folded edge almost invisibly to another folded edge or to a flat piece. Because the thread is not exposed, it is very durable.

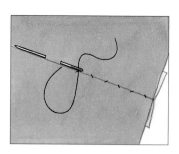

1 To join two folded edges, working from right to left, hide the knot in one folded edge, bringing the needle out through the folded edge. Now insert it into the other folded edge just 1–2mm (¹⁄₁₆in) further along. Slip the needle through the fold and bring it out again 6mm (¼in) along. Repeat on the opposite edge, and continue in this way.

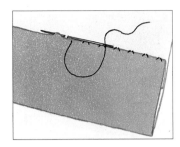

2 To sew a folded edge to a flat piece, bring the needle out through the folded edge, then insert it in the flat piece 1–2mm (¹⁄₁₆in) further along, picking up only about three threads. Insert the needle into the folded edge 1–2mm (¹⁄₁₆in) further along and slip the needle through the fold, bring it out 6mm (¼in) along. Repeat. This is also called *slip hemming*. A variation, in which the stitches are about 2cm (¾in) long, is known as *ladderstitch* and can be used as a tacking stitch when matching patterns (see page 44).

HEMMING STITCH
This is the quickest hemming stitch but it is not very durable. It is worked from right to left.

1 Bring the needle up through the edge of the hem. Holding the needle diagonally, pick up one or two threads from the flat fabric, close to the hem edge and about 6mm–1cm (¼–³⁄₈in) to the left of the thread.

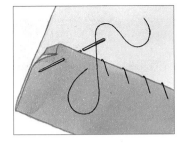

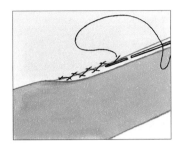

2 Pass the needle through the hem edge and then pull it through. Repeat.

HERRINGBONE STITCH
This strong hemming stitch is useful for heavy, bulky or stretch fabrics or for joining wadding. Because it neatens the raw edges at the same time, it means you don't have to turn under the raw edge beforehand.

1 Working from left to right, bring the needle up through the hem edge. With the needle always pointing to the left, take a small backwards stitch in the flat piece just above the hem edge and about 6mm–1cm (¼–³⁄₈in) from the point where the thread emerges.

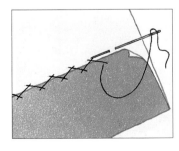

2 Now take a small backwards stitch in the hem, 6mm–1cm (¼–³⁄₈in) from

the last stitch. Repeat both steps. Avoid pulling the thread too tight.

BLIND HERRINGBONE STITCH

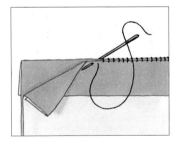

This hemming stitch is hidden under the hem. It is worked just like herringbone stitch except that the hem edge is folded back, so that the stitches are taken on the wrong side of the hem.

OVERHAND STITCH

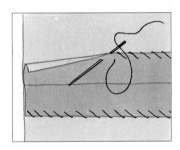

These tiny vertical stitches can be used to hold two edges together. Working from right to left, bring the needle out at the front edge. Holding the needle diagonally, insert it in the back edge immediately behind the thread, and bring it out through the front edge.

WHIPSTITCH

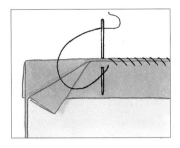

This is similar to overhand stitch but the stitches are larger and slanting. The needle is held at a right angle to the fabric, and it is inserted to the left of the thread rather than immediately behind it.

OVERCAST STITCH

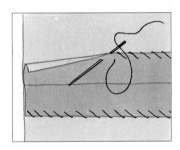

Also known as oversewing, this is used for finishing raw edges by hand. It can be worked from either direction. Hold the needle diagonally and take even stitches about 3mm (¹⁄₈in) wide and 6mm (¼in) apart.

SEE ALSO

SEAMS

Seams are the means of joining fabric pieces together, and will, therefore, determine the structure of an item. Seams fall into two broad categories – plain seams and self-enclosed ones.

PLAIN SEAMS

A plain seam is the one most often used in soft furnishings, particularly when joining fabric widths for large items like curtains or bed covers. The stitching is not visible on the right side. For bulky fabrics, this is the flattest seam.

1 Place the two fabric pieces with right sides together and raw edges even. Pin together, placing the pins at right angles, with the heads towards the raw edges. The pins will need to be closer together on an intricate, curved seam or bulky fabric than on a long, straight seam or thin fabric.

2 Hand tack close to the seamline if necessary. (Tacking is useful for tricky seams: if you are a beginner, you may prefer to tack all seams, as it makes them easier to stitch smoothly and evenly.) If you tack the seams, the pins can then be removed.

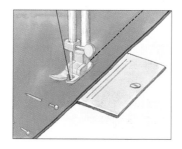

3 Set the stitch length and width. With the raw edges on the right, stitch the seam at the desired distance from the raw edges – usually 1.5cm (⅝in). Use the stitching guide on the machine if there is one. If not, attach either a separate magnetic gauge or a piece of tape the correct distance from the needle. If the seam is not tacked, remove each pin as you come to it unless your machine can stitch over pins. At each end, stitch a few stitches in reverse to fasten the threads.

4 Remove any remaining pins or tacking. Neaten the raw edges (see Neatening Raw Edges, page 17), if necessary.

5 When stitching on a curve, work slowly and carefully, and use a shorter stitch. Take care to stitch exactly on the seamline.

6 To stitch around a corner, stop stitching when you are the width of the seam allowance from the end. With the needle in the fabric, raise the presser foot and pivot the fabric to bring the new edge in line with your stitching guide. Lower the presser foot and continue stitching. Using small stitches on each side of the corner will help to reinforce it.

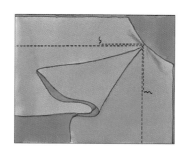

7 To join an inward corner to a straight edge or outward corner, first stitch along the seamline for about 2cm (¾in) each side of the corner. Clip into the seam allowance at the corner. Spread it out so both edges align with those of the other piece. Stitch along the seamline with the clipped side up, pivoting at the corner.

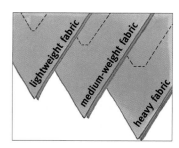

8 On a sharp corner, make one to three stitches across the point, to produce a better point.

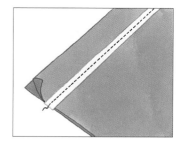

9 To prevent seams in very stretchy fabrics from being too elastic, stitch narrow tape into the seams.

TIP

If a long, straight seam shows signs of puckering, keep the fabric taut by pulling equally on the front and back as you stitch. Do not actually stretch it – it should still feed through the machine on its own.

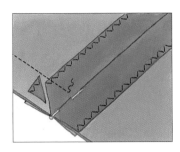

10 When stitching a seam where two other seams meet, you'll need to trim, neaten and press the other two seams first before beginning this one. When pinning, pin right through both seamlines to ensure they will align. After stitching, trim off the corners of the previous seam allowances.

11 When you are joining two edges that are slightly different in length, the longer edge has to be *eased* into the other. Distribute the fullness evenly, avoiding puckers, and pin closely.

TRIMMING, GRADING AND CLIPPING SEAMS

Often you will need to trim, grade and/or clip seams. (If you have to do them all, that is the correct sequence in which to do them.) Be sure to use small, sharp sewing scissors for this.

Note that the instructions in this book for stitching seams do not stipulate pinning and tacking first, nor exactly what trimming, grading or clipping is necessary each time. Therefore, follow the detailed guidelines given here to make sure you do not omit an important step.

1 It may be necessary to trim away part of the seam allowance to reduce bulk. (Remember, however, that it also reduces the strength of the seam.) This may just be a simple matter of cutting away half of each seam allowance. Note that fabric which frays cannot be trimmed as closely as other fabrics, and loosely woven fabrics should not be clipped a great deal.

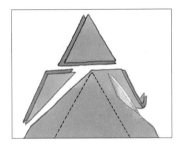

2 On a very sharp corner, trim away the seam allowances on both sides of the point, then taper them. On other corners simply trim the allowances diagonally on outward corners, or clip into the seam allowance on inward corners.

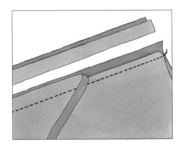

3 When seams form an edge or are enclosed, *grading* – also known as *layering* – is advisable. After trimming away half of each seam

allowance, trim a little more off the seam allowance that will be further away from the item itself. Grading is also advisable when seams consist of several layers.

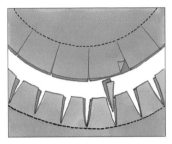

4 Curved seams need to be clipped to make them lie flat and smooth. This is done after neatening (see below). For outward (convex) curves, cut slits into the seam allowances. For inward (concave) curves, snip away wedge-shaped notches. For both types, use only the tips of the scissors, being careful not to cut through the stitching itself.

NEATENING RAW EDGES

If you plan to wash the item often, or if the fabric frays easily, you will need to neaten the raw edges of the seam. Seams are usually neatened after stitching, but on a large project with long, straight edges that won't be trimmed or graded, you could neaten the edges prior to stitching the seams.

If you have a three-, four- or five-thread *overlocker machine*, also known as a *serger*, the seams are stitched, trimmed and neatened simultaneously.

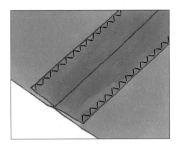

Otherwise, one of the simplest and most effective methods is zigzag stitching the edges using a medium stitch width, and a short length.

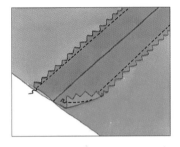

Cutting the edges with pinking shears – *pinking* – will not prevent fraying, but *stitching and pinking*, which involves running a line of stitching 6mm (¼in) from the raw edge before pinking, is fairly effective.

PRESSING

Plain straight seams are pressed *before* the edges are neatened, but plain curved seams are pressed *after* the edges have been neatened and clipped. On the wrong side, press the seam flat first, to embed the stitches in the fabric, and then press it open, unless the instructions say otherwise. Try to avoid ever using a bare iron on the right side of a seam.

TOPSTITCHED SEAMS

For a decorative effect that makes a plain seam a little more durable, it can be topstitched (see Topstitching, page 13).

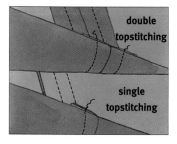

For *single topstitching*, the seam is pressed to one side then topstitched through all three layers about 6mm (¼in) from the seamline. For *double topstitching*, the seam is pressed open and then topstitched through both layers about 6mm (¼in) to each side of the seamline.

WELT SEAM

This is the same as a single topstitched seam except that the underneath seam allowance is trimmed to 6mm (¼in) prior to topstitching.

SELF-ENCLOSED SEAMS

With self-enclosed seams, the raw edges are enclosed during construction of the seam, so the neatening stage is not necessary. These seams are hard-wearing and are particularly useful if the item will be washed often. The seam allowance is the usual 1.5cm (⅝in).

FRENCH SEAM

In this neat, hard-wearing seam the raw edges are enclosed and no stitching is visible on the right side. It is not suitable for curves.

1 Join the fabric pieces with *wrong* sides together, taking a 1cm (⅜in) seam. Trim the seam allowances to 3mm (⅛in) and then press the seam open.

2 Turn the fabric so that the right sides are together and the stitched line runs along the fold; press.

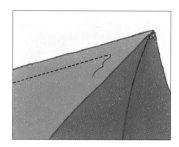

3 Stitch a 5mm (¼in) seam, making sure that the raw edges from the previous seam do not protrude at all. Press the seam to one side.

MOCK FRENCH SEAM

This looks similar to a French seam but can also be used where there are curves, corners or joins between seams.

1 Join the fabric pieces with *right* sides together, taking a 1.5cm (⅝in) seam. Trim the seam allowances to 1.2cm (½in).

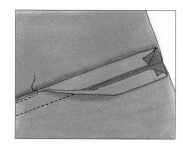

2 Turn in 6mm (¼in) on each seam allowance, and stitch these folded edges together. Press the seam to one side.

FLAT FELL SEAM

Another very hard-wearing seam, this is flatter than the French seam. It can be made so that either one or two lines of stitching are visible on the right side of the fabric.

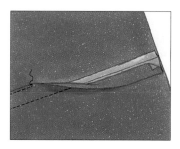

1 For a flat fell seam with two visible lines of stitching, join the fabric pieces with *wrong* sides together, taking a 1.5cm (⅝in) seam. Press both seam allowances to one side. Trim the underneath seam allowance to 3mm (⅛in). Turn under 6mm (¼in) on the upper seam allowance. Press. Stitch the upper seam allowance to the main fabric near the fold, keeping the stitching parallel to the first line of stitching.

2 For a flat fell seam with one visible line of stitching, follow step 1 but join the fabric pieces with *right* sides together.

SEE ALSO

Machine stitching   13

SHAPING FABRIC

There are various ways of shaping fabric in order to create fullness precisely where it is needed. The main methods of doing this are pleats, darts, tucks and gathers.

PLEATS

Pleats are folds of fabric held in place at the top. They can either be pressed along the folds, which gives a crisp, tailored look, or they can be left unpressed, which creates a softer look. Only fabrics that will hold a sharp crease are suitable for pressed pleats, but most fabrics can be used for unpressed pleats. All pleats will hang better if folded on the straight grain.

Pleats can be used all the way across the top of an item (such as a bed valance) or just at the corners (for example, on a fitted tablecloth) or individually (down the back of a loose chair cover, for instance).

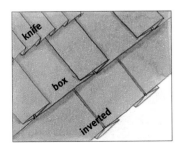

TYPES OF PLEAT
There are three main types of pleat: knife, box and inverted.

Knife pleats are the most basic type, with the folds all facing in the same direction. They are generally used in groups rather than individually.

Box pleats each consist of two knife pleats with the folds facing away from each other on the right side. The inner folds may meet at the back but this is not essential. In soft furnishings, box pleats are most often used in groups.

Inverted pleats each consist of two knife pleats whose folds face each other on the right side, meeting in the centre of the pleat. (From the wrong side, an inverted pleat looks like a box pleat.) Inverted pleats are often used individually.

MAKING PLEATS
All three types of pleat are made in much the same way, by folding the fabric along a *foldline* and bringing this outer fold over to a *placement line*. Hemming is generally done before pleating.

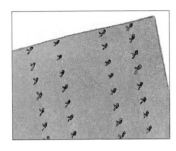

1 Decide on the size and placement of the pleats. (In this book, these aspects are covered under each project.) Take into account the fabric pattern, if any; for example, vertical stripes could be pleated so that one colour is always inside the pleat and the other colour on top. Mark the foldlines and placement lines on the right side of the fabric using lines of tailor tacks.

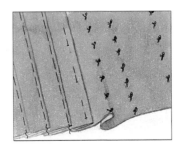

2 Still on the right side, fold each pleat along the foldline and bring it over to the placement line. Pin each pleat

in place from top to bottom, matching the horizontal pattern if there is one. Tack next to each foldline through all three thicknesses.

3 Using a pressing cloth, press the pleats, first from the right side and then from the wrong side.

4 Stitch across the top edge. Remove the tacking.

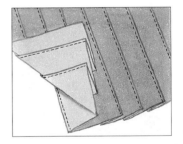

5 To make pressed pleats hang better and to avoid having to re-form them after laundering the fabric, you can, if you wish, extend each pleat away from the fabric and *edgestitch* (ie, topstitch next to the edge) from the bottom up, very close to the inner and/or outer folds, taking particular care to keep the lines straight when stitching through the hem.

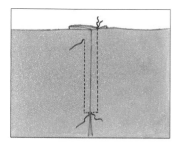

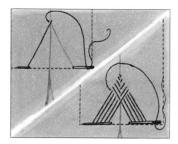

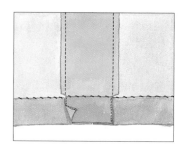

6 Inverted pleats are often topstitched part of the way down the seam, through all thicknesses. The point where the topstitching ends and the pleat begins is called the *release point*. When topstitching, work from the right side, starting in the centre of the pleat at the release point. Because this starting point is not within a seam allowance, do not backstitch at the beginning; instead, tie the threads on the wrong side after the topstitching is completed. Make a few stitches across the pleat, then pivot and stitch along one side to the top. Start again in the centre and stitch across the pleat in the opposite direction, pivot and finally stitch along that side to the top of the pleat.

7 If you want to edgestitch a seam to be topstitched, edgestitch the seam before topstitching, but only as far as the release point.

8 Hand-embroidered *arrowheads* are sometimes used just above the release points of topstitched pleats. These are not only decorative but also practical, as they strengthen the pleat. Mark a triangle with 1cm (⅜in) sides on the right side of the fabric using tailor's chalk. Using buttonhole twist or embroidery cotton, bring the needle up from the wrong side through the lefthand corner at the base of the triangle. Take a very small stitch across the top point of the triangle from right to left. Pull the thread through. Now insert the needle at the righthand corner of the base and bring it up at the lefthand corner, just to the right of the previous stitch. Continue making stitches in this way within the triangle until it is filled. Fasten off on the wrong side.

INVERTED PLEATS WITH SEPARATE UNDERLAYS
If desired, an inverted pleat can have an underlay of a separate – possibly contrasting – fabric. Here, the pleat is constructed from the wrong side, and the hemming cannot be done till the pleating is finished.

1 Mark the foldlines and a parallel line halfway between them on the wrong side. Cut along the marked central line.

2 Bring together the two foldlines for the pleat, right sides together, and tack along this line. Press the tacked seam open, forming the *pleat extensions*.

3 The width of the underlay should be the same as the distance between the raw edges of the pleat extensions, and it should also be the same length as the extensions. Lay the underlay on top of the extensions, with the right sides together and the raw edges even.

4 Join the underlay to the pleat extensions along the raw edges, taking 1.5cm (⅝in) seams. Be sure to stitch only through the pleat extensions and underlay. Press the seams flat on both the wrong side and the right side, using a pressing cloth on the right side. Trim and neaten the seams above the hemline. Stitch across the top edge through all thicknesses. Remove the tacking.

5 Turn up the hem on the entire lower edge of the item, then snip into the seamlines of the pleat just above the hem edge. Oversew the bottom of the seam allowances above the snips. Edgestitch the seams of the pleat within the hem area.

DARTS
....

Darts are a useful means of shaping fabric around a curve, as on loose chair covers. Usually they are stitched wedges of fabric that taper to a point at one end.

MAKING DARTS

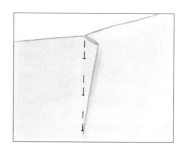

1 Mark the dart on the wrong side of the fabric. With right sides together, bring the two stitching lines together and pin along the line. Tack, then remove pins.

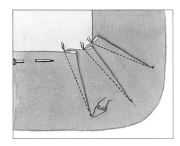

2 Starting at the wide end, stitch along the stitching line, tapering off by sewing very close to the fold at the pointed end. Tie the thread ends. Remove the tacking.

3 Unless the dart is very wide or the fabric is bulky, press the dart flat (as stitched) to one side. For very wide darts, press it so that the dart is centred over the stitching line. For bulky fabric, cut along the centre fold almost to the point, then press open.

DOUBLE-ENDED DARTS

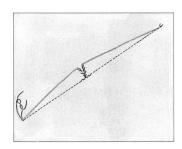

These do not begin at the fabric edge; instead, they taper to a point at each end. Pin and tack as in step 1, then stitch, starting at the widest part and finishing at one point. Turn the dart over and repeat for the other half. Clip into the centre, and oversew the cut edges. Press.

TUCKS

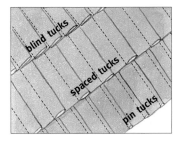

Tucks are stitched folds on either the right side or the wrong side of the fabric. They may either meet (these are known as "blind tucks") or have spaces between them, and can be used as decorative trim for a wide range of soft furnishings, including cushion covers, blinds, chair covers, curtains and tablecloths.

Very narrow tucks are known as pin tucks. They can be stitched as for plain tucks, but if you have a "tucker foot" for your sewing machine, you can stitch them automatically. Tucks that extend the full depth of an item are purely decorative, but released tucks (see below) are a method of controlling fullness.

PLAIN TUCKS

1 On the straight grain of the fabric, mark stitching lines on either the right side (using tailor tacks) or the wrong side (using a fabric marker). For each tuck, the distance between the two stitching lines should be twice the desired width of the tuck. Space the tucks equally.

2 Join pairs of stitching lines on either the right side or the wrong side. Press the tucks flat then all in the same direction, using a pressing cloth on the right side.

CORDED TUCKS

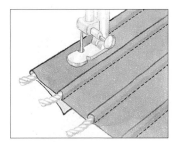

Make these raised tucks as for plain tucks, but insert piping cord (slightly narrower than the tuck) inside the fold, then stitch using a zip foot.

CROSSED TUCKS

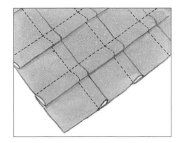

Make plain tucks on the straight grain, then, with these tucks facing downwards, stitch tucks on the crosswise grain. Be careful not to allow the first tucks to twist when you are stitching the second set. Press as for plain tucks.

RELEASED TUCKS

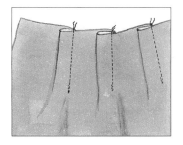

These tucks are stitched only as far as *release points*. Sometimes known as *dart tucks*, they are used to control fullness at a particular point in much the same way as darts are (see page 20). Unlike darts, however, they do not taper. Each tuck may have one or two release points.

1 Make as for plain tucks, but stop the stitching at the release point, fastening off by either reverse stitching or tying the threads.

2 Alternatively, instead of stopping at the release point and fastening off, pivot the needle and stitch across the tuck to the fold, at right angles to the first stitching, or at a sharper angle.

TIP

To prevent your fabric from rippling, stitch the central tuck first, then stitch the ones on each side in the opposite direction. Working outwards, continue stitching in opposite directions.

GATHERS

Gathering involves drawing up fabric into tiny, soft folds, using lines of stitching. It is done after completing any seams in the fabric to be gathered.

If your machine has a gathering foot, you can use this to gather fabric automatically as you stitch. Gathering can also be done automatically on an overlock machine.

When gathering a very long area, it is best to work in sections of no more than about 60–90cm (2–3ft) so that the gathering threads are less likely to break. Similarly, because it is difficult to gather fabric at seams, it is a good idea to stop the stitching just before any seams and resume stitching just beyond them.

1 Use your longest machine straight stitch. You may also need to loosen the upper tension – check your machine manual. In the bobbin use a strong thread such as a heavy duty synthetic thread, or buttonhole twist if it can be used on your machine. Working from the right side of the fabric, make two parallel lines of stitching within the seam allowance. One line should be just inside the stitching line and the other about 6mm (¼in) inside that. If the fabric is quite heavy, a third row, just outside the seamline, is advisable; this

row will need to be unpicked at the end. Leave ends at least 10cm (4in) long on the threads. If you are gathering a small area or a lightweight fabric, you could work two or three rows of running stitch by hand instead of using the machine – use a double length of thread, and line up the stitches to help the gathers to lie straight.

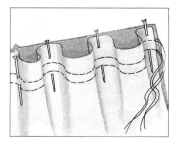

2 If you are joining this fabric piece to another piece at this stage, mark the centres of both. If the fabric you will be gathering is quite long, also mark the quarter points or even smaller segments. With right sides together and raw edges even, pin the two pieces together at these markings.

3 At one end, secure the bobbin threads by wrapping them around a pin in a figure-of-eight shape. At the other end, carefully pull the two bobbin threads at once to gather up the fabric. (If you have used hand stitches, this refers to all the threads at each end, since there is no bobbin thread.) Gently slide the fabric along the threads as you pull. When half the section has been gathered and is the correct length, repeat the process from the other end. Distribute the gathers gently and evenly. (On small pieces, the gathering can all be done from one end, in which case the threads at the other end should be fastened off.)

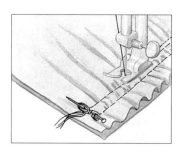

4 When joining the gathered fabric to an ungathered piece, pin the two pieces together all along the seamline at frequent intervals between the points at which they are already pinned. Tack if desired, removing the pins. Stitch the seam with the gathered fabric on top, so that you can keep the gathers straight and even as you

stitch. Holding the fabric on each side of the presser foot will help prevent any tiny pleats from forming.

5 Trim any seam allowances that cross this seam. Press flat (as stitched) then open out the two pieces of fabric and press from the wrong side. Press only within the seam allowance, so that you won't crease or flatten the gathers.

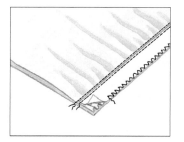

6 Finish the seam allowances together with zigzag stitching (unless the project requires them to be pressed open). Alternatively, position seam binding on top of the gathered seam allowance, with the binding edge next to the seamline. Straight stitch just inside the seamline through both seam allowances and the binding, then trim the raw edges of the seam allowance even with the binding, and zigzag stitch all three edges together.

SEE ALSO

Headings 84

EDGINGS

Because of the long edges often found in soft furnishing projects, the way in which you finish the edges on a particular item is an important consideration.

HEMS

Hems may be hand or machine stitched. Machine stitched hems are quicker to do and stronger, but they normally show on the right side of the fabric. Hand stitching is used where the hem is deep or needs to be invisible, such as on lined curtains, and machine stitching is used when the hem is long, narrow and inconspicuous, as on frills or on bed valances.

If your machine has a blindstitch foot, you can have a quick and inconspicuous hem. Follow the instruction manual for this. Similarly, narrow hems with straight or zigzag stitching are possible using special hemmer feet on the sewing machine. Rolled hems for table linen can be produced with an overlock foot or using an overlocker machine.

NARROW HEM
Use this hem on tablecloths, frills and curved edges. The hem allowance should be 1.5cm (⅝in). (If your machine has a hemmer foot, it will do the folding for you and the hem will be narrower. In that case, a 6mm (¼in) hem allowance is enough.)

1 Turn up 1.5cm (⅝in) on the edge to be hemmed, and press the fold.

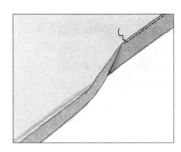

2 Turn under the raw edge inside the hem to meet the crease; press. Pin and stitch next to the upper fold.

WIDE PLAIN HEM
Wide hems are useful when the way that the fabric hangs is important.

1 First neaten the edge of the hem, either by zigzag stitching, or, if the fabric isn't bulky, by turning under 6mm (¼in) and machine stitching. For very thick, loosely woven fabrics, you might have to oversew the edge by hand using large stitches.

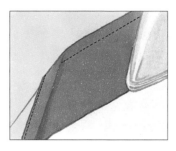

2 Turn up the hem by the required amount and press in position.

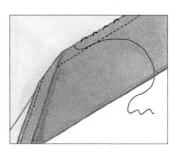

3 Sew the hem in place close to the neatened edge, either by hand (using slipstitch, hemming stitch, herringbone stitch or blind hem stitch) from the wrong side, or by machine from the right or wrong side. If you machine stitch, you may need to pull the fabric gently from the back with your left hand and from the front with your right hand as you stitch; known as *tensioning* the fabric, this technique will help prevent it from puckering.

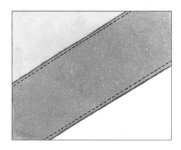

4 If you have machine stitched the hem, you may wish to make a feature of this and stitch again close to the lower edge. Alternatively, working from the right side, stitch with a decorative machine embroidery stitch along the stitched hem line.

WIDE DOUBLE HEM

The most frequently used hem for soft furnishings, the wide double hem is neat and smooth. It is ideal for fabric where a narrow hem turning under a wider one could create a ridge, and for sheer fabric. The extra weight also helps the item to hang well.

The specified size of a double hem refers to the depth of the finished hem. The hem allowance is twice this. For example, for a 5cm (2in) double hem you need to allow a 10cm (4in) hem allowance. Suitable hem depths are specified in the instructions for projects.

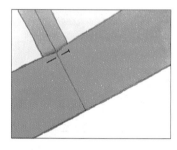

1 Turn up and press the lower edge of the item by the depth of the finished hem. Turn up and press the same amount again. (If the edge is longer than your ironing board, turn up both amounts for one section before moving the fabric along.) Check that the line looks straight – you might have to vary the depth slightly to achieve this, especially across seams. If possible, put the item in its eventual position, and check the length, adjusting the depth of the hem if necessary.

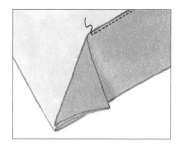

2 Tack if desired. Then either hand sew in place or machine stitch, as for a wide plain hem (step 3).

MITRING HEMS AT CORNERS

Mitring is a neat, smooth way of finishing corners. The technique you use depends upon what you are mitring (hems, bands, trims). Here is how to mitre a corner where two hems meet. The exact method depends on the type of hem.

MITRING NARROW HEMS OF THE SAME WIDTH

1 Unfold both pressed sides and fold the corner in diagonally so that the creases line up; press.

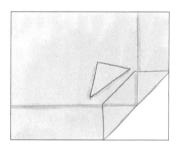

2 Trim off the corner, leaving a 6mm (¼in) seam.

3 Refold the hems, and slipstitch the mitre.

MITRING WIDE PLAIN HEMS OF THE SAME WIDTH

1 Unfold both pressed sides. Fold the corner in diagonally so that the creases line up; press, then open it out again.

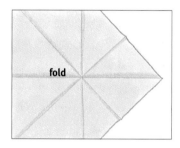

2 With right sides together, fold through the centre of the corner, so that the neatened edges are even.

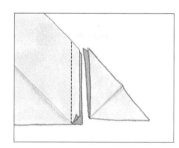

3 Pin and stitch at right angles to the foldline. Trim off the point, leaving a 1cm (⅜in) seam allowance, and snipping into it at the folded end. Press the seam open.

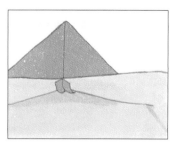

4 Turn the mitred corner right side out and press.

MITRING HEMS OF DIFFERENT WIDTHS (UNEVEN MITRE)

1 Mark with a pin where each folded edge comes to on the other edge when that edge is unfolded.

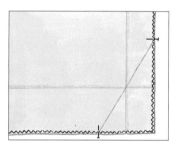

2 Draw a line between these points and fold the corner in along it, then proceed as for mitring narrow hems of the same width (steps 2–3).

MITRING WIDE DOUBLE HEMS

1 Make the first fold on each side; press the folds.

2 Leaving both edges folded, proceed as usual with the second folds and the mitre.

HEMMING IN POSITION

Sometimes it is necessary to pin up a hem after the item – such as a curtain – has been hung in position. In that case, pin it up so that it is an equal distance from the floor all along the hem, then press the finished hem line, removing pins and adjusting it as you press to make it smooth and straight.

For a double hem, open out the hem after pressing, and bring the lower edge to the pressed hem edge, pressing the fold. Refold and pin.

Hang up the item again to check the length. Adjust if necessary, then remove the pins, trim the hem allowance to make it even, and finally machine or hand stitch.

FUSED HEM

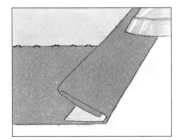

Instead of hand or machine stitching a straight hem, you could fuse it with fusing tape.

1 After pressing in the fold, open out and iron fusible tape to the wrong side of the hem allowance, following the manufacturer's instructions. Allow to cool.

2 Remove the paper backing and refold the hem. Iron the tape to fuse the hem in position. It can also be used on a double hem – open out the second fold and fuse to the fabric in the same way as for single hems.

SELF-FRINGED HEM

This is an attractive hem for table linen and throws. It works best on a loosely woven fabric.

1 Make sure the edge is exactly on the straight or crosswise grain. Cut on a pulled thread to straighten an edge if necessary.

2 Pull a thread (see page 11) to mark where the fringe will begin. Machine stitch (using either short straight stitches or narrow, short zigzag) along this line in order to prevent the edges of the fabric from fraying.

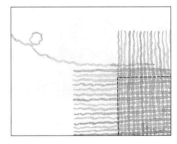

3 Pull out the threads that are parallel to the edge, stopping when you get to the stitching. The threads that remain, at right angles to the edge, form the fringe.

FACINGS

A facing is a separate piece of fabric that is the same shape as the edge of the item. It is stitched to the edge in order to neaten it. Facings are useful for edges with tight curves, corners or angles that would be difficult to hem or for straight edges in which other pieces (such as ties) are inserted into the seam.

If the fabric is heavy, choose a lighter fabric for the facing. Otherwise, it's optional whether you use the same fabric or a cotton or lining fabric for it.

A faced edge does not need a hem allowance – it only needs a seam allowance.

1 On paper, draw around the edge to be faced. Draw the other edge of the facing about 6.5cm (2½in) away, following the same shape. Mark the straight grain of the main fabric on it with a long double-ended arrow. Also mark several points around the edge of both the pattern and the wrong side of the main fabric.

2 Place this paper pattern on the facing fabric so the grain line marking matches the grain of the fabric. Cut out the facing. Transfer the markings onto the wrong side of the facing. Neaten the raw edge that will not be stitched to the main fabric.

3 With right sides together and raw edges even, stitch the facing to the main fabric around the edges. Grade the seam, clip or notch any curves and snip off any corners. Press the seam allowances towards the facing.

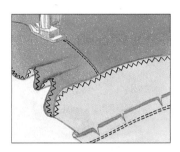

4 *Understitching* is not essential but it will help prevent the facing from rolling out to the right side. Open out the main fabric and facing, with the right sides up. With the seam allowances towards the facing, stitch 2mm (a scant ⅛in) away from the seamline, through the facing and the seam allowances.

5 Turn the facing to the wrong side of the main fabric. Press so that the seamline is just inside the edge. Depending on the project, either hand sew the facing to the main fabric as for a hem, or attach the facing only to the seam allowances that it crosses.

BINDING

Another way of finishing raw edges is to bind them. Either make your own as shown here, using the same or contrasting fabric, or use ready-made binding.

For straight edges you can use binding cut on either the straight grain or the bias, but for curved edges only bias binding is suitable. This is because bias binding will stretch to fit curves easily, while seam binding (binding cut on the straight grain) will not. Bias binding can also be used to make piping.

The instructions here are for binding one layer of fabric, but two or three layers are bound in the same way.

When estimating fabric amounts for bias binding, bear in mind that 1m (1yd) of 90cm (35in) wide fabric will produce approximately 21m (23yd) of binding cut to a width of 3cm (1¼in), or about half that amount of binding if cut to a width of 6cm (2¼in). Similarly, 1m (1yd) of 140cm (54in) wide fabric will produce about 34m (37yd) of the narrower binding or about 18m (20yd) of the wider one.

MAKING BIAS BINDING (CONVENTIONAL METHOD)

This is the simplest method for making small amounts of bias binding.

1 Decide on the finished width of the binding (ie, what is seen from the right side after it is attached), and multiply this by 4. This is the cut width.

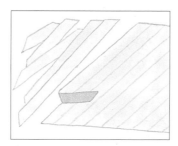

2 Find the true bias by folding the fabric diagonally (see page 12) and press along the fold. Draw lines parallel to this fold, with the distance between them the desired cut width of the binding. Cut out.

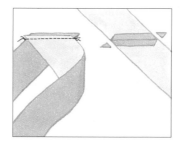

3 Join strips on the straight grain as shown, with the seams all slanting in the same direction. Trim off the points that extend beyond the edges.

4 If you have made your own binding, fold the two long edges in to meet the centre; press. (You can buy metal devices that do the folding automatically.) For binding that will be used for piping, this is not necessary.

MAKING BIAS BINDING (CONTINUOUS STRIP METHOD)

This method avoids having to make lots of individual seams, so is useful if you are making a large amount of binding.

1 From your fabric cut out a rectangle in which the length is at least twice the width. The longer side can be on either the lengthwise or crosswise grain. Fold each end along the true bias. Press and then cut out along these lines. You can use the two triangles to make separate strips of binding if desired.

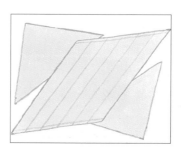

2 Mark cutting lines parallel to the slanting ends, with the distance between them equal to the desired width of the binding. Also mark seamlines that are 6mm (¼in) from the long edges of the fabric piece.

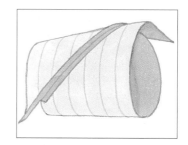

3 Fold the fabric as shown, right sides together, with the corner of the raw diagonal edge even with the first cutting line. Pin along the seamline, so that you have a tube with a diagonal seamline, in which one strip overhangs at each end. Check that the cutting lines match exactly all the way down, then stitch along the marked seamline. Press the seam open.

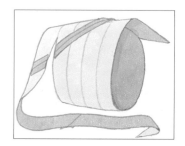

4 Finally, cut around the line spiralling around the tube. Press as in step 4 of the conventional method.

ATTACHING A HEM FACING

If you are using bias binding as a hem facing, ready-made hem facing tape that is either 2.5cm (1in) or 5cm (2in) wide is suitable.

1 Trim the hem allowance of the project to 6mm (¼in). Open out one folded edge of the binding, turn in the end and pin it to the hem edge with right sides together and raw edges even. Stitch along the foldline.

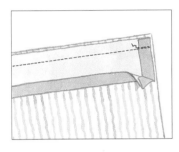

2 If the other end meets the first one, overlap the second one (without turning it under). If there is a finished edge on the item, turn under the end of the binding before stitching it.

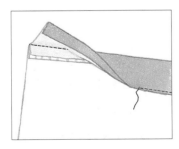

3 Press the binding to the wrong side of the fabric. Stitch the other folded edge in place by hand or machine.

Slipstitch any turned-under ends of the binding.

BINDING AN EDGE (TWO-STAGE METHOD)

This method allows you to bind an edge without the stitching being noticeable.

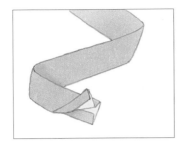

1 Fold the binding lengthwise, wrong sides together, so that the fold is slightly off-centre (ie, nearer one lengthwise fold than the other). Ready-made bias binding is already folded in this way.

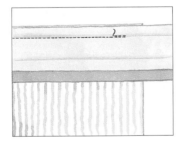

2 Open out the folded edge on the narrower side of the binding and pin it to the fabric edge with right sides together and seamlines matching. (The raw edges will align only if the seam allowances are the same.) Stitch along the fold line. Treat ends as for a hem facing.

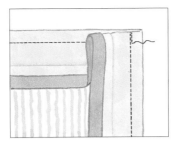

3 To mitre any corners, stitch along the edge until you reach the stitching line of the adjacent edge, then backstitch to secure the thread. Fold the binding back on itself, forming a 45-degree angle. Now fold it so the seamline of the binding is aligned with the adjacent seamline of the fabric. Backstitch, then stitch along the new edge, from the top.

4 When the first stitching is complete, trim the fabric seam allowance so that it falls just short of the binding fold-line; this will give a nice plump edge. If the fabric is bulky, trim the fabric seam allowance to slightly less than 6mm (¼in).

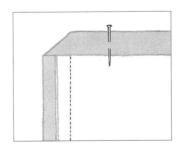

5 Bring the binding over to the wrong side of the main fabric; pin the other folded edge of the binding over the stitching. At corners, fold the extra binding into mitres.

6 Tack the edge if desired. Now either slipstitch in place from the wrong side, or "stitch in the ditch" (machine stitch in the groove just alongside the binding) from the right side. Slipstitch the diagonal folds at the corners.

BINDING AN EDGE (ONE-STAGE METHOD)

This method is quick, but the stitching is visible on the right side.

1 Fold the binding as for the two-stage method (step 1).

2 Trim the seam allowance of the main fabric to just under the finished width of the binding, unless the fabric is quite bulky, in which case trim the seam allowance to 6mm (¼in).

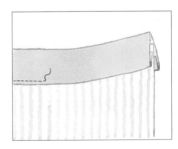

3 Slot the fabric edge into the folded binding, with the wider side of the binding on the underside. Pin and then topstitch through all thicknesses along the turned-under edge of the binding.

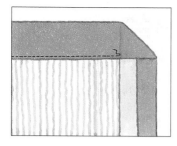

4 At corners, stitch as far as the adjacent side, fold the binding diagonally on both the top and underside and then continue stitching along the next side; slipstitch the folds of the mitres.

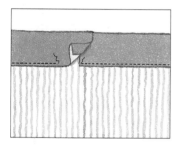

5 Where ends of the binding meet, turn under one end and lap it over the other; slipstitch the folded end.

DOUBLE BINDING

This method is good for lightweight fabrics, as it creates a double-thickness binding. Ends are turned under and corners mitred as for the two-stage method.

1 Cut binding that is six times the desired finished width. Do not press it in the usual way – instead, with wrong sides together press it in half lengthwise, then press it in thirds lengthwise. Unfold the thirds so it is folded in half once again.

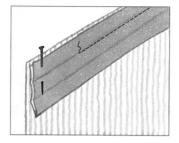

2 Trim the fabric seam allowance to the desired finished width of the binding. With right sides together and raw edges even, stitch the folded binding to the fabric along the nearest foldline. Press the binding towards the seam allowance.

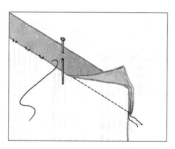

3 Pin the other folded edge of the binding to the wrong side of the fabric, just covering the stitching line. Slipstitch the binding in place from the wrong side.

SELF BINDING

On items like bed covers that have a backing, this is a quick and easy method of binding the edges.

1 Cut the backing so that it is larger all around by the desired width of the binding plus 6mm (¼in). Tack the backing to the front, wrong sides together.

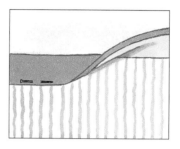

2 Press under 6mm (¼in) on all the raw edges of the backing. Bring each edge over to the front, folding it along the raw edge of the front fabric; press. Topstitch along the inner folded edge of the binding all around.

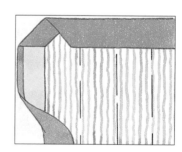

3 Mitre the corners as for narrow hems of the same width (see page 24).

A band is an extension of the fabric, generally in a contrasting fabric. It can be used on all manner of soft furnishings, including curtains, bedspreads, tablecloths, placemats, napkins, cushions and chair covers. A border looks very similar to a band but does not extend beyond the fabric.

A band can be applied to just one edge – say, the leading edge of a curtain, or the hem of a chair loose cover – or it may go around more than one edge. In that case, the corner is mitred, a decorative feature in itself. When four sides are banded, for example on a cushion, a fabric with a directional pattern, such as a stripe, can look good.

SINGLE BAND

This type of band can be used on a cushion cover or placemat that will be backed with fabric.

1 Cut the band to the desired width plus 3cm (1¼in) for seam allowances. The length should be the length of the fabric edge (including seam allowance); if there are any corners, add a mitring allowance equal to the finished width of the band, for every corner.

2 Pin the band to the main fabric with right sides together and raw edges even.

BANDS AND BORDERS

At a corner, the fabric should extend beyond the main fabric by the mitring allowance. Stitch up to the seamline of the adjacent edge. Repeat for that edge, stitching up to the seamline of the previous edge.

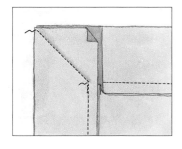

3 At the corner, fold the projecting part of each strip along a line running between the inner and outer corners. With right sides together, pin and stitch these together along this line. Trim and press open.

4 The remaining raw edges of the band are stitched when the banded fabric is joined to its backing.

DOUBLE BAND
Use this type of band on items in which the reverse side of the band will not be covered up.

1 Cut the bands to twice the desired finished width (ie, what will be visible from the right side) plus 3cm (1¼in) for seam allowances. The length should be equal to the length of the edge you are attaching it to (including the seam allowances) plus a mitring allowance for each mitred corner. Calculate the mitring allowance by adding 1.5cm (⅝in) to the finished width of the band. If, for example, the width of the band is to be 7.5cm (3in), the cutting width should be 18cm (7¼in); the mitring allowance for each corner would be 9cm (3⅝in).

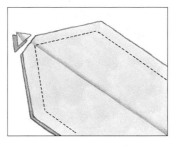

2 Mitre any corners before attaching the band. To do this, fold each band with wrong sides together and press. With the band still folded, fold the end to be mitred over diagonally, so that the end is even with the lengthwise fold; press. Trim along the diagonal crease through both layers. Unfold, revealing a pointed end. Now join the pointed ends of the two bands, with right sides together and raw edges even; take a 1.5cm (⅝in) seam and stop and start 1.5cm (⅝in) from the edge. Trim the seam and snip off the corner. Press the seam open, turn right side out and refold along the old lengthwise lines. Press.

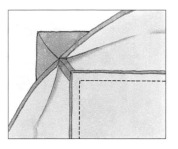

3 You can now either stitch both layers of the band to the main fabric at once, leaving the seam allowance visible, or stitch one layer at a time (as shown here), like binding an edge in two stages (page 27). The unstitched parts of the mitre will open up to allow the band to fit onto the corner. Stitch a 1.5cm (⅝in) seam, stitching into the corner rather than around it and pressing the excess band fabric out of the way.

FABRIC BORDER
This looks like a band but it is in fact constructed more like a facing.

1 Cut the borders as for a single band, step 1. Mitre any corners before attaching the border, folding the end of one strip diagonally to the wrong side; press, then trim 1.5cm (⅝in) from the fold. Press under 1.5cm (⅝in) along the shorter long edge of this strip, and one long edge of the adjacent strip. Open out the folds, and pin the strips right sides together along the diagonal fold.

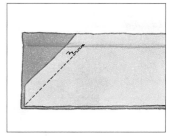

2 Stitch, but only as far as the fold on the long edges, reinforcing the stitching at this point. Trim the other seam allowance even with the first. Press the seam open.

3 Press under a 1.5cm (⅝in) seam allowance on one long edge (or in the case of strips already joined at the corner, re-press the turned-under edge). With raw edges even, pin the other edge of the border to the raw edge of the fabric, with the right side of the border facing the wrong side of the fabric. Stitch a 1.5cm (⅝in) seam.

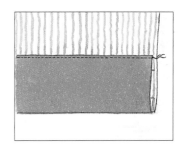

4 Press the border away from the fabric, and then to the right side of the fabric so that the seamline runs along the bottom. Pin and then topstitch along the folded edge of the border.

TRIMMINGS

Braid, ribbon, lace, fringing or other trimmings are usually topstitched or hand sewn to the right side of the fabric.

Try to apply trimmings before stitching seams so that the ends can be caught in the seams. If this is not possible, turn under the ends. Where two ends meet, turn under one end and lap it over the other, preferably in an inconspicuous place. On bulky fabrics, however, butt up the raw ends and either whipstitch them together or coat the ends with seam sealant.

Trimmings on which machine stitches would be too noticeable, or which might be flattened by machine stitching, or which simply wouldn't go through the sewing machine (such as decorative cording) should be sewn on by hand with tiny, inconspicuous stitches.

TOPSTITCHED TRIM WITH TWO STRAIGHT EDGES

1 Tack the trim right side up (using hand stitches, fusible web, tacking tape or even a glue stick) just inside the placement line or the finished edge of the fabric. Topstitch along one edge close to the edge of the trimming, turning under the ends. Then topstitch the other edge in the same direction to prevent puckering.

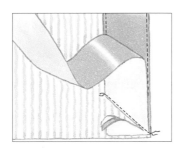

2 To mitre a corner, stop the inner stitching short of the next placement line by the width of the trim. Fold the trim back on itself and finger press the fold even with the new placement line. Now fold the trim diagonally so that it is right side up with the outer edge running along the new placement line; press. Lift the trim up and stitch along the diagonal crease through all layers. Trim along the diagonal seam, leaving a 6mm (¼in) seam allowance on the underside.

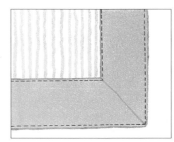

3 Refold the trim along this stitched mitre and resume topstitching along the new outer and then inner edges.

TOPSTITCHED TRIM WITH ONE STRAIGHT EDGE

1 Tack the straight edge of this trim just outside the placement line. Topstitch along this edge.

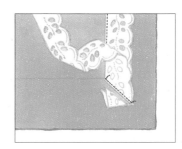

2 To mitre a corner, topstitch as far as the placement line of the adjacent edge. Fold and stitch the mitre in the same way as for topstitched trim with two straight edges (step 2) but with the inner, rather than the outer, edge of the trim against the placement line, and stopping the stitching at, rather than before, the next placement line.

PIPING

Piping is a folded strip of bias fabric that is inserted into a seam. Cording is usually included inside the piping, in which case it is technically known as corded piping. Usually, though, it is just referred to as piping. It can be made from the same fabric as the rest of the project (sometimes called self piping) or a contrasting one. Not only does it lend a professional finish and add definition to the lines of soft furnishing items, but it also strengthens them because it protects the seams from wear.

Piping cord comes in various widths – choose one to suit the fabric and the scale of the item being piped. Make sure it is pre-shrunk – if necessary, pre-shrink it beforehand by placing it in boiling water for three minutes; dry thoroughly before use.

PLAIN PIPING

For most piping, the cord is covered with bias strips that are either home-made (see Bias Binding, page 26) or ready-made.

1 To work out the width of bias binding that you'll need, pin a strip of fabric around the cord – you will need this width plus two 1.5cm (⅝in) seam allowances.

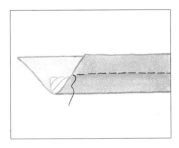

2 To cover the cord, wrap the bias strip (right side out) around it so that the raw edges are even. Pin and then machine tack next to the cord, using the piping foot or zip foot on your machine.

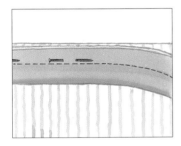

3 Pin the covered piping to the right side of the fabric around the edge, with the piping facing inwards. (If you are piping an edge where a straight strip will be attached to the sides of a rectangle, such as on a box cushion, the piping should be attached first to the side where it will need more control – in other words, to the rectangle rather than the straight strip.) The tacking on the piping should be barely within the seam allowance of the main fabric. If the seam allowances of the piping and the main fabric are the same size, the raw edges will be even.

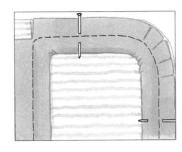

4 Clip into the piping seam allowances at any corners. This will allow the seam allowance at an outer corner to open up and fit smoothly around the corner, and at an inner corner to overlap and fit into the corner. On curves, clip into the seam allowance at frequent intervals so that it will lie flat.

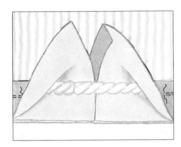

5 With the piping foot or zip foot on the machine, machine tack the piping in place along the previous tacking line. Make ends meet at an inconspicuous place, preferably on a straight edge rather than a curve or corner. Leave 5cm (2in) unstitched at each end, unpick some of the tacking on one end of the piping and pull back the bias binding. Trim the cords so the ends butt up. Turn under the end of the bias strip and wrap it around the cord ends. Tack to the fabric.

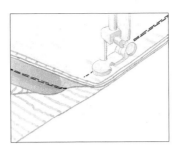

6 Now lay this piece of fabric on top of the other piece, with right sides together and raw edges even. With the piping foot or zip foot still on the machine, stitch through all four layers very close to the cord to hide the tacking completely. Grade the seam allowances.

GATHERED PIPING

This piping is more unusual but can look striking on something like a cushion. Here, the fabric is cut on the straight grain.

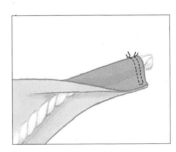

1 Cut the fabric strips on the straight grain, not the bias, to twice the length of the edge to be piped. (Calculate the width as for plain piping, step 1.) Wrap it around the cord, with the right side out and raw edges even. Now stitch twice across the end, through both the binding and the cord.

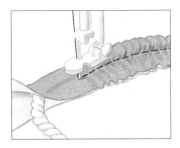

2 With the piping foot or zip foot on the machine, machine tack next to the cord for about 15cm (6in). Now, with the needle in the fabric and the zip foot raised, gently pull on the cord, gathering up the fabric.

3 Lower the foot and repeat until you have covered a sufficient amount of cord for the project.

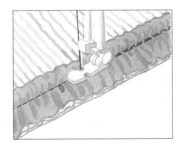

4 Attach this piping in the same way as for plain piping (steps 3–6).

TIP

Where piping is to start or finish in the middle of an edge, or where the end of the fabric will be turned under, a good way to neaten the end of the piping is to twist it so it is at right angles to the seamline and the raw end is hidden in the seam allowance. Tack and stitch across cording.

FRILLS

These strips of gathered fabric add a feminine touch to the edges of soft furnishings, whether in the same or a contrast fabric.

Frills can be cut either on the straight grain (for a crisp effect) or on the bias (for a softer look). The fullness depends on the weight of the fabric and the width of the ruffle. Allow for a fullness of 1½ to 2½ times (three times for sheers).

SINGLE FRILL
This consists of one layer of fabric with a narrow hem.

1 Cut the fabric to the desired width of the frill plus a seam allowance of 1.5cm (⅝in) and a hem allowance of 1.2cm (½in).

2 Join strips with French seams. If the ends of the frill will need to be joined, do this now, using a French seam.

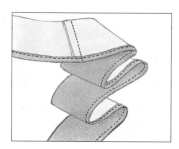

3 Hem the edge, and the ends if not joined, with a narrow hem or bind them.

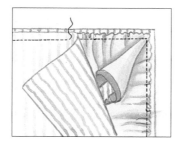

4 To insert a frill in a seam, gather it up and stitch it to one side of the main fabric with right sides together and raw edges even, taking a 1.5cm (⅝in) seam (see Gathering). Allow extra fullness at corners so that the frill will fit around them when the fabric is turned right side out. Join the second fabric piece to this one, again with right sides together and raw edges even, and taking a 1.5cm (⅝in) seam. Trim the seams, turn the item right side out and press.

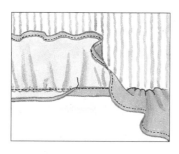

5 To attach a frill to a single fabric panel, gather up the frill and join it to the fabric (see Gathering, page 22) with right sides together and taking only a 6mm (¼in) seam. Trim the seam allowance of the frill only, to 3mm (⅛in). Turn under 3mm (⅛in) on the fabric seam allowance. Fold it over again, enclosing the frill seam allowance. Stitch along the folded edge. Press the seam towards the fabric.

DOUBLE FRILL
This consists of one strip of fabric folded in half lengthwise. Because of the extra weight, heavy fabrics are not suitable for double frills.

1 Cut the fabric to twice the width of the frill plus twice the seam allowance.

2 Join strips together with flat seams. If the ends are to be joined, do this now. Otherwise, finish the ends by folding the frill in half lengthwise and stitching across the ends, then turning right side out and pressing.

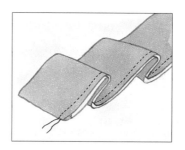

3 Fold the strip in half lengthwise, with wrong sides together and raw edges even. Machine tack along the seamline.

4 Attach as for a single frill (steps 4 and 5).

DOUBLE-EDGED FRILL
Frills with two finished edges have gathering between the edges, often down the centre.

1 Join the ends with French seams, then make a narrow hem on all the edges. Gather down the centre of the frill (or off centre) using two rows of stitching.

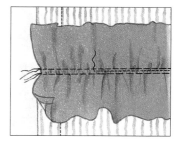

2 Pin the wrong side of the frill to the right side of the fabric, and topstitch down the centre of the gathers.

3 Unpick the gathering stitches, or conceal by topstitching ricrac, ribbon or narrow flat trim over it.

READY-MADE FRILLS
Ready-made frilled edgings have a firm binding on one edge, which may be inserted into the seam as for single frills. Or, the edging may be hand sewn to a finished project.

SEE ALSO

FASTENINGS

Fastenings enable a cover to be removed for cleaning. They can be completely concealed, like zips, or made into a decorative feature like covered buttons or ties.

DECORATIVE FASTENINGS

BUTTONS AND BUTTONHOLES

These can be an intrinsic part of the design of a cushion cover. Most sewing machines make buttonholes semi-automatically using a buttonhole foot, so follow the instructions in your manual.

COVERED BUTTONS

Covered buttons give a smart, professional look to projects such as cushions, pleated curtain headings and tiebacks. You'll need a covered-button kit for this.

1 Cut a circle of fabric to the size specified in the kit (or cut two circles if the fabric is very thin and see-through).

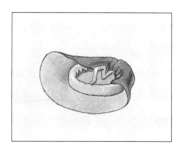

2 Place the button on the wrong side of the fabric circle, in the centre. Stretch the fabric over opposite sides so that it catches on the tiny hooks. Do the same for the other sides. (Running a hand gathering stitch around the edge and pulling it up makes this easy.)

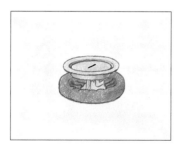

3 Smooth out any bumps around the rim so it is smooth all round, then press the back plate in position.

EYELETS

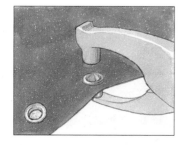

Large eyelets threaded with cord are now often used in soft furnishings, particularly for curtains and cushions.

Eyelets, whether large or small, are often made using a tool rather like a pair of pliers.

These come with metal eyelets in kits. Although the instructions vary, one typical method is to make a hole in the fabric, insert the pointed end of the tool, place an eyelet over it and then clamp the pliers together.

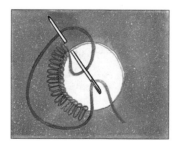

For hand sewn eyelets, make a hole in the fabric with a stiletto, sewing in a circle around it with tiny running stitches. Work closely spaced buttonhole stitches all around the hole between it and the running stitch.

ZIPS

These are mainly used on cushion covers and loose covers. There are various methods of inserting a zip, but the centred application shown here is the quickest and easiest. Try to insert the zip early in the making of the project, when you can still open the fabric out flat.

Insert the zip in a seam with seam allowances of at least 1.5cm (5/8in), and preferably 2.5cm (1in), which will make the insertion stronger.

1 Mark the opening for the zip on the seamline; it should start 6mm (1/4in) above the top stop and finish just below the bottom stop. Join the fabric along this seamline with right sides together and raw edges even, stitching the portion of the seam that is not part of the opening. Backstitch securely just before the opening and then machine tack along the opening. If the seamline continues on the other side of the opening, backstitch at the beginning of it then stitch the seam as before. Neaten the edges of the seam allowance and press the entire seam open.

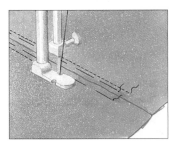

2 On the wrong side of the fabric, centre the closed zip, face down, over the seamline within the opening. Tack in place using either hand tacking, tacking tape or a glue stick.

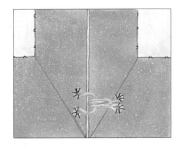

3 With the zip foot on the machine, topstitch the zip down one side – about 6mm (¼in) from the opening edge, across the end, down the other side again 6mm (¼in) from the opening edge, and across the other end if there is one. (If you are working on fabric that has a tendency to creep, it's safer to stitch the second side in the same direction as the first.) Be careful not to stitch into the zip stops. Rather than backstitching, tie the threads on the wrong side. Remove the zip tacking and also the tacking along the seamline.

SINGLE FASTENERS

These are useful for a concealed fastener in a specific spot.

PRESS STUDS AND POPPERS

A press stud consists of a "ball" which fits into a "socket". Whipstitch the ball to the underside of the overlap, and the socket to the top side of the underlap, so that they align.

Poppers also have two halves but they do not require sewing. Both halves are cleated into the fabric and secured with clips at the back.

HOOKS AND EYES

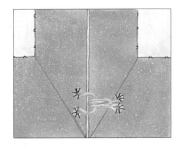

Use these individually on openings with either butted edges or lapped openings. The hook and the eye are each

whipstitched to one side of the opening. On openings with butted edges, the hook is attached so it is even with the folded edge, while a round eye is sewn on so as to project slightly beyond the edge.

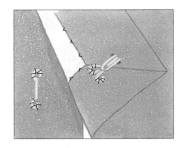

On lapped openings, the hook is whipstitched to the underside of the overlap, and a straight eye is attached to the top side of the underlap.

TOUCH-AND-CLOSE FASTENERS

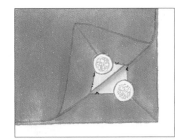

These are small, precut dots or squares of touch-and-close tape (see page 35). There are two types – the sew-on type and the self-adhesive type.

TAPE FASTENERS

There are three types of tape fastener, corresponding to the three types of single fastener (see left). They are generally stitched down all four edges, with the ends caught into the ends of the opening.

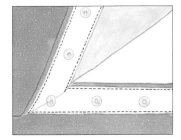

PRESS STUD OR POPPER TAPE
This type of tape consists of a row of press studs or poppers spaced at regular intervals. Often used on duvet covers, it must be sewn into a lapped opening, with the ball strip on the underside of the overlap and the socket strip on the top side of the underlap (like single press studs).

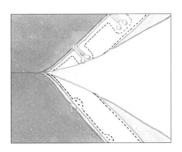

HOOK-AND-EYE TAPE

This has regularly spaced hooks on one strip and eyes on the other. Stitch the tapes to the underside of the opening so that the hooks are even with the folded edge and so that the eyes extend slightly beyond the other folded edge.

TOUCH-AND-CLOSE TAPE

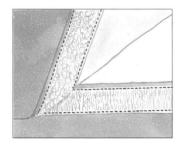

Touch-and-close tape, such as Velcro, consists of two interlocking strips, one with tiny hooks and the other with tiny soft loops. The two strips are pressed together to close an opening and pulled apart to open it. It has to be used in a lapped opening. The hook strip goes on the top side of the underlap and the loop strip on the underside of the overlap.

As well as the sew-on type, in which both strips are stitched to fabric, there is a second type; in this, one strip is sewn onto the fabric and the other stuck to a hard surface. This is very useful for fixing curtains and valances to a wall.

TIES AND TABS

TIES

Ties are used in a variety of places – including at the back of chair covers and squab cushions, at the openings of scatter cushions, and as part of tie-on curtain headings.

1 For each tie, cut a strip on the lengthwise or crosswise grain. It should be four times the finished width, and the finished length plus 6mm (1/4in).

2 With wrong sides together, turn in one end by 6mm (1/4in). Fold in the long raw edges so they meet in the centre; press. Now fold in half lengthwise and press again.

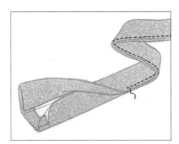

3 Edgestitch across the folded end and down the long edge. When making the project, tack each tie to the right side of the main fabric with raw edges even, before stitching the seam. (If the end is not to be inserted in a seam, turn it under as for the other end.)

TABS

These are often used at the tops of curtains in the same way as ties, or as decorative closures on cushions.

1 For each tab, cut two strips of fabric to the desired width and length plus 1.5cm (5/8in) seam allowances all around.

2 On the wrong side of one piece, mark the seamline 1.5cm (5/8in) from the edge along two long edges and one end. At this end mark the centre point on the seamline, and draw a straight line from here to the point on the side seamline where you'd like the point to begin tapering. Repeat for the other half of the fabric piece.

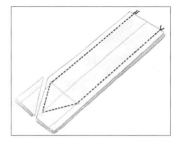

3 With right sides together and raw edges even, stitch the two fabric pieces together along the marked lines, pivoting at each corner and the point. Trim the seam to 6mm (1/4in), and snip off the corners in the tapering portion.

4 Turn right side out through the unstitched end, and press. When making the project, tack each tab to the right side of the main fabric with raw edges even, before stitching the seam.

SEE ALSO

Pleated fitted cover   176

BELOW ~ *Curtain headings are just one of the uses for tabs.*

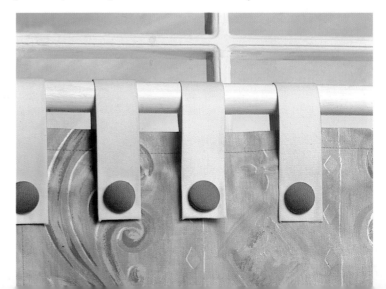

FABRIC

CHOOSING FABRIC

When choosing furnishing fabric, take into account aesthetic factors like the fabric's colour, pattern and texture, its weight and draping qualities, and whether it will suit the style or mood of your decor.

However, looks are not the only factor. The width the fabric comes in may be important too. Furnishing fabrics are at least 115–120cm (45–48in) wide, and the majority are 137–150cm (54–60in) wide. A few even come in 229cm (90in) or 305cm (120in) widths. These large widths will either be economical or impractical, depending on whether your project is very large or very small.

There are other practical considerations, too – such as where and how the fabric will be used, how much wear it will get and how often it will need to be cleaned.

A fabric's fibre content, along with the weave structure and the finishing process are the main factors determining how the fabric will perform. This information can generally be found on the fabric label.

FIBRES

Fibres are either natural, man-made or synthetic. (Sometimes man-made and synthetic fibres are treated as one category.)

NATURAL FIBRES
These come from vegetable and animal sources and include cotton, linen, wool and silk. They are resistant to dirt but may shrink when washed. Cotton, linen and silk will crease, and silk in particular is prone to fading and rotting in the sun.

MAN-MADE FIBRES
These fibres have been regenerated from natural materials and chemically treated. Acetate and viscose rayon, both made from cellulose, are the main examples of man-made furnishing fabrics. These are easy-care, they do not shrink and they are resistant to mould. Because of their silky feel, lustre and draping qualities, and because they are less likely to rot in the sun, man-made fibres are often used in place of silk.

SYNTHETIC FIBRES
Derived from chemicals, these fibres include acrylic, nylon and polyester. Stronger than natural fibres, they will not shrink or crease, but they do attract dirt.

BLENDS AND MIXTURES
Fibres are made into yarns, from which furnishing fabrics are woven. Often fibres are blended, or yarns are mixed, in order to take advantage of the best qualities of each fibre

without its drawbacks. For example, acrylic, which resists sunrot, is often blended with cotton or wool, which are both very prone to it, but which hang better than acrylic. Linen is frequently combined with cotton (called linen union) and/or synthetic fibres to make it resist wrinkles and creasing better.

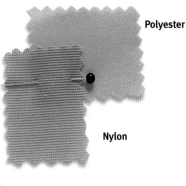

Polyester

Nylon

Silk

Cotton

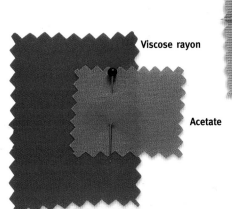

Viscose rayon

Acetate

WEAVES

The weave structure determines the texture of the fabric. Here are some of the weave structures most commonly found in furnishing fabrics.

PLAIN WEAVE

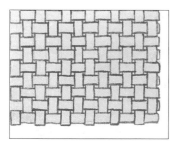

In *plain* weaves the *weft*, or *woof* (crosswise threads), goes under one and over one *warp* (lengthwise thread). Plain weaves include gingham, canvas, voile and muslin (all made from cotton) and taffeta (which is made from silk or silk-like fibres).

TWILL WEAVE

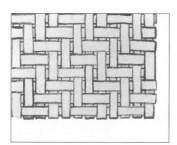

A *twill* weave (in which the weft moves one step to the left or right with each line) produces the diagonal texture of tartan.

SATIN WEAVE

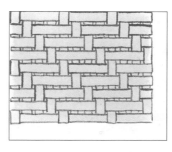

A *satin* weave (in which the weft threads are "floated" over

more than one and under one warp thread) has a smooth, lustrous surface.

JACQUARD WEAVE

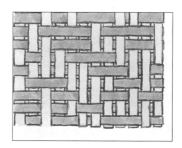

A *Jacquard* weave has complex patterns produced by combinations of plain, twill and satin weaves on a plain or satin-weave background. It is manufactured on a Jacquard loom. Examples of this weave include damask, brocade and tapestry fabric.

DOBBY WEAVE

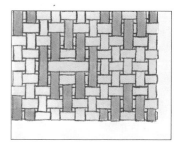

A *dobby* weave is made on a plain-weave loom with a dobby attachment. This skips warp threads, producing small-scale geometric designs such as the one shown here.

PILE WEAVE

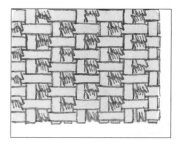

A *pile* weave such as velvet has an extra filling or warp thread, which is drawn up into loops that are cut or sheared, or left as loops.

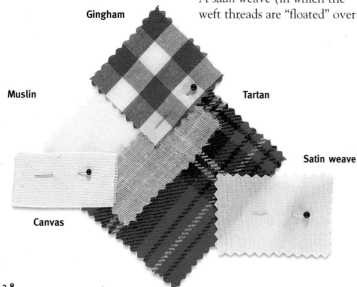

Gingham
Muslin
Tartan
Canvas
Satin weave

Jacquard
Dobby
Velvet

FINISHES

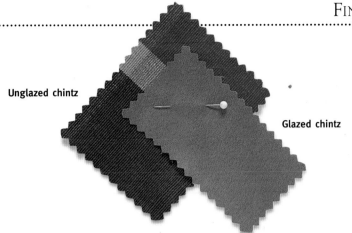

Unglazed chintz

Glazed chintz

Most furnishing fabrics have been given special finishes to improve the look, feel or care requirements. Glazing is one of the best-known, imparting a sheen to chintzes. Other common finishes include treatments to make a fabric resistant to sun, mildew, dirt, stains or creasing. Sizing, or dressing, is often used to give a fabric body, and most furnishing fabrics have been treated with flame retardants.

Washing generally removes special finishes, so dry cleaning is preferable unless you actually wish to remove it.

PERFORMANCE FACTORS

Before buying a fabric, borrow or purchase a large sample and take it home to see what it looks like in all lights.

If at all possible, buy all the fabric from one bolt to avoid potential problems with dye-lot variations. If you do have to buy from more than one bolt, it's a good idea to keep them apart.

When purchasing the fabric, examine it for flaws or other unacceptable marks.

CURTAINS

Check the care instructions when you choose a fabric. Unroll the bolt part way and gather the fabric up in your hand. Now look to see how well it drapes and what the pattern looks like when pleated. Make sure that it is straight, and that any pattern is not badly off-grain. Test it too for stretchiness, and crush it to see how much it creases.

ABOVE ~ Before buying, check what a fabric looks like when pleated or draped.

UPHOLSTERY AND LOOSE COVERS

Flame resistance is a legal requirement for fabrics used on sofas and chairs, so check that the fabric complies with regulations. If it doesn't you will have to use a fire-resistant interlining.

Upholstery fabric must have a strong, firm, even weave so that it will be hard-wearing. Avoid very thick fabrics. Bear in mind that plain fabrics and light or dark colours show dirt more than patterned or textured materials and medium colours.

LEFT~ *A fabric's draping qualities and translucency are the most important factors for curtains, but durability is the key consideration for upholstery and loose covers.*

SEE ALSO

SPECIAL FABRICS

Certain furnishing fabrics require special treatment when cutting out or sewing. So long as you know what to do, they should present no particular problem.

SILKS AND SHEERS

When pinning delicate sheers and silks, use very fine pins so that you won't damage the fabric. Place them only within the seam allowances, and remove them as soon as possible.

To make the fabric easier to cut, cover the cutting surface with a sheet so that it won't slip. Make sure your scissors are very sharp.

If the seams or the fabric catches on the machine or the seams pucker when you are stitching, place tissue paper or stabilizer between the machine and the fabric, removing it afterwards. If the two layers slip when you are stitching, place the tissue paper or stabilizer between the layers. Use narrow French seams.

RIGHT~ *It is worth taking particular care with sheer fabrics, as they are sometimes quite delicate.*

VELVET AND CHENILLE

Use only very fine pins in the seam allowances, and remove them as soon as possible. When cutting out, cut all pieces so they run in the same direction. Cut out one layer at a time, wrong side up (or right side up if you are matching a pattern). Cut in the direction of the pile.

Tack seams before stitching, to help prevent the fabric from shifting. A walking foot or even-feed foot on the machine also helps prevent slipping. Stitch in the direction of the pile, holding the fabric taut. If the fabric slips or the seam puckers, stitch with tissue paper or stabilizer between the layers. Avoid topstitching. Be sure to grade the seams. Press from the wrong side, with a towel on the ironing board. If you do have to press from the right side, use a wool pressing cloth, and press with the pile.

LACE

If the lace has decorative borders, place these at the edges or hemline, and do not hem them. Use French seams.

Use a roller foot or wrap transparent tape around the tips of the presser foot in order to prevent snags.

PVC AND OTHER PLASTICS

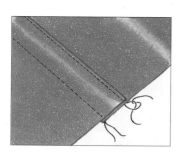

These fabrics can be used for tablecloths and placemats, shower curtains, even toaster covers. They have no grain and are easy to clean with a damp cloth, but they cannot be washed or dry-cleaned. They do not fray, but they tear easily and also tend to form permanent creases if left folded for any length of time. Avoid using pins, as they will leave permanent holes – use masking tape, a glue stick or paperclips instead. (Let the glue dry before stitching over it, and avoid stitching through the tape.)

Stitch with a long stitch and do not backstitch – tie the threads instead. If you find the fabric sticking as you stitch, place tissue paper above and below it and remove after stitching. The best seam for this is a lapped seam, in which you trim off

PRE-QUILTED FABRICS

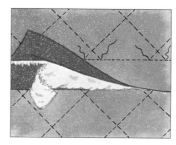

Fabrics that come pre-quilted are useful for bedcovers, pelmets, tiebacks, placemats, and items like computer covers. To avoid bulk in seams, unpick the quilting in the seam allowances after stitching, and trim the wadding back to the seamline, as shown above. For hems, stitch along the hemline and then unpick the quilting and trim the wadding away below this line before hemming.

one seam allowance and lap it over the other piece by the width of the remaining seam allowance, with right sides up, so that the cut edge aligns with the seamline. Stick together with glue stick or fusible web, then topstitch along the overlapping edge and again 1.2cm (½in) away from it, as shown.

Turn up the hem only once, finger press it and topstitch (or omit a hem altogether if the PVC is heavy).

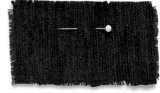

Chenille

Lace

PVC

Pre-quilted fabric

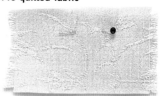

Damask

Velvet

ONE-WAY FABRICS

Many fabrics must be cut so that all the pieces lie in the same direction. On one-way patterns, the pattern is not the same if turned the opposite way up. On pile or nap fabrics, either the pile or a finishing process means that the fabric looks different depending on which way up it is. Pile fabrics like velvet look richer if the pile feels smooth when stroked from bottom to top. Shiny fabrics like satin also look different according to which way up they are.

The nap is not always obvious, so treat all fabrics as though they had a nap. Mark which way up by drawing an arrow on a piece of tape stuck on the wrong side of fabric.

RAILROADING

On projects like curtain valances and bed valances, where the cut length is shorter than the cut width, fabrics are often "railroaded" (cut with the lengthwise grain running horizontally). However, this may not be possible on a patterned fabric, since many designs will not look right if turned sideways.

RIGHT~ *Fabrics with a one-way pattern must all run the same direction in use.*

PATTERN MATCHING

On soft furnishings, even small patterns look better matched, and it is of course essential with large patterns, both vertically and horizontally. If you are making curtains for more than one window, large patterns will also need to match from window to window.

On full-length curtains, there should be a full repeat (the vertical distance between each complete part of the pattern) just below the heading, which is seen first.

On sill-length curtains, the bottom is more noticeable, so place the pattern with the full repeat ending at the hem.

If you are using sill-length and full-length curtains in one room, place the full repeats just beneath the headings on all windows so that they match.

The fabric label will give the fabric repeat, or you can measure it for yourself. For how to use this in calculating fabric requirements, see page 73.

Most patterns match at the selvedges. If trimming off the selvedge (which is usually recommended for curtains, to prevent the seam from puckering) would affect the pattern matching, simply clip into the selvedge every 10cm (4in) or so instead.

Curtains are not the only project where pattern matching is crucial: virtually all soft furnishings require it. Be particularly careful when mitring corners on fabric with a large check or stripe. If your mitre is not precise, the lines will not meet. Using a protractor to measure the 45-degree angle can help here.

LADDERSTITCH

When joining seams, the best way of accurately matching the pattern is to use ladderstitch. A variation of slipstitch, this hand stitch allows you to see the pattern as you tack the seam.

1 Press under one seam allowance and lay this along the seam allowance of the other piece. The right sides of both pieces should be uppermost, and the pattern matching. Pin.

2 Bring the needle and thread up through the folded edge. Holding the needle vertically, insert it into the unfolded piece along the seamline, next to the thread.

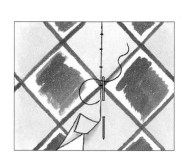

3 Bring it up 2cm (¾in) further down the seamline. Pull the thread through, then insert it into the folded fabric on the seamline, next to the thread, and bring it out 2cm (¾in) down. Continue in the same way. When the whole seam has been tacked, fold the fabric with right sides together, ready to stitch.

LININGS

Curtain lining fabrics are most often sateen, a tightly woven cotton with a slight sheen. Sateen is commonly available in white, cream and ivory but also comes in a range of colours, in various qualities and prices. Expensive linings retain their body after cleaning, while cheaper ones become limp after the dressing disappears.

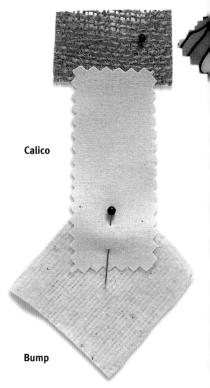

Buckram

Calico

Bump

LININGS AND INTERLININGS

RIGHT ~ *A coloured lining that contrasts or coordinates with the curtain fabric can be a decorative feature in itself.*

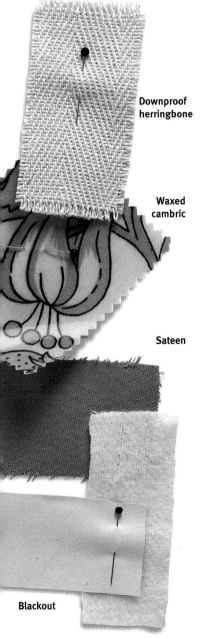

Downproof herringbone

Waxed cambric

Sateen

Blackout

Natural domette

An alternative to sateen would be a fabric that coordinates with the main fabric in colour or texture. An aluminium-coated lining reflects heat and cold, providing extra insulation. Blackout lining, which comes in cream or white, blocks out all light and so can be useful in the bedroom or nursery.

Calico, waxed cambric and downproof herringbone are all plain-woven cottons used for cushion pads.

Interlining may be used inside curtain linings. Domette is a lightweight brushed cotton suitable for interlining curtains, pelmets and swags and tails. Bump is a thicker, loosely woven cotton, suitable for interlining heavy curtains.

Buckram, made from cotton or jute, is used to stiffen curtains with hand-pleated headings, tiebacks and pelmets. It comes in many different widths and weights. Various forms of extra-firm interfacing can also be used for these very successfully.

SEE ALSO

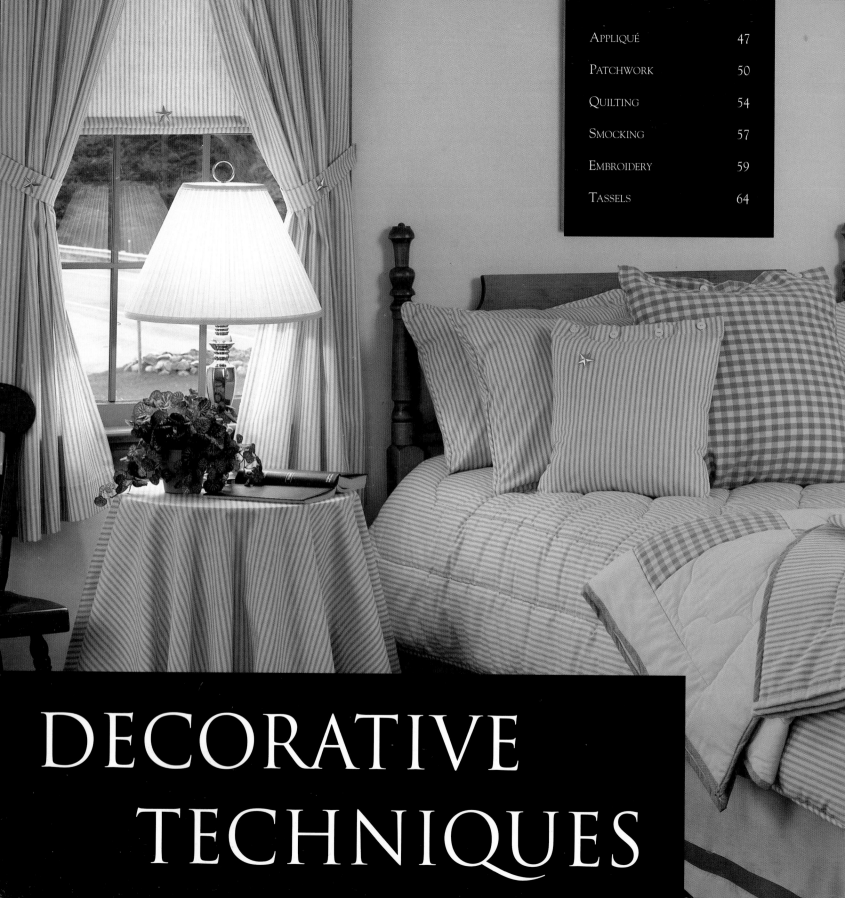

DECORATIVE TECHNIQUES

APPLIQUÉ

Appliqué, which involves applying cut-out fabric motifs to another piece of fabric, can be used to decorate virtually any soft furnishings, from table napkins and bath towels to duvet covers and curtains.

BASIC APPLIQUÉ TECHNIQUES

There are two main techniques. In traditional turned-edge appliqué, the raw edges of the fabric shape are turned under and stitched in place, usually by hand. In machine appliqué, the raw edges are not turned under but simply covered with zigzag stitching. An amalgam of these, raw-edge appliqué, can be used for felt or closely woven wool, neither of which will fray, or for a project in which frayed edges are a design feature.

Most fabrics are suitable for appliqué, but light- to medium-weight cotton is especially good for beginners because it does not fray badly. Felt is easy to appliqué too.

When planning your design, consider decorating the appliqué motifs with machine embroidery. The two crafts complement each other well – leaves for appliqué, for example, can be machine embroidered with veins.

TURNED-EDGE APPLIQUÉ

1 Draw out your design on paper, incorporating only straight edges and gentle curves if you are a beginner. Use a dotted line to indicate areas where pieces overlap. Make templates for the motifs, without adding a seam allowance to them.

2 Cut out your fabric base (if using), making it a little larger than the required size. If the design is complex, lightly draw it on the right side of the fabric base, using the templates from step 1 and a fabric marker.

3 Draw around the templates on the right side of the motif fabric(s) with the fabric marker, leaving at least 1.2cm (½in) between pieces.

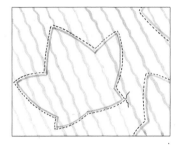

4 If desired, staystitch just outside the seamline of each motif using a hand or machine straight stitch, to help the edges turn under more readily.

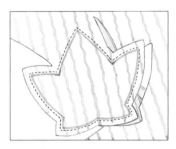

5 Cut out the shapes, leaving a 6mm (¼in) seam allowance around each shape, except where it is overlapped by another piece.

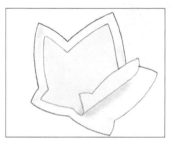

6 If you are using flimsy fabric or if you want crisp edges, you may wish to interface the motifs. Draw around the templates in reverse on lightweight fusible interfacing, but do not add a seam allowance. Cut out, centre on the wrong side of the motif and iron on.

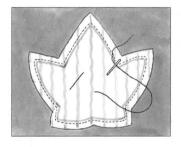

7 Pin, tack or glue (with fabric glue) the motifs to the background fabric, positioning the underneath ones first. Secure only the centre of each motif, and do not turn under the edges at this stage.

47

8 Use your needle to roll under the seam allowance for about 5cm (2in), pressing it with your fingers, and hand stitch in place. Continue needle turning and finger pressing the seam allowances as you stitch, remembering not to turn under the edge on any underlaps.

9 Slipstitch is often used for appliqué but blanket stitch, hemming stitch, stab stitch, feather stitch, cross stitch, running stitch or machine stitching can be used instead.

10 On an outward corner, fold down the tip of the point, then fold down each side, as you stitch. On an inward corner, or valley, snip into the seam allowance before turning under each side and stitching. As you work your way around, clip into seam allowances on inward curves, and notch them on outward curves.

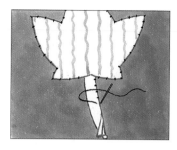

11 For appliqué stems in a flower design, either cut thin curving strips of fabric or use straight pieces of bias binding (home-made or ready-made) and stretch it into a curve. Turn under the edges, stitch the inward curve first, then the outward curve, and finally press it.

12 When the stitching of the motif is complete, remove any tacking.

TIPS

If precise positioning is important in your design, pre-basting is a good idea. Instead of using the needle-turning method in step 8, turn under the seam allowances and tack them in place before positioning each motif on the base fabric.

Alternatively, try this trick. Iron fusible web onto the back of the fabric for the motif, cut out the motif, then use your iron to warm the motif. Now quickly peel off the backing paper and turn under the seam allowances all around with your fingers – they will stick to the fusible web. (You can then use the fusible web on the rest of the motif to hold the motif in place instead of having to tack it to the base fabric – just lay it in position right side up and warm with your iron.)

MACHINE APPLIQUÉ

1 Prepare your fabric base and templates as for turned-edge appliqué (steps 1 and 2). If using flimsy fabric for motifs, it can be interfaced if desired, but do it prior to cutting out the motifs.

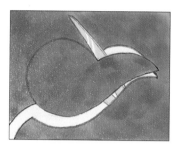

2 Using a fabric marker, draw around the templates on the right side of the motif fabric(s), but do not add a seam allowance. Cut out the motifs along these lines.

3 Fusible web gives a smooth appliqué and is especially useful for large motifs. Draw around the templates in reverse onto the backing paper, then cut them out, making the web shapes slightly smaller. Following the manufacturer's instructions, iron fusible web to the wrong side of the cut-out motifs, being careful not to get any adhesive on the iron. Remove the paper backing and iron the motifs in position on the base fabric.

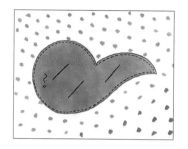

4 Alternatively, if you don't wish to use fusible web, pin, tack or glue the motifs in place, and machine straight stitch close to the edge. (If you have trouble stitching close to the edge, particularly on small pieces, you could cut out the motifs with a seam allowance then trim away the seam allowance after stitching.)

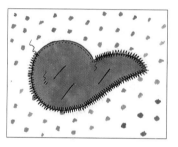

5 Cover the raw edges, and any straight stitching, with zigzag or machine satin stitch (see page 63). You could also decorate the appliqué with machine embroidery. Remove any tacking.

RAW-EDGE APPLIQUÉ

1 Prepare the fabric base and templates as for machine appliqué (step 1, see page 48).

2 Using a fabric marker, draw around the templates on the right side of the motif fabric(s), but do not add a seam allowance. Cut out the motifs along the outlines.

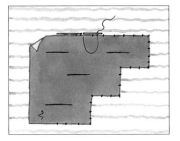

3 Pin, tack or glue in position, or use fusible web as for machine appliqué (step 3). Now hand stitch in place as for turned-edge appliqué (step 9). Remove any tacking.

APPLIQUÉ TOWELS

Appliqué can be used for fabric motifs on ready-made items such as towels or a bathmat. Choose a washable fabric for the motifs – perhaps one from which you can cut out selected motifs, like the seahorse, shell and starfish in the photograph shown here. The entire fabric – or a similar one, as here – could be used for a blind or curtains. Or use towelling fabric in a contrasting colour for the motif. Either the turned-edge or machine-appliqué method is suitable.

Sheets, duvet covers, napkins, placemats, tablecloths, plain cushions and even shower curtains are potential candidates for appliqué and provide an ideal opportunity for personalizing ready-made soft furnishings.

LEFT~ *Appliqué shapes on the towels reinforce this bathroom's marine theme.*

PATCHWORK

Patchwork is an absorbing craft used mainly for soft furnishings. Although devotees often spend many enjoyable hours constructing intricate designs, it is possible to create stunning effects quite quickly.

BASIC PATCHWORK TECHNIQUES

Patchwork designs are well suited to quilting, but this is by no means essential. The designs can also be successfully combined with appliqué.

FABRIC

Choose fabrics that do not stretch or fray, and that are the same weight, thickness and fibre content. Natural fibres are easier to work with and will look better than man-made or synthetic fibres. Scraps can, of course, be used too, but bear in mind that they will probably wear out sooner than new fabrics.

Fabric from specialist patchwork shops and mail-order companies is available not only by the metre or yard but

TIP

Also invaluable is a quilter's ruler. This is a see-through plastic ruler with lines calibrated over its width.

Always remember to replace the protective guard on the rotary cutter whenever you lay it down, even just for a moment – the blade is lethal.

in a convenient size known as a "fat quarter", which is half a yard cut in half crosswise – in other words, 46×56cm (18×22in).

CUTTING OUT WITH A ROTARY CUTTER

Whereas templates have traditionally been used for cutting out patchwork shapes, it is quicker to cut simple shapes with a rotary cutter on a self-healing cutting mat. Several layers can be cut at once, with great speed and accuracy. Because this equipment can be used for cutting out fabric for other soft furnishing projects as well, it is a good investment. If you haven't used a rotary cutter, practise on fabric scraps before cutting into fabric.

1 Place the fabric squarely on the cutting mat, lining it up with the grid lines. Lay the quilter's ruler over the fabric, with the right-hand edge of the ruler on the inner line of the left-hand selvedge.

2 Pull away the protective guard on the cutter. With your right hand holding the

cutter at a 45-degree angle to the cutting mat, and flat against the ruler, place your left hand on the ruler (away from the blade) and press down hard on the ruler. (Reverse these instructions if you are left-handed.) Push the cutter forward, away from you, trimming off the selvedge from the bottom edge to the top edge. Lift up the ruler and remove the selvedge without moving the main fabric.

3 To cut strips of fabric, line up the left-hand edge you trimmed in step 2 with the line on the ruler corresponding to the width of the strip. The strips will need to be 1.2cm ($\frac{1}{2}$in) wider than the required finished width, to allow for the seams. Cut, lift, remove and reposition as before.

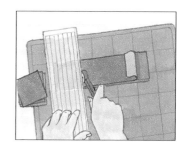

4 To cut the strips into squares or rectangles, stack several strips together with the left-hand, top and bottom edges even and lined up with the grid on the cutting mat. Repeat twice, so that you cut through a few piles at one time. Using the quilter's ruler, line up the appropriate line on the ruler with the left-hand edge, and cut as before. Continue in this way along the strips.

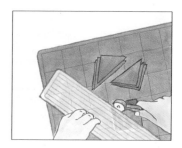

5 To cut squares into triangles, stack several squares so the raw edges are even and

lined up with the grid. Place the ruler on the diagonal of the square. Cut as before.

CUTTING OUT WITH SCISSORS

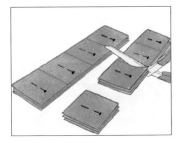

If you don't have a rotary cutter, a self-healing cutting mat and a quilter's ruler, measure and draw the lines on one layer of fabric using a metre ruler (yardstick) and a sharp fabric marker. Cut out with sharp shears. Depending on your fabric, you may be able to cut more than one layer at a time if you pin them together at regular intervals.

SEAMS

Some traditional patchwork, known as the English method, involves tacking individual patches to papers cut to the same shape, minus the seam allowance, then hand sewing the edges of the patches together and removing the tacking and papers.

However, for simple shapes, the technique known as the American method is faster. The pieces are joined with right sides together, and stitching can be by hand running stitch or machine straight stitch. The latter is

obviously more practicable for large projects. It's important that the seams, which are normally 6mm (¼in) wide, are exactly the same width. Many sewing machine manufacturers offer a special patchwork foot that allows you to stitch seams of precisely this width.

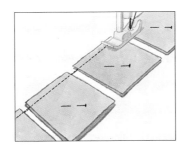

When joining pieces, it saves time to stitch them in a a chain, then cut them apart later, rather than continually stopping and starting.

PRESSING

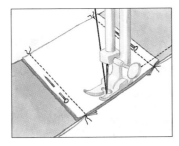

After stitching, the seams are normally pressed to one side, usually towards the darker side. Press as you go, since seams always have to be pressed before other seams are stitched across them. When joining rows, press matching seam allowances in opposite directions to reduce bulk.

BLOCKING

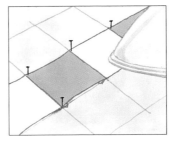

Strips of patches should be blocked to straighten them. Draw a grid on your ironing table, then pin all of the edges into the padded surface, so that they are in line with the grid. Press with a steam iron, using a pressing cloth if the fabric is delicate.

PIECING

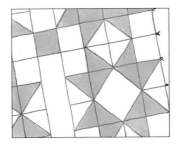

The type of patchwork most suitable for soft furnishing projects involves *piecing* – joining one or more simple shapes, like squares, rectangles

and/or triangles, into larger and larger units. The patches can be joined at random, or they can form an overall pattern.

Often patches are joined into repeating "blocks", or sometimes long strips, which are then stitched together. They may be joined edge-to-edge or separated by fabric strips known as sashes.

STRIP PIECING

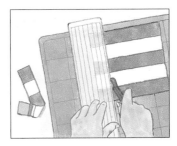

Another way of speeding up the piecing process is to join horizontal strips, rather than patches, together then cut these rectangles into vertical strips. The technique can be used only where a sequence is repeated at least a few times, or where the sequence does not matter. The comforter shown in the photograph here uses strip piecing throughout.

COLOURFUL SQUARES COMFORTER

This comforter is simple to make, as it is built up entirely from 6cm (2½in) squares in five colours, machine stitched together and finished with a 15cm (6in) deep edging. Each patch is 5cm (2in) square after stitching, so a 210 × 270cm (7 × 9ft) comforter, to fit a single bed, would be 36 patches wide and 48 patches long within the edging.

The block in the diagram represents one-eighth of the whole comforter, because two blocks fit across the width and four blocks along the length. The top half of the block is a repeat of the bottom half but turned around. Therefore, you can save yourself a lot of work by using the strip-piecing technique.

If you wish to make a comforter for a 137cm (4ft 6in) wide double bed, add half of one block to the width, and increase the number of strips by 25 per cent. For a comforter to fit a king-sized bed, add a whole block to the width, and increase the number of strips by 50 per cent.

The colours given in the instructions relate to those in the photograph but you could substitute colours of your choice.

For a comforter measuring 210 x 270cm (7 x 9ft) you will need the following: 115cm (45in) wide fabric for patchwork and edging: 4.2m (4⅝yd) of blue, 1.3m (1½yd) of white, 1.1m (1⅛yd) of green, 1.4m (1½yd) of red and 80cm (⅞yd) of paisley. In addition, you will need a 230 x 290cm (92 x 116in) rectangle of blue for backing and self binding; plus a 225 x 285cm (90 x 114in) rectangle of wadding.

1 Using a rotary cutter, self-healing cutting mat and quilter's ruler, and cutting several layers at a time, cut out the following 96 × 6cm (40 × 2½in) strips: 48 blue (B), 20 white (W), 16 green (G), 12 red (R) and 12 paisley (P).

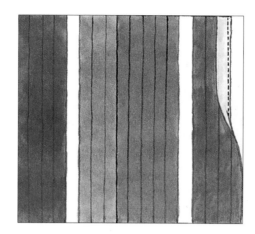

2 With right sides together and taking exactly 5mm (¼in) seams, join the strips along the long edges, making six different rectangles of 18 strips each in the following sequences:
Type 1: BBBBWPPPGGGGGWBBBB
Type 2: WBBBBWRRGPRRWBBBBW
Type 3: PWBBBBWRGPRWBBBBWG
Type 4: PRWBBBBWGPWBBBBWRG
Type 5: PRRWBBBBWWBBBBWRRG
Type 6: GGGGWBBBBBBBBWPPPG

3 Press the seam allowances towards the darker fabric. Label each rectangle with its number from the chart so you won't forget which is which.

4 Using the rotary cutter, cutting mat and quilter's ruler again, cut each rectangle across the seams into 16 multicoloured strips, each 6cm (2½in) wide. With a steam iron, block the strips to straighten them. Keep the strips from each rectangle together, still labelled.

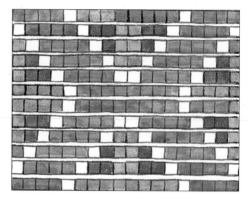

5 Join twelve strips – two from each rectangle – in the following sequence (starting at the top): type 1, 2, 3, 4, 5, 6, and then upside down 6, 5, 4, 3, 2, 1. The patches will be in the arrangement shown in the above diagram, which is one block.

6 Repeat step 5 for the other seven blocks. Block with a steam iron as before, then join the blocks in pairs along the side edges. Finally, join these along the top and bottom edges.

7 Measure the patchwork – it should be 181 × 241cm (72½ × 96½in). Cut and join together, end-to-end, enough 6cm (2½in) wide red strips to make two red strips each as long as the width of the patchwork. Repeat to make four blue strips to this length. With right sides together and taking 5mm (¼in) seams, join these to the top edge in the following order: blue, red, blue. Repeat for the bottom edge.

8 Repeat the cutting and joining in step 7 to make two red and four blue strips, each the length of the patchwork with the edging on the ends. Join them to the sides in the same way as the strips for the ends.

9 Make a "quilt sandwich" with the patchwork, backing and wadding, and quilt with hand running stitches (see Quilting). Bind the edges with self binding (see page 28).

LEFT ~ *This patchwork comforter can be made by the quick "strip piecing" method.*

SEE ALSO

QUILTING

In soft furnishings, quilting – by either hand or machine – is useful not only for bed covers but also for cushions, placemats, curtain tiebacks and even curtain pelmets.

BASIC QUILTING TECHNIQUES

WADDING
Although old blankets were once used as filling in quilts and still are sometimes used, these days wadding is generally preferred. Polyester wadding, which is washable and comes in sheets, is available in 60g (2oz), 115g (4oz), 180g (6oz), 220g (8oz) and 350g (12oz) weights. The thinnest one – 60g (2oz) – is the easiest to stitch. Cotton wadding is also available, but it must be closely quilted to prevent it from forming lumps, and it is not washable.

Domette, a lightweight woven curtain interlining, is a good filler for wall hangings, because it is quite flat.

"QUILT SANDWICH"
Before the three layers are quilted together, they need to be temporarily joined so that they will stay flat and smooth, with the edges even, while you quilt.

1 Spread the backing out, wrong side up, on a clean surface. Lay the wadding on top of the backing.

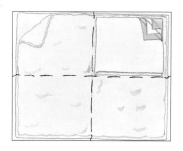

2 Centre the quilt top over the wadding. To make it easier, mark the centre of the wadding with lines of dark thread, fold the fabric in quarters right sides together, then place it over the centre before unfolding. The backing and wadding should be 7.5–10cm (3–4in) larger all around than the top.

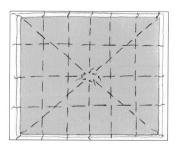

3 Either safety pin or hand tack the layers together. To tack, start at the centre and work outwards to each corner, then work horizontal and vertical lines at intervals.

4 A much quicker method of preparing the layers for quilting is to spray the wadding all over with spray adhesive, then place the fabric on top. The backing is secured in the same way. This will not affect your fabric or how well it washes. However, it is essential to protect the floor or other work surface with plastic sheeting and to work in a well-ventilated room.

QUILTING PATTERNS
The quilting pattern can be produced in various ways. All the approaches described and illustrated here can be done by hand or by machine.

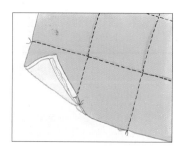

The least conspicuous quilting for patchwork is to "stitch in the ditch" – ie, just alongside the seamlines of patchwork or appliqué, on the side with no seam allowance. If the seamlines are too far apart in places, you can combine this with other stitching lines, such as rows of parallel diagonal lines.

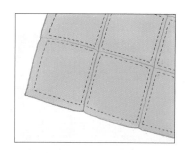

Alternatively, stitch about 1cm (⅜in) inside the seamline on each patch – this is known as "contour stitching".

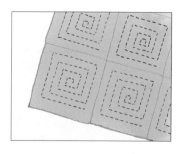

"Echo quilting" incorporates quilting lines that echo the shapes of the patchwork or appliqué design over the whole surface of the quilt.

A simpler approach, for non-patchwork, is to follow the lines of the fabric pattern, as in the quilt shown here, creating an appliquéd effect.

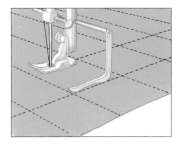

Or you can do "background quilting" in a simple overall pattern such as diamonds; masking tape guidelines on the fabric, or a seam guide-bar on the machine walking foot (see Machine Quilting, page 56), will be useful for this.

ABOVE ~ *Quilting around the pattern of the fabric creates a patchwork effect on this comforter.*

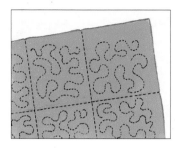

A different style of quilting is "motif quilting", which uses a water-removable fabric marker and a quilting template to create an intricate stitch pattern that is unrelated to the fabric. Yet another approach is freehand quilting, where the stitching is at random over the quilt top.

MACHINE QUILTING

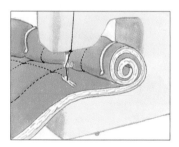

This is the fastest way of quilting (though it is unfortunately not feasible for thick, large comforters or king-sized quilts). If possible, use a walking foot, also known as an even-feed foot, on the machine, to prevent the fabric from puckering or pulling. Set the machine for a medium straight stitch. Keep the bulk of the fabric on the left-hand side, and roll up the excess fabric on the right-hand side as tightly as possible, holding it in place with quilting clips (or even bicycle clips).

Stitch in a pattern that requires you to stop and start as little as possible.

An alternative is to quilt with free embroidery (see page 63).

HAND QUILTING

You can do this in your lap or in a large quilting hoop or frame. Hold one hand above and one beneath the quilt, and wear a thimble. Use a single 45cm (18in) length of quilting thread at a time, and small, even running stitches along the line of the pattern. Take several stitches before pulling the needle and thread through each time.

TIED QUILTING

This is a good way to join the layers of large or very thick quilts and is much quicker than stitching. Join the layers temporarily as for conventional quilting. Use either a strong, natural-fibre thread or an embroidery cotton such as coton à broder, stranded cotton, pearl cotton or crochet cotton.

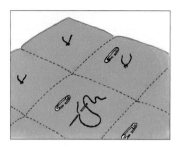

Starting at the top, with the thread unknotted, take two small stitches, one on top of the other, then tie the ends in a reef knot (not too tightly or the fabric might tear). Trim the ends to the same length. If desired, use a pin to separate the two ends of the knotted thread.

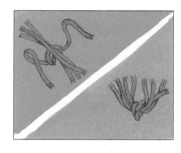

Alternatively, for a fluffy tuft, either thread the needle with a few strands of thread, or cut three short strands of the thread, place them over the reef knot while tying the second half of the knot, then cut all the ends evenly.

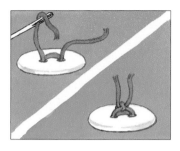

Buttons can be tied or sewn on too for a decorative effect. Use a needle to take the thread through the holes of the button, then tie the ends in a knot.

FINISHING

Trim the edges of the backing and wadding even with those of the front. Bind the edges, and remove any tacking thread or safety pins. If you have used a fabric marker, spray the quilt top lightly with water in order to remove it, following the manufacturer's instructions.

SMOCKING

A decorative and highly traditional way of gathering fabric, smocking makes an attractive fixed curtain heading, valance or shelf edging and can also be used for cushions.

USING SMOCKING IN THE HOME

Smocking consists of a series of tiny, even gathers held together by embroidery stitches. Any fabric can be smocked, but cotton, linen, wool and silk look especially nice. Gingham and other fabrics with a small, regular pattern are easy to smock because the pattern can be used when gathering.

BASIC SMOCKING
This technique can be adapted to whatever item you are smocking. The fabric needs to be about three times the desired finished width, though less is required with thick fabric.

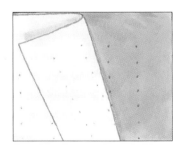

1 If you are not using the fabric pattern as a guide, iron transfer smocking dots to the wrong side of the fabric. The dots are usually 6mm–1cm (¼–⅜in) apart, and the rows are about

1–1.2cm (⅜–½in) apart. The finer the fabric, the closer together they should be.

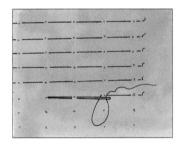

2 Using strong thread, work hand running stitch evenly from the wrong side of the fabric. Sew from right to left, knotting the thread and taking a backstitch at the beginning. With your needle, take up about one-third of the depth of each pleat. At the end, leave the ends loose. Make sure that each row of stitches exactly aligns with the previous rows.

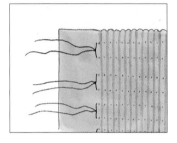

3 Pull up the gathers to form tiny, even pleats. Tie the threads in pairs at the end.

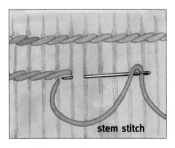

stem stitch

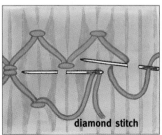

diamond stitch

4 Use one or more embroidery stitches to smock the pleated area, working from the right side and leaving the seam allowance free of embroidery.

Two popular smocking stitches – stem, or outline, stitch and diamond stitch – are shown here.

SMOCKED GINGHAM CURTAINS WITH SELF FRILL
Smocking tape is available for curtain headings (see page 88) but this only gives a smock-like effect. A genuine smocked heading is sewn completely by hand. Use it for a valance or for curtains where the heading can remain closed, since the curtains will not draw back satisfactorily. Allow for a curtain fullness of about 2½–3 times.

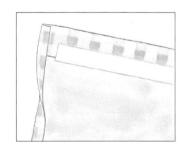

1 Cut out and join widths of gingham as for unlined curtains (see page 74). At the top of each curtain, press 7cm (2¾in) to the wrong side, and tack in place. Position a strip

of 5cm (2in) wide fusible interfacing over the raw edge so that the interfacing is 4cm (1½in) from the top and 5cm (2in) in from the side edges. Iron in place. Stitch 2.5cm (1in) double hems at the sides and a 7.5cm (3in) double hem at the bottom.

2 Work eight rows of running stitch, starting 3cm (1¼in) from the top and spacing the rows 1cm (⅜in) apart. Use the gingham as a grid, taking the needle over the white checks and under the coloured ones, so that the coloured areas will be at the front when gathered up. Fasten the thread at the beginning of each row securely with a knot and a backstitch, and leave a long tail at the end of the row.

3 Gather up the rows to form even pleats. Tie the threads in pairs.

4 Using six strands of floss, work diamond stitch over the pleats (see page 57) starting 4cm (1½in) from the top. Remove the gathering stitches.

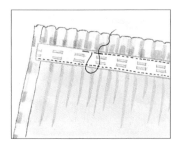

5 Hand sew standard curtain tape to the back of the heading, centring it over

RIGHT ~ Smocking makes a very elegant fixed heading for curtains or a valance.

interfacing and turning under both ends. Use a double row of backstitch to make it secure. Insert curtain hooks, but do not gather up the tape.

TAILORED SMOCKED CURTAINS
This style looks very elegant on wool curtains but can be used for other fabrics too.

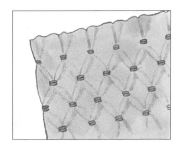

1 Make curtains with a stiffened heading (see Hand-made Headings, page 90). Use transfer dots to make the gathers on the wrong side. Work the rows of running stitch and the smocking near the top edge.

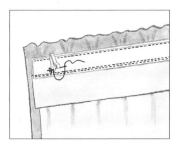

2 Cut a length of 2.5cm (1in) wide webbing tape as

long as the curtain width after smocking. Using a lapped seam, stitch the back of it to a strip of lining fabric that is the same length as the tape and is twice the width.

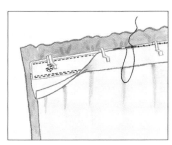

3 Hand sew the webbing to the back of the smocked heading 1.2cm (½in) from the top edge, using backstitch and picking up the buckram but not the main fabric in the stitches. Now hand stitch sew-on hooks to the webbing.

4 Turn under the raw edges of the lining and fold it up over the webbing, leaving the hooks projecting over the top. Slipstitch the top edge and both ends.

SEE ALSO

EMBROIDERY

Use hand and machine embroidery to add decorative detail to a wide range of soft furnishings, from tiebacks and table linen to pillowcases and towels.

HAND EMBROIDERY

Beautiful examples of crewel work bed hangings, whitework bedlinen, cutwork table linen and needlepoint cushion covers have been produced for centuries. Along with hand-worked samplers, these items are works of art in themselves. On a less ambitious scale, hand embroidery can be used to create small motifs and borders on soft furnishings very quickly.

THREADS
A variety of cotton embroidery threads can be used for hand embroidery, including stranded embroidery cotton (the six strands of which can be separated and used singly, in pairs or in threes if wished), coton à broder, pearl cotton (available in three thicknesses) and matt embroidery thread. Linen, silk and metallic threads are also available from specialist shops. Embroidery wools such as crewel, Persian and tapestry wools are employed too.

EQUIPMENT
Use a crewel needle, which is small and sharp, for freehand embroidery; a chenille needle, which is larger but still sharp, for embroidering with heavy threads; and a tapestry needle, which is blunt, for counted-thread embroidery. They all come in various sizes.

A frame or a hoop is also essential, as it will hold the fabric taut and square, preventing distortion.

When hand embroidering, use a thread no longer than 38–50cm (15–20in) so that it won't fray or tangle. Avoid using knots – weave the ends into the back instead. (At the very beginning, you *can* knot the thread, taking the needle through from the top, about 5cm (2in) away from where the first stitch will be, and in the path of the subsequent stitches. Once the end is covered with the stitching, snip off the knot.)

STITCHES
Embroidery stitches are worked using either the "stabbing" method, in which the stitch is done in two stages, with one hand above

satin stitch

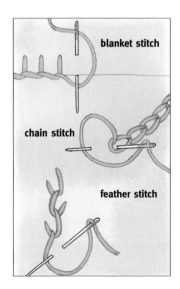

blanket stitch

chain stitch

feather stitch

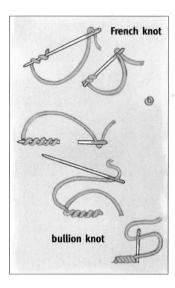

French knot

bullion knot

and one below the fabric; or the "sewing" method, in which the stitch is done in one scooping movement. The sewing method is faster, but the stabbing method produces a more even tension.

Embroidery stitches are grouped into four types, according to how they are

constructed. The best-known *flat stitches* are running stitch and backstitch (see Hand Stitching, page 14), stem stitch (see Smocking) and satin stitch. *Crossed stitches* include herringbone stitch (see Hand Stitching, page 15), basic cross stitch (see overleaf) and a number of variations of these. Blanket stitch, chain stitch and feather stitch are common *looped stitches*. The best-known *knotted stitches* are the French knot and the bullion knot.

Hand embroidery falls into one of two categories: counted thread embroidery, which is worked over a particular number of threads, or freehand embroidery, which is worked independently of the background.

COUNTED THREAD EMBROIDERY

This is traditionally worked on an evenweave fabric, which has the same number of weft (horizontal) threads as warp (vertical) threads, ranging from 11 to 32 threads per 2.5cm (1in). You can often use evenweave fabric, which is generally cotton or linen and comes in different colours, for a soft furnishing project. However, other fabrics can be used instead, if they have an inherent grid in the surface pattern; a checked or polkadotted fabric, for example, works well.

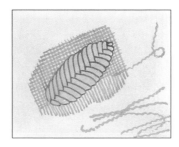

To work counted thread embroidery on fabric with no inherent grid, use "waste-canvas". This evenweave fabric is tacked to the right side of the main fabric, and the embroidery is worked through both layers. The waste canvas is then removed, one thread at a time, from the embroidery.

Counted thread embroidery is worked from charted designs, with each square in the grid representing one stitch. Thread colours are indicated by colours or symbols in the squares.

BLACKWORK

Traditionally embroidered in black silk thread on white linen, blackwork was originally used to decorate bed linen. It is perfect for borders or single motifs and can look very striking when filling in outlines made from stem or chain stitch. It consists of geometric patterns built up from straight stitches like backstitch or running stitch, worked vertically, horizontally or diagonally. The spacing of the stitches creates tonal effects in the design.

COUNTED CROSS STITCH

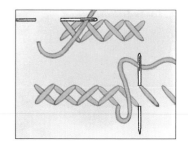

The best-known type of counted thread embroidery, this is often used for mono-grams and decorative borders and is well suited to naive, folk-art designs. It may be worked over any number of threads, though two is the norm. The diagonal stitch on the top of each cross should always slope in the same direction. Cross stitch can be worked horizontally, vertically or diagonally, and either by

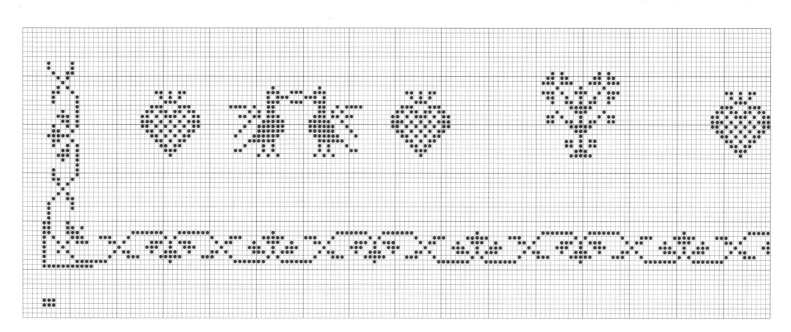

ABOVE ~ *Use this chart to work the repeat embroidery motif on the bed linen shown opposite. It is worked in cross stitch using two strands of embroidery thread on waste canvas with 12 threads per 2.5 cm (1 in).*

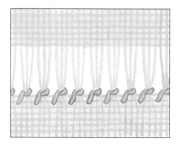

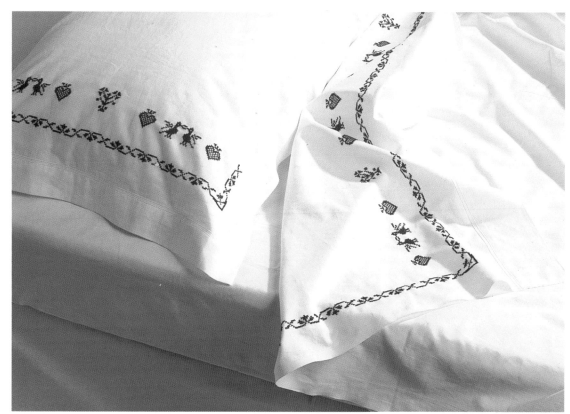

ABOVE ~ *Work counted cross stitch on waste canvas to embroider bed linen and table linen. The chart for this is shown opposite.*

3 Hemstitch looks like this from the right side. If you prefer the look of the stitches in the previous step, work them from the right side instead of the wrong side.

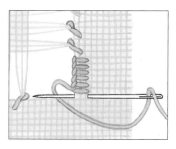

4 At corners, both warp and weft threads are removed, and the edges reinforced with blanket stitch.

completing one cross at a time, or by working a row of diagonals in one direction and then working the other diagonals.

DRAWN THREAD WORK

Generally used to decorate tablecloths and placemats, this openwork technique involves removing some of the warp and/or weft threads then embroidering over some of the remaining threads, most often with hemstitching. A coarse evenweave fabric is the easiest for beginners. The most basic drawn thread work is done as follows.

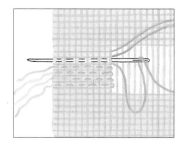

1 Mark the centre and tack the area from which the threads will be removed. With sharp embroidery scissors, cut the horizontal threads to be removed and ease them out to each side with a tapestry needle. With the same needle, darn the ends into the wrong side of the fabric at the edges, trimming away the excess.

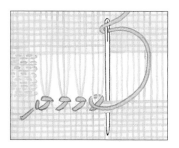

2 Hemstitch the edge as shown, working from the wrong side. If you hemstitch the opposite edge as well, binding the same threads, this is known as ladder stitch.

OTHER OPENWORK

Other openwork techniques include *hardanger embroidery* (with groups of satin stitch enclosing cut-away areas), *pulled thread work* (in which embroidery stitches pull some threads together and others apart) and *cutwork* (floral motifs created by outlining with buttonhole stitch and running stitch, then cutting away portions of the fabric next to the outline). All of these techniques are mainly used for table linen.

FREEHAND EMBROIDERY

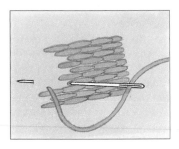

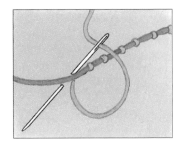

All the stitches referred to here, including cross stitch, can be used in freehand embroidery. Some, such as running stitch, backstitch, stem stitch and chain stitch, are best for outlining, while others – including satin stitch and long-and-short stitch (shown above) – are ideal for filling in an outline.

CREWEL WORK

One of the oldest and best-known forms of freehand embroidery, traditionally on linen, this is worked in very fine wool, known as crewel wool. The free-flowing design is usually based on flowers, trees and animals. The outlines are embroidered in a simple outline stitch and filled in with a variety of stitches.

One type of filling often used for crewel work is known as *laidwork*, in which "couched" lines are laid side by side. (*Couching* involves laying a thread – often thick, textured or metallic – on the surface and anchoring it with small stitches.)

BLOCKING AND PRESSING

When the embroidery is complete, press it lightly on the wrong side, covered with a pressing cloth. If the shape has become badly distorted, you'll need to block it. Soak it in cold water, roll in a towel, then lay it, right side up, on a board covered with plastic or cotton. Stretching it taut, pin it at the corners, then at 2.5cm (1in) intervals along the edges, starting at the centre of each edge. Leave until dry. (If the fabric or thread is not colourfast, block it without wetting it first.)

MACHINE EMBROIDERY

Lively and dramatic effects in brilliant colours are quickly achieved with machine embroidery and look sensational on fabrics like velvet, silk and satin. It is also an ideal way to decorate appliqué.

Although some state-of-the-art sewing machines can embroider a vast number of patterns automatically, even the most basic machines can be used to create a multitude of embroidered effects. Initially, try something small like curtain tiebacks or a cushion, then after you have become familiar with the technique, larger projects such as a pelmet or a bedspread could be feasible.

THREADS

A variety of threads can be used, including lustrous rayon and glittering metallic threads, as well as shaded threads that change colour at intervals. Subtle effects are possible too, worked in cotton threads on, say, calico or linen. Many of the most interesting effects depend on using a different thread on the bobbin from the one on the top (such as tapestry or crewel wool, chenille, cotton embroidery thread or even shirring elastic).

USING A HOOP

To keep fabric taut, it's a good idea to place it in an embroidery hoop whenever you are doing machine embroidery, and it is essential for some types of free embroidery.

Choose one about 20cm (8in) in diameter that is thin enough to fit under the presser bar when the presser foot is removed. If the hoop doesn't have a screw to adjust the tightness, bind the inner ring with a woven tape (such as lampshade binding tape) to prevent the fabric from slipping. Lay the fabric right side up over the outer ring (this is different from hand embroidery) and push the inner ring down into it.

SIMPLE MACHINE EMBROIDERY

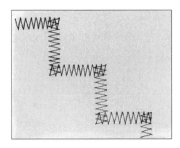

The simplest technique is machine embroidery using straight or zigzag stitching with the presser foot (or an open embroidery foot, which will give clearer visibility) on the machine. Nevertheless, surprisingly interesting and varied effects are possible. Altering the tension creates different textures, such as a beaded effect or even a looped stitch. Changing the stitch width and length also adds variety. Crosshatching, with straight stitch or zigzagging, can look dramatic, as can machine couching produced by zigzagging over cord or thick thread.

Zigzag stitching with a very low stitch length creates a machine satin stitch. This is quite a difficult technique, since it is difficult to get the stitch even and smooth. Both stitches are used for covering the raw edges of machine appliqué, but the zigzag stitch is the easier one.

For both zigzagging and machine satin stitch, you need to take special care at corners, points and tight curves. On outward corners, turn the corner by pivoting with the needle on the outside. On inward corners, pivot with the needle on the inside. On points, adjust the stitch width gradually so that the zigzagging tapers, then pivot and gradually increase the stitch width again. On tight curves, stop and pivot often, with the needle on the narrower side of the curve.

FREE EMBROIDERY

Lowering the machine feed dog prevents it from feeding fabric through automatically, which allows you to control the speed and direction of the stitching. This technique is known as free embroidery.

When the feed dog is lowered, you need to remove the presser foot and then stitch either with a darning or freehand embroidery foot or with no foot at all (keeping your fingers well away from the needle). If you use no foot, be sure to use a hoop around the fabric. Experiment with free embroidery by following these steps.

1 Remove the presser foot. Put the fabric in the hoop and slip it under the presser bar. Fit the darning or freehand embroidery foot if using. Lower the presser bar, even if you are not using a foot. Set the stitch width to 0.

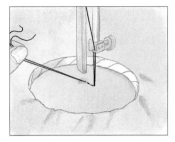

2 Holding the thread with your left hand, turn the hand wheel to bring up the bobbin thread. Pull out the end and hold both threads while you stitch a few stitches. Now cut off the ends.

3 With your fingers on the edge of the hoop, guide it in the required direction as you stitch, always keeping it moving evenly. Try out the effects you can achieve from varying the tensions, altering the speed at which you move the fabric, changing direction or altering the stitch width. Zigzag stitch can be used in free embroidery too.

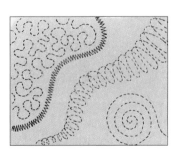

4 Experiment with outlining shapes and filling in with close lines of free running stitch. Try building up thick areas of stitching, and overlapping stitching. Make spirals of free running stitch, with some so tight that they become solid dots. Embroider concentric circles and other geometric or linear shapes. Create "contour lines" with gently curving free running stitch. Other machine feet such as a tailor tack foot, a pin-tucking foot and a braiding foot will also create some interesting effects.

5 To move to another part of the fabric, raise the needle, lift the presser bar, move the fabric and hoop, then lower the needle and presser bar and continue. Cut off the loose thread when you have finished stitching.

6 To finish, move the embroidery hoop slowly to make several small stitches, and snip the threads.

SEE ALSO

TASSELS

Tassels are a fun way to embellish cushions, swags, tiebacks, blinds, even cupboard doors. Make your own at a fraction of the price of bought ones, and match the colours and scale to the rest of the project.

SIMPLE YARN TASSEL

1 Cut two pieces of card to the desired length of the tassel. Place them together and wind one or more colours of wool or silk yarn (or embroidery cotton) around the card at least 20 times.

2 When it is the desired thickness, slide a separate length of yarn between the pieces of card and tie tightly in a knot around the loops of yarn. Trim the ends, and hide the knot inside the loops.

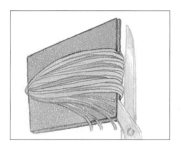

3 Slide the scissors' blade between the pieces of card and cut the loops at the other end. Remove the card.

LEFT ~ *Tassels provide the finishing touches to soft furnishings. To make these, see the variation for Simple Yarn Tassel (opposite).*

4 If desired, pad the head of the tassel by pushing tiny pieces of wadding or cotton wool inside. Bind about one-fifth of the way down with a separate length of yarn.

5 Thread both ends of the binding yarn through a tapestry needle and take them through the top of the tassel at the centre. Use these to attach the tassel to the project.

VARIATION

For a decorative tie like the one in the photograph opposite, make the simple yarn tassel but, in step 5, secure and cut off the ends of the binding rather than bringing them out through the top. When the tassel is complete, sew the end of a length of twisted cord to the top of the tassel, working the end of the cord into the tassel.

BALL TASSEL

This tassel is topped with a small ball (either a wooden bead or a cotton ball) covered with pearl cotton embroidery thread.

1 If using a cotton ball, enlarge the central hole with a knitting needle.

2 Thread a tapestry needle with pearl cotton. Tie a small loop at the end – do not cut the other end yet. Thread the needle through the ball or bead, then take it through the loop; pull tight.

3 Wind the cotton around and through the hole again. Repeat until the entire ball or bead is covered to the desired thickness. Fasten off on the underside.

4 Make a tassel from the same pearl cotton, following the instructions for the simple yarn tassel left. After threading one of the ends of the binding thread out of the top of the tassel, thread it through the ball and back down over the side of the ball and inside the tassel. Once again thread it up through the top of the tassel and through the hole in the ball or bead. Repeat for the other end of the binding thread. Use the ends of the thread to attach the tassel to the project.

VARIATION

For a tassel with a decorative tie, omit step 4 and sew the end of a length of twisted cord to the top of the tassel and take this through the centre of the wrapped ball. Glue the ball to the tassel.

FRINGED BALL TASSEL

1 Cover a medium and a small-sized bead or ball as for the ball tassel (steps 1–3).

2 Coil a 23cm (9in) length of 5–7.5cm (2–3in) wide fringe; glue or sew the end in place. Glue the covered medium-sized bead or ball to the top, and then glue the small one on top of this.

3 Glue a length of narrow braid over the join between the bead and the fringe, or wrap twisted cord around the join, butting up the ends and gluing them in place. Sew or glue a hanging loop to the top.

SEE ALSO

CURTAINS

HARDWARE

Because of the growing interest in attractive curtain fittings, an enormous – and sometimes rather bewildering – range of tracks and poles is available today.

TRACK

Curtain track was originally intended to be hidden behind a pelmet, but some tracks today are designed to be seen, though they do not show when the curtains are closed. Their streamlined look makes them better-suited to a modern decor than a traditional one.

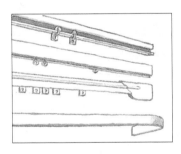

Track is either plastic, steel or aluminium; steel is recommended for heavy curtains. or

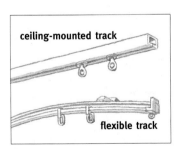

Track can be mounted on the wall, in a window recess

or on the ceiling. Flexible track can be bent to fit an arched, bay or bow window (tight corners may need to be dealt with professionally). Hinged track is also available which will fit neatly into corners of bay windows or windows that meet in a corner.

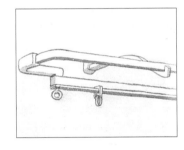

Combination track will hold both a curtain and valance or swag and tails.

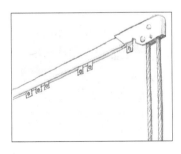

Tracks are either corded (whereby a cord is pulled to open or close the curtains,

preventing the leading edges from getting grubby or worn) or uncorded. They are designed for a two-way draw (opening two curtains in the conventional way) but can be adjusted for a one-way draw (a single curtain).

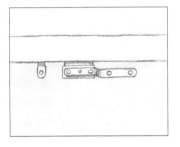

Electronic versions can be operated automatically on a time switch or from an armchair. Cording sets are

also available, which can be fitted to existing tracks. Some tracks can have overlapping arms if desired, so that the curtains overlap in the centre.

Curtains are hung from the tracks by means of curtain hooks attached to the back of the curtain. The hooks are inserted into gliders that slide along the track. On uncorded tracks, endstops keep the outer edges of the curtains in position.

It's important that the curtains hang clear of any obstruction such as a window ledge or architrave. If necessary, mount the curtain track on a batten fixed to the wall in order to increase the distance between the curtains and the wall.

POLES

Curtain poles look good with either traditional or modern furnishings. They come in wood, brass and cast iron and are visible even when the curtains are closed. Unlike tracks, they are not meant to be hidden behind pelmets.

LEFT ~ *A wide variety of poles are available today, including brass as shown here.*

Poles cannot be used with pelmets, swags or blinds.

Although poles cannot be curved around a bay window, it is possible to obtain curved pieces to join two straight poles so they will go around a corner.

Poles are supported on cornice brackets (which they rest on) or rod sockets (which they slot through) fixed to the wall. Short poles do not need a central socket.

The ends of a pole are finished with decorative finials. Ceiling fixings are also available, and poles used in recesses can be slotted into side-wall fixings.

The curtain hooks fit into small eyes at the bottom of rings that slide along the pole. Alternatively, the curtains may be sewn to the eyes on the rings, or slotted directly onto the pole without rings (see pages 92 –96).

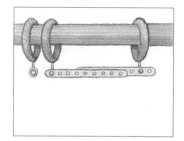

To allow the curtains to overlap at the centre, a cross-over arm can be fixed to the central rings.

Poles are positioned at least 5cm (2in) above the window and extend about 15–40cm (6–16in) to each side, depending on the thickness of the curtains and the amount of wall space (see page 72). If there is enough room, there should be about 10cm (4in) between the outer edge of the bracket and the inner edge of the finial, with a ring between them to hold the outer edge of the curtain in position.

If the brackets do not project far enough for the curtains to clear a window architrave, mount the brackets on blocks of wood fixed to the wall, or buy special extension brackets designed to bring the pole further away from the wall.

FALSE POLES

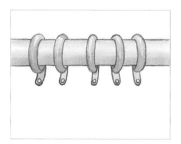

It is possible to get curtain track that looks like a pole but has track in the base and is corded. The "rings" are actually half-round ring-slides.

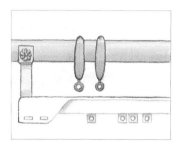

It is also possible to buy double rods with a lower track for sheers.

SPECIALIST FITTINGS

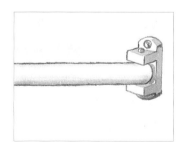

For a deeply recessed or dormer window, hinged dormer rods can be used. When closed, the curtains are

held against the window, then to open them they are swung back to the walls of the recess (see page 101).

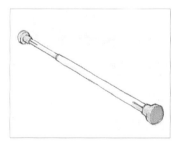

The expandable tension rod is also designed for use in small recessed windows. This plastic or metal rod is slotted through a cased heading. An internal spring tension mechanism holds the rod in place against the window inside the recess, without the need for fittings.

The casings of sheer curtains can be slotted onto a slightly expandable plastic-sheathed curtain wire. Eyelets are screwed into the ends of

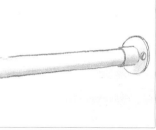

A hollow plastic drop rod can be slotted into the cased heading of sheer or light-weight curtains and screwed to a small window frame.

the wire and attached to the window frame or the wall with cuphooks.

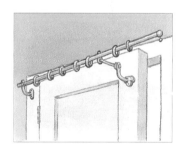

A portière rod is used over a door. It fixes to the door and opens when the door opens.

LEFT ~ *Today, the hardware is often as important a part of the window treatment as the curtains.*

SEE ALSO

ACCESSORIES

Accessories can make all the difference to the look of curtains. They range from the decorative to the invisible, but all of them are very useful.

HOLDBACKS

Also known as ombras, holdbacks are brass, wooden or gilt arms or bosses which curtains can be draped over. They should be chosen to match the style of the curtains, poles and room decor.

DRAW-RODS

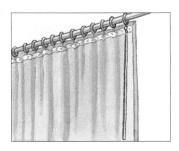

A draw-rod attached to the inner ring or glider of each pole or track allows the curtain to be opened and closed without affecting the fabric or pulling at the curtain pole. The draw-rod hangs at the back inside the fold, where it is not visible.

CLIP-ON RINGS

These rings grip the top of the curtains and so do not need hooks. They can only be used on lightweight curtains but are invaluable for creating quick, stylish curtains using a rectangle of fabric, such as antique lace that you do not want to cut into or stitch.

HOOKS

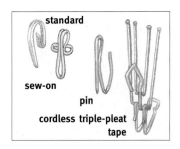

Most heading tapes use standard one-prong hooks, which can be plastic, brass, aluminium or nylon. Metal ones are recommended, except for sheers or lightweight curtains (which can take any).

Hand-stitched headings use either pin hooks, which have sharp prongs that are pushed into the backs of the pleats, or sew-on brass hooks.

Hooks for cordless triple-pleat tape have long prongs, which slip into the pockets of the tape and are pinched together to form triple pleats. (These tapes are no longer widely available, having largely been superseded by corded triple-pleat tapes.)

CORD TIDIES

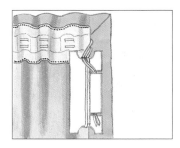

Cord tidies are used with corded heading tape. The excess cord, which is never cut off, is wrapped around a cord tidy, which then hangs at the outside corner. (The alternative is simply to let the string hang down the edge of the curtain at the back, which is not a great deal more conspicuous.)

LEAD WEIGHTS

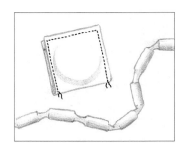

These improve the hang of curtains. They are available in two forms: buttons, which should be encased in fabric and sewn to the hem; and leadweight tape, in three weights and sold by the metre.

TIP

If you are making a lot of curtains, sew the casings for the lead weights all at once. Join two pieces of lining fabric along opposite edges then stitch double lines 6mm (¼in) apart in one direction, with the pairs just a little further apart than the diameter of the weights. Insert the weights into these channels. Stitch double lines at right angles to the first lines, between the lead weights. Cut between each pair of lines.

SEE ALSO

Tapes   84

CURTAIN FABRICS

The wonderful range of curtain fabrics available today is inspiring enough to motivate anyone to start making curtains. The choice has never been better.

FABRIC WEIGHT

Lightweight fabrics such as muslin, lace, voile and net are generally used as sheer curtains, in combination with heavier ones, to filter sunlight and provide privacy when the heavier curtains are open. They are not lined.

Medium-weight fabrics are the ones most often used for curtains. Incredibly versatile, they include furnishing cottons (which are heavier than dressmaking cottons). They are often lined but it is not essential.

Heavyweight fabrics are used for elegant, formal curtains and include brocade, damask and velvet. Not only do they hang beautifully, but they are also good insulators. They should be lined and, ideally, interlined.

PRACTICAL ASPECTS

In addition to the way a fabric looks, you need to think about certain practical aspects relating specifically to curtains.

Loosely woven or open-textured fabrics will sag unless you use a medium-weight lining. Even that may not completely prevent the problem, however, as they may pull and pucker at the sides. Heavy, tightly woven fabrics provide better insulation than loosely woven materials. Similarly, heavily textured fabrics are better for sound insulation than lighter, smoother materials.

Dark fabrics cut out more light, especially if they are thick and tightly woven. In young children's rooms, this may prevent early waking in the spring and summer, but it can also be gloomy.

POPULAR FABRICS

Here are a few watchpoints and tips regarding some of the best-known curtain fabrics.

Brocade and *damask* are traditionally made from silk but today are available in less expensive versions – brocade in cotton or synthetic fibres and damask in cotton, linen or wool fibres. They still offer the elegant look, but at a fraction of the price.

Calico can look very stylish if used lavishly in a bold treatment, but anything less could look insipid. Take care when washing it – it creases badly and shrinks. (Pre-shrinking and pressing while damp may help.)

Chintz has a distinctive glaze that adds body and gives this cotton fabric a luxurious sheen. However, it will wash out sooner or later, so be sure only to dry clean it. Crushing will affect the finish too, and the glaze makes it more prone to creasing.

Cotton, though not luxurious, is tough and practical. Easycare cotton has been given a polished finish that makes it feel soft and silky, and it will drape and wash well.

Dupion is a term used for both real and artificial silk. The man-made version (made from acetate and viscose) looks rather like silk but is less expensive. Some dupions are heavily slubbed. It drapes well but will need to be lined and interlined. Like real silk, it will fade in the sun.

Linen union, a blend of linen and cotton, has the look of linen but is less prone to creasing and more supple. It is still a bit too springy for short curtains, however, so should be reserved for full-length ones instead.

Moiré is a watermark effect applied to fabric as a finish. Also known as watered silk, it was traditionally used on silk taffeta, but today it is more often a cotton and viscose mixture. Water will not only remove the effect but will also cause staining. Dry cleaning too will eventually make it fade. Because it reacts to changes in temperature and humidity, it should be stitched with a loose tension.

Silk drapes beautifully and has a wonderful lustre, but it is very vulnerable to fading and rotting in the sun. If you do decide to use it in a sunny window, protect it with under-curtains or blinds. Thai silk is the most expensive, but lightweight silks from India or China cost considerably less.

Velvet was originally made from silk, but that is extremely expensive so cotton velour is the best quality to use. It is heavy and drapes particularly well, so is suitable for short curtains as well as full-length ones. Acrylic velvet, which is often used for upholstery, does not really drape well enough for use as short curtains.

MEASURING AND CUTTING OUT

The measuring and cutting out stage is the most important – and nerve-racking – part of curtain making. Get this right and the rest ought to come together smoothly.

MEASURING AND CALCULATING

Always use a steel (or wooden) tape measure to measure for curtains, and ask someone to help you.

Plan for the curtains to be cut on the lengthwise grain. The fabric will hang best this way and is less likely to sag.

PLAIN FABRIC

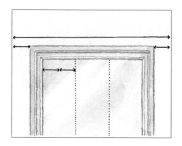

1 First decide how much stackback you want. This is the distance by which the track or pole extends on each side of the window. It is determined by the amount of wall space, the width of the window, the thickness of the fabric and how much of the window you want the curtains to overlap. For fabrics of average thickness, allow one-third the width of the glass for the stackback. For paired curtains, half this allowance

goes on each side. For a single curtain, it all goes on one side. If your fabric is quite thick, add 2.5cm (1in) per width to the stackback.

2 Install the track or pole, then measure the width. Be sure to include the ends, known as the returns, in the measurement if the curtains will go right around the corners. (Some, but not all, tracks have returns; poles do not.)

3 Multiply the track or pole width by the desired fullness. This is generally determined by the heading you are using (see page 84) and ranges from about 1½ to 3.

4 Add an allowance for a centre overlap, if any (for example, on a fixed heading, a track with an overlap or a pole with a cross-over arm) which is usually about 10–15cm (4–6in). There is no need to add an allowance for seams, but you do need to add an allowance for side hems, ranging from 15cm (6in) to 25cm (10in) on a pair of curtains depending on the method of construction. This figure is the *total width*.

5 Divide the total width by the fabric width, and round it up or down to the nearest whole number. This is the *number of fabric widths* you will need. If you are making a pair of curtains, half the number of widths will be used for each curtain. If the total number of widths is an odd number, you'll have to use a half-width on the outside edge of each curtain.

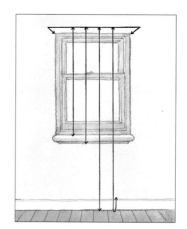

6 Next, decide where you want the curtains to finish: just above sill length for a curtain in a recessed window or where the sill projects too far for the curtains to hang clear of it; just below sill length if there

is a radiator beneath the window; just grazing the floor; or pooling onto the floor, for which you need to allow an extra 5–10cm (2–4in).

7 Measure from the hook suspension point on the track or rod down to the finishing point. This is the *finished length* of the curtains. Add a hem allowance and a heading allowance (both will depend on the curtain construction, and are specified on the following pages) and also an allowance of 2.5cm (1in) for squaring the ends. This figure is the *cut length* of each fabric width.

8 Finally, multiply the number of fabric widths by the cut length. This is the amount of fabric you'll need in centimetres (inches), so divide by 100 (36) to get the number of metres (yards).

TIP

If there is a sofa or other piece of furniture beneath the window, the curtains will probably look better extending down to finish just above it rather than at the sill.

PATTERNED FABRIC

For patterned fabric, you'll need extra material unless the pattern is so tiny it does not need to be matched. Follow the steps for plain fabric, adapting them as follows.

1 Check that the crosswise pattern matches at the selvedges. If it doesn't, work out how much fabric you will lose by making it match. Deduct this amount from the fabric width, and substitute the new figure, called the *usable width*, for the fabric width when calculating your fabric requirements.

2 Decide where the lengthwise pattern repeats should fall (see Pattern Matching, page 44). Measure the *repeat height* or check the fabric label.

3 Work out the number of pattern repeats in each cut length by dividing the repeat height into the cut length (see step 7 of Plain Fabric) and round up if the answer contains a fraction. Now multiply this number by the repeat height, to get the

adjusted cut length. This is the length each piece will be cut to, so that whole repeats appear on the curtain.

4 To calculate the amount of fabric, multiply the number of fabric widths by the adjusted cut length, as for plain fabrics (step 8).

5 Now carefully double-check your measurements and calculations before proceeding any further!

RIGHT ~ *Taking care with this stage always produces a better result.*

CUTTING OUT

1 Lay the fabric out on a large working table or a clean floor. Prepare the fabric as directed on pages 11–12. Use a set square placed against a metre ruler to mark the first cutting line of the fabric. Remember to start in the appropriate place if it is a patterned fabric.

TIP

If you want to be really safe, mark the entire fabric into lengths and then, once you know you haven't measured it incorrectly, cut it out.

2 Measure along both selvedges and mark a distance equal to the cut length (or the adjusted cut length if using patterned fabric). Draw a line between the marks. Use the set square to check that the line is square. Check your

measurements, then cut out. Mark the top right side of the fabric with thread.

3 Repeat step 2 until the correct number of widths has been cut out.

SEE ALSO

MAKING UP

This part of curtain making is not difficult, although it can sometimes become tedious.
The main skill is to be able to stitch a straight line.

JOINING WIDTHS

UNLINED CURTAINS

If your curtains will consist of more than one width per panel, the widths will be stitched together at this stage. If you are joining a partial width to one or more full widths, the partial width should always go on the outside edge.

If the fabric needs to be straightened and you were unable to do so prior to cutting out the widths, try to straighten it at this stage (see page 11).

Unless the pattern repeat is affected (see page 44), trim off the selvedges, or clip into them at frequent intervals. (If the selvedges contain any writing that is likely to show through to the front of the curtain, then trimming the selvedge off is your only option.)

PLAIN FABRIC

1 Use flat fell seams to join the widths of unlined curtains, and use plain seams to join the widths of curtains that will be lined.

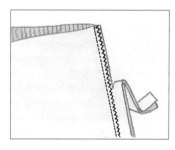

2 For curtains that will be lined, hold a piece of main fabric with a piece of lining fabric up to the light. If the seam allowances will show through, you can, if you wish, zigzag the seam allowances together, 3mm (⅛in) away from the stitching line, then trim the seam allowances next to the zigzag stitching.

PATTERNED FABRIC

When you are matching two pieces of patterned fabric, use the tacking stitch known as *ladderstitch*. It allows you to see the pattern as you tack.

1 Press under one seam allowance and lay this along the seam allowance of the other piece. The right sides of both should be uppermost, and the pattern matching. Pin.

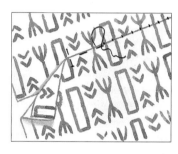

2 Now hand sew as for slip hemming (see page 15), with stitches 2cm (¾in) long.

3 When the whole seam has been tacked, fold the fabric with right sides together, ready to stitch.

SHEER FABRIC

Because the seams would show through sheer fabric, it is generally better to treat each width as a separate panel when making sheer curtains. Otherwise, use French or flat fell seams.

Unlined curtains are the easiest ones to make and are suitable for either lightweight fabrics or for sheer fabrics.

1 Cut out the fabric. Double 3cm (1¼in) side hems and a double 7.5cm (3in) lower hem are allowed, but these could be reduced to about half those sizes if desired; or the lower hem could be increased to a double 10cm (4in) hem for full-length curtains (in which case, allow for this when calculating the total width and cut length). For sheer curtains, use double 1cm (⅜in) hems for sides; the 7.5cm (3in) lower hem should be double or even triple. Join widths if necessary.

2 Turn under, press and pin a double 3cm (1¼in) hem down each side and a double 7.5cm (3in) hem along the lower edge.

3 For fabric that isn't sheer, each corner should be mitred as follows. Open out the second fold of the lower hem but do not open out the first fold. Do not open out the side hem at all. Mark with a pin on the outside (folded) edge of the lower hem where the side hem comes to. Now open the second fold of the side hem and refold the lower hem. Mark with a pin where the lower hem comes to on that edge.

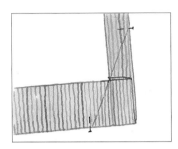

4 Unfold the second fold of the lower hem again and draw a line between the pins. With the second fold of both hems opened out, fold the corner in along this line; press. Refold both hems, forming the mitre, and pin them in place.

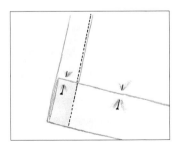

5 Mitring is neither necessary nor suitable for sheer or very lightweight fabrics, so the lower hem will just be folded over each side hem neatly and then stitched after the side hems are stitched (step 8).

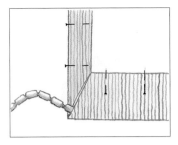

6 Weighting the hem is important to make unlined curtains hang well. Insert leadweight tape along the bottom of the hem, hand sewing it in place at each end.

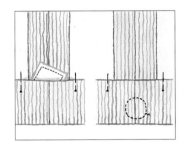

7 Alternatively, for a heavier fabric, use individual weights, stitching each into a little bag, before hand sewing in place underneath each mitre and also at the bottom of any seams joining widths.

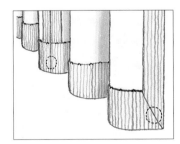

8 Either slipstitch or machine stitch the side hems in place. Slipstitch the lower edge and each mitre. Alternatively, use fusing tape

ABOVE ~ *Unlined curtains suit today's informal window treatments.*

(see page 25) or, if you have a blindstitch foot for your machine, you can machine blindstitch the hems.

9 Make the heading of your choice. (If you are using a loose-weave fabric, or are hanging curtains in a position where the length has to be exact, such as over a radiator, it's a good idea to apply the heading *before* hemming it and then allow it to hang in place for a few days prior to actually sewing the hem.) Hang and "dress" the curtains (see page 79).

DETACHABLE LINING

Made with a special heading tape, a detachable lining gives you the best of both worlds, because it can be removed from the curtain for washing or in the summer. Another advantage is that the lining does not have to be as full as the curtain, because it hangs separately. The tape can be used with all conventional curtain heading tapes.

1 Make the curtains as for unlined curtains. Make the lining in the same way, but with a fullness of about 1½ times (or 1¼ times if you are using a blackout lining or thermal lining) and about 2.5cm (1in) shorter than the curtain. Use machine stitching for all the hems.

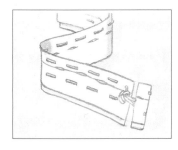

2 Cut a length of lining tape about 1.2cm (½in) longer than the width of the hemmed lining. Knot the two cords together at one end, and trim off the excess tape.

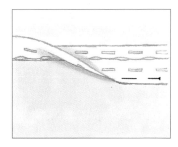

3 Slip the heading tape over the top edge of the lining, with the right side of the lining and the corded side of the tape uppermost and the tape extending beyond the lining a little at each end. The raw edge of the lining should be sandwiched between the divided "skirt" of the tape. Turn under the knotted end of the tape. Pin.

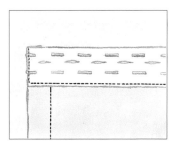

4 Stitch along the turned-under end and the lower edge of the tape. Because the underneath layer of the "skirt" is slightly deeper than the top one, the stitching will not miss it. Turn under the other end of the tape, leaving the cords free, and then stitch across the end.

5 Pull up the cords, distributing the gathers evenly until the lining is just slightly less than the width of the curtain. Knot the ends but do not cut off (see page 84).

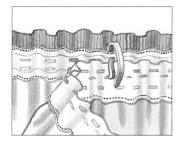

6 Place the curtain and lining with wrong sides together. Push the curtain hooks through the slots at the top of the lining tape then through the pockets on the main curtain heading tape and finally through the gliders or rings on the track or pole.

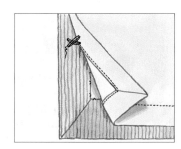

7 To keep the lining in place, either make long catch stitches at intervals down the sides, as shown, or slipstitch the edges together, or sew press studs or touch-and-close dots at intervals to the hem allowances.

Apart from lightweight curtains, most curtains will be improved by being lined. There are two types of lining: tube lining (sometimes known as sewn-in lining) and locked-in lining. Locked-in lining is the only suitable method for curtains that are very wide or long and heavy, or will be interlined (see page 78). When a contrast lining is used, the best method is to cut the fabric and lining to the same size, then join them with right sides together around the side and lower edges.

TUBE LINING

Quicker than locked-in lining, tube lining is attached only at the top and sides of the curtain. The side edges are actually self facings because the lining is cut narrower than the curtain, and so even though they are machine stitched the stitching does not show on the right side.

1 For the curtain, allow an extra 7.5cm (3in) on the width for self facings (which are instead of side hems) and an extra 15cm (6in) on the depth for the lower hem. (See step 1 of Unlined Curtains for possible adjustments to the hem allowances.) The upper hem allowance will depend on the heading you use. Cut out the fabric, joining widths if necessary.

LINED CURTAINS

2 The lining should be the finished width of the curtain less 2.5cm (1in), and the finished length of the curtain (with no upper hem allowance) plus the lower hem allowance. Cut out the lining and join widths.

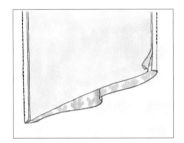

3 With right sides together and lower edges even, stitch the lining to the main fabric along both sides. Take 1.2cm (½in) seams and stop 25cm (10in) from the lower edge. Press the seams towards the lining, pressing the unstitched seam allowances at the lower sides as well.

ABOVE ~ *Full-length formal curtains should generally be lined.*

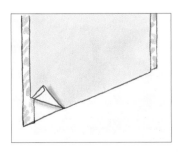

4 Turn right side out. Press the side edges, making sure that there is the same amount of fabric – ie, 2.5cm (1in) – on both sides.

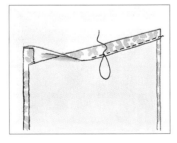

5 Fold the curtain over the lining along the top edge; tack. The raw edge of the curtain will be covered when the heading is complete.

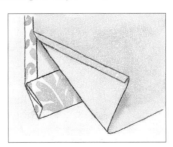

6 Turn up a double 7.5cm (3in) hem along the lower edge of the main fabric, mitring the corners by turning in the corner diagonally

before turning up along the second fold; pin. Turn up the lining so that the lower edge is 2cm (¾in) above that of the curtain. Make a 7.5cm (3in) double hem in the lining, trimming off the extra 2cm (¾in); press. Machine stitch the lining hem.

7 Slipstitch the side and lower hems in place, sewing lead weights to the corners, and at the base of any vertical seams (see page 75, step 7). Slipstitch the mitres and slipstitch the lining to the curtain at the lower sides. Make the heading of your choice, and hang and "dress" the curtain (see page 79).

LOCKED-IN LINING

This is the professional method. It involves a lot of hand sewing, but undoubtedly looks much better than either tube lining or a detachable lining. Because the lining is attached right across the curtain, it cannot separate from the curtain fabric.

1 For the curtain, allow an extra 10cm (4in) on the width for side hems, and 22.5cm (9in) on the length for the upper and lower hems. For the lining, allow an extra 2.5cm (1in) on the depth; the width should be the same as the finished curtain. Cut out the curtains and lining, joining widths if necessary.

2 Turn under and press a single 5cm (2in) hem on each side edge of the curtain and a double 7.5cm (3in) hem on the lower edge of the curtain, mitring corners (see pages 74–75, steps 3–4). Sew lead weights into the hem (see page 75, step 7), then herringbone stitch the hems in place all around. If you are making a hand-pleated heading, end the stitching 25cm (10in) from the top; insert stiffener (see page 90) then complete the stitching. Slipstitch the mitres.

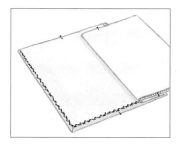

3 Machine stitch a single 5cm (2in) hem on the lower edge of the lining. Mark the centre of the curtain and of the lining. Place the curtain and lining wrong sides together, with the lining on top and the centres matching. The lower edge of the lining should be 2.5cm (1in) above that of the curtain. Turn in 2.5cm (1in) on one side edge of the lining, 2.5cm (1in) from the curtain edge; slip-stitch the lining to the curtain. Pin the lining to the curtain in a vertical line 40cm (16in) from the edge. Now fold the lining back on itself along the line of pins.

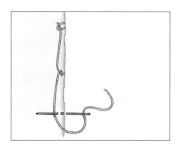

4 Lockstitch the lining to the curtain along the fold. To lockstitch, cut a very long length of thread and bring the needle and thread out through the folded edge at the top. Holding the needle horizontally, pick up only two or three threads of the curtain fabric, just next to the folded lining. Pull the thread through, but do not pull it tight – leave a loop. Take the needle through the loop then make a second stitch about 10cm (4in) below the first, again keeping the thread loop under the needle before pulling it through. Continue in the same way, without ever pulling the thread tight.

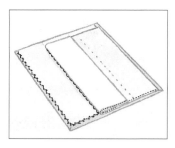

5 Repeat to work other rows of lockstitching about 40cm (16in) apart, or at least every half-width. If there are any seams joining widths, work the lockstitching along the seams.

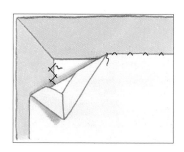

6 Turn in the edges of the lining by about 2.5cm (1in) along the remaining side, leaving 2.5cm (1in) of curtain exposed. Turn in the top edge of the curtain by 7.5cm (3in) and the top edge of the lining by 2.5cm (1in), leaving 2.5cm (1in) exposed. Mitre all the corners and slip-stitch the lining to the curtain all around.

7 Make the heading of your choice, and hang and "dress" the curtain carefully (see page 79).

INTERLINED CURTAINS

These require time and patience, and ideally a large work table, but they are worth the effort. Interlined curtains look wonderful and provide excellent insulation. If your curtain fabric is expensive, omitting the interlining would be false economy.

Use bleached interlining for white curtains, and cream for all others. If you are also making a pelmet or valance, it should be interlined in the same colour. If possible, buy interlining the same width as the lining so that the seams will align.

1 Cut out and join widths of fabric for the curtain and for its lining as for curtains with locked-in lining (see page 77), step 1.

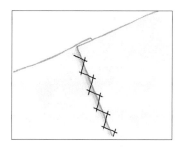

2 The interlining should be the same size as the finished curtain (ie, without the hem allowances all around). If necessary, join widths by overlapping them by 2.5cm (1in) and then herringbone stitching.

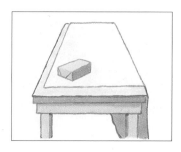

3 Lay the curtain wrong side up on your work

table, lining up a side edge and the lower edge with the edges of the table. Lay the interlining on top, with the edges along the foldlines of the curtain. Smooth out any wrinkles, and anchor with a brick covered with fabric or other heavy weight.

4 Pin the interlining to the curtain down the centre. Fold the interlining back on itself along the line of pins. Lockstitch along this line (see Locked-in Lining, step 4) from top to bottom. Repeat across the curtain, lockstitching every 40cm (16in) or each

half-width, finishing along the side edges of the interlining, which should be aligned with the foldline of each curtain side hem. Now lockstitch along the lower edge of the interlining, which should be aligned with the foldline of the curtain lower hem.

5 Turn the side, top and bottom hems over the interlining, mitre the corners. Sew lead weights into the lower hem. Herringbone stitch the hems to the interlining. (For hand-pleated headings, see Locked-in Lining, step 2.)

6 Complete the curtains as for lined curtains, steps 3–7, lockstitching the lining.

VARIATION

For a luxurious look, pad leading edge. Cut a strip of interlining the length of the finished curtain. Roll lengthwise and slipstitch the long raw edge. Lockstitch interlining to the curtain, sew with tiny stitches.

LEFT ~ For professional-looking curtains such as these Italian - strung curtains with a goblet heading, interlining is a must.

HANGING AND DRESSING CURTAINS

This is an important part of the curtain-making process and will make all the difference to the look of your curtains. "Dressing" the curtains (steps 3–5) is not always necessary for informal, lightweight curtains that are not meant to hang in pleats, but all other curtains need it. Be sure to dress curtains straightaway, before they get into any bad habits.

1 If using a corded tape heading, pull it up to the correct width and insert hooks before hanging, to minimize the time spent up a ladder. Make sure the number of hooks you have inserted or sewn on corresponds to the number of rings or gliders (including end stops) on the pole or track.

2 Use a stepladder and enlist someone's help in holding it and supporting a heavy curtain. Carry the curtain over your shoulder, so that the weight will not distort the heading as you hang it. Insert the hooks at the centre of the curtain first and work outwards so the weight will be more evenly spread. Starting with the overlap arm (if there is one) would cause it to bend.

curtain hanging from a pole, all the pleats should be forward and the fabric between them folded evenly, behind the pleats. For a curtain hanging in front of a track, the fabric between the pleats should be in front of the pleats. Make sure the edges of the curtain are pointing to the window/wall. Adjust any pleats that are not in the right position. For unpleated headings, adjust the folds so that they are even.

ABOVE ~ *"Dressing" the curtains is essential if you want even pleats like these.*

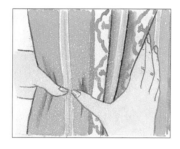

4 Stand on the floor and continue adjusting the same pleats, then kneel and adjust the pleats at the lower edge. The aim is to have them all straight and even, from top to bottom. At the lower edge, finger press the pleats at the hem to prevent wrinkles (especially important for interlined curtains). If the curtains are very long, so that they pool onto the floor, keep them in their pleats but bend the whole bundle neatly out to the side.

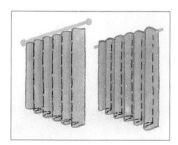

3 After the curtains are hung, continue standing on the stepladder to begin "dressing" each one. The heading should be at your eye level. With the curtain drawn back into the "stackback position", check that the heading is correctly arranged. For a pleated heading on a

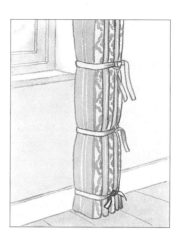

5 Tie fabric strips or long, thin scarves around the curtains at 30cm (12in) intervals along the whole length. They should be tied tight enough to hold the folds in place and not fall off, but not so tight as to crease the curtains. Carefully adjust any pleats that look twisted or uneven. Leave the curtains like this for several days before removing the ties.

CURTAINS WITH CONTRAST BANDS

Contrast bands make plain curtains look very smart and up-to-date. The band can be just along the lower edge, or the top edge, of each curtain; or only down the leading (centre) edges; or along the base and one or both side edges. Any corners should be mitred.

For a light-coloured band on a leading edge, it is advisable to use a corded track or draw rods (see page 70) to stop the band from getting grubby.

If you are using a one-way or patterned fabric for a band on two or more adjacent edges, one piece will have to be cut on the lengthwise grain and the other on the crosswise grain. In that case, if the curtain is made from more than one fabric width, the seam joining widths on the horizontal band should align with that of the curtain.

The band is attached in one stage for the lined curtains. However, the resulting raw edge makes this method unsuitable for unlined curtains, so the band is attached in two stages for them.

LINED CURTAINS WITH BAND

1 Make a double band (see page 29) as long as the length of the curtain, and the desired width. You'll need to allow for the width of the band when working out the size of the curtain and also the lining. Cut out the curtain and join widths, as for lined curtains (step 1).

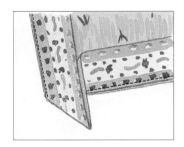

2 With right sides together and raw edges even, position the band along the edge of the curtain. Pin and stitch through all three layers (both layers of the band, plus the curtain), taking a 1.5cm (⅝in) seam. If there is a mitred corner, stitch *into* the corner from both sides, stopping at each seamline. Trim the corner. Press the seam towards the curtain so the band extends out from the edge.

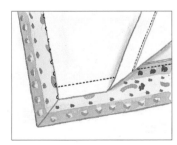

3 Complete as for lined curtains, treating the band as part of the curtain and covering the raw edges of the seam with the lining.

TIP

Use a contrast border as an inset near the lower edge, to lengthen a pair of curtains that are too short. Cut the curtain parallel to the lower edge, zigzag the cut edges, then position braid trim or a fabric border (which has been cut on the straight grain, with the edges turned under) so the edges overlap the zigzagged edges. Topstitch. Alternatively, simply attach a double band to the edge.

UNLINED CURTAINS WITH BAND

1 Make a double band as in step 1 of lined curtains with band. When stitching the pointed ends, start and stop 2cm (¾in) from the front edge and 1cm (⅜in) from the back edge, rather than 1.5cm (⅝in) from each. Cut out the curtain and join widths. Note that instead of a hem on each banded edge, you will need to allow for a 2cm (¾in) seam allowance.

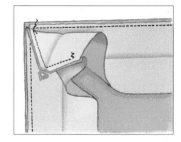

2 With right sides together and raw edges even, pin the border front to the curtain, pulling the back of the border out of the way. Stitch through the two layers, taking a 2cm (¾in) seam. If there is a mitred corner, stitch into the corner from both sides. Trim the corner. Press the border and seam allowance away from the curtains.

3 Turn under 1cm (⅜in) on the other raw edge of the border, and take it over to the wrong side of the curtain. Pin and tack in place on the wrong side so that the border is flat. Now "stitch in the ditch" (in the groove just alongside the first seamline) from the front. Alternatively, slipstitch the border in place on the wrong side.

4 Hem any remaining edges, and complete the curtains as for unlined curtains (page 74).

LEFT ~ *The decorative "bands" down the sides of this curtain are printed on the fabric, but the band along the bottom has been cut out and stitched on.*

CURTAIN TRIMMINGS

An attractive fringe, or other trimming can dress up the simplest curtain fabric. If desired, it can be echoed in trimmings applied to tiebacks, pelmets and valances.

Use braid along the edges of the curtain, for a crisp, graphic effect. Narrow satin ribbon looks pretty on voile or muslin curtains and petersham ribbon on gingham. Cording can be looped along a fixed heading, or covered buttons sewn onto the pleats of a heading.

An incredible variety of fringes are available, including bobble, beaded, fan-edged, bullion, tasselled or plain. Apply fringe or another edging to the leading edges of curtains that have a fixed heading (see page 87), to emphasize the curve. Or add a frill in the same fabric (or a contrasting plain fabric) to the leading edges of curtains with a fixed heading.

ATTACHING BRAID OR RIBBON

1 Cut out the curtain. On the right side, use a fabric marker and metre ruler to draw a placement line for the trim, the desired distance from the edge. (Don't forget to allow for the width of the hem when measuring.)

2 Starting at the raw edge of the curtain, pin the trim along the placement line so that it just covers it. Tack and then topstitch along one edge of the trim. If you are only trimming one edge of the curtain, stitch the trim to the curtain all the way to the end. If you will be turning the corner and continuing along the adjacent edge, stop stitching when you get to the next placement line.

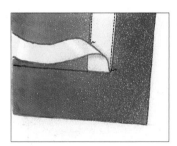

3 Now go back and topstitch the other edge in the same way. It's important to stitch in the same direction, otherwise the trim may not lie flat. If you will be turning the corner, stop the width of the trim away from the placement line

of the next edge, mitre the corner (see page 30) and then continue along the new placement line. Otherwise, simply stitch to the end.

4 Make up the curtain in the usual way. The raw ends of the trim will be covered up at the same time as the raw edges of the curtain.

ATTACHING A FRILL

Single, double and double-edge frills are all suitable for curtains. Make up a frill and stitch it to the curtain edge as shown on page 32. If on the leading edge, it should extend all the way to the top of the curtain. If you are attaching it to both the leading edge and the lower edge, you could round off the corner.

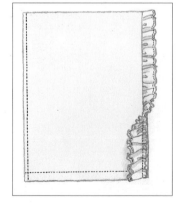

Attach a frill after hemming the other edges of the curtain but before making the heading. (An edge with a frill is not hemmed.) If the curtains are

lined, attach the lining after stitching the frill, bringing it right up to cover the seam.

RIGHT ~ Use tassels, rope or a variety of other trimmings to accentuate the design of your window treatment.

HEADINGS

The heading determines the style of curtains, and also the amount of fullness and the way they hang. Hand-pleated headings look professional, while tapes are also very smart – and faster.

TAPES

These offer the simplest method of making a pleated or gathered heading. They are stitched to the top of the curtain after the interlining and lining, if any, are attached and after the hems are completed. Apart from cordless triple pleat tape, curtain tapes are corded – after attaching them, you simply pull up the cords to form the pleats or gathers, then tie the cords.

A wide variety of tapes is available, in different styles, widths and weights. The wider tapes generally have two or three rows of pockets, one of which the hooks are hooked through; the row that is used determines the height of the curtain relative to the track or pole. (If the hooks will not be flush with the top, you'll need to allow for this in the curtain length.)

When making a pair of curtains, always start with the leading edge of the curtain – in other words, the one that will be in the centre.

APPLYING CORDED TAPE: BASIC METHOD

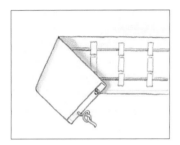

1 Turn under 6mm (¼in) at the top edge of the fabric (except for gathered tapes – see page 85). On the tape leading edge, pull the cords free for 4cm (1½in). Knot them individually, and trim the cord ends to 3mm (⅛in). Trim off excess tape 1cm (⅜in) from the knots. Turn under the tape and the knots.

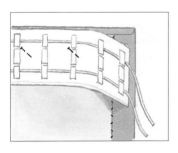

2 Make sure that the tape is the right way up (some have yellow lines to indicate the bottom) and is facing you (with the pockets on top). Pin the tape to the wrong side of the curtain at the top, 2–3mm (a scant ⅛in) from the leading edge and the same from the top edge (except for gathered headings – see page 85). At the other end, free about 2.5–5cm (1–2in) of cord. Turn under 1cm (⅜in) of tape, leaving the cords free.

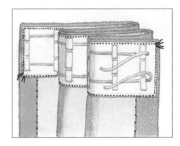

3 Stitch across the first end and then along the top edge, along the stitching lines if any. Tie the threads at the back rather than backstitching. Now stitch in the same direction along the lower edge of the tape and across the other end, being careful not to stitch over the free cords at that end. Again tie the threads at the back.

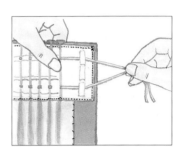

4 For gathered and pencil pleat headings, pull the cords to draw up the fabric, pushing the fabric along the cords, until the curtain is the desired width. For pleated headings with space between the pleats (ie, cluster, triple and goblet pleat tapes), hold your thumb in front of the first cluster and push the pleat into position. Push the next cluster into position in the same way, then go back and redo the first ones, which will no longer be pleated. Continue in this way until the whole heading is pleated.

5 Tie the cord ends in a slip knot, looping the loose cords around a cord tidy if desired. (Do not cut them, because the curtain will need to be pulled flat for cleaning.)

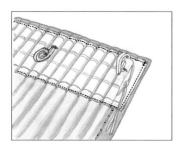

6 Insert the appropriate hooks (see chart on page 89) in the pockets at the ends and either behind each pleat or at 8cm (3in) intervals, depending on the type of tape. Cartridge hooks have two prongs, which should be inserted into adjacent pockets. If the tape has more than one row of pockets, use the top row if the curtains are to hang below a track or pole, and the bottom row if the track is to be covered.

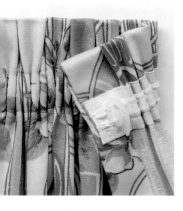

ABOVE ~ *Gathered tape is an easy way of creating gathers.*

TIP
....

If your curtains are very wide, pull up the heading tape cords by looping them around a doorknob.

GATHERED TAPE

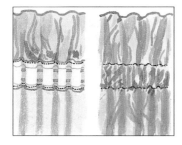

Also known as standard tape, this makes a plain gathered heading. The amount of fullness is about 1½–2 times the track width. Normally it's better to err on the side of too much rather than too little fullness, but with this tape, sometimes skimpy curtains are more suitable. Not only do they look simple and fresh, but also, if the curtains are to go in a recessed window, they will not reduce the amount of light coming in quite so much as fuller curtains.

This type of heading does not look very good hanging under a track or pole (although it can be used if a valance or pelmet covers it up) – it needs either partially or completely to cover the track instead. The amount by which it does this is determined by how far from the top you position the tape. The lower it is positioned, the deeper the self frill that forms above it. Although 2.5cm (1in) is the conventional depth of the frill, 6.5–7.5cm (2½–3in) can look nicer on crisp cotton.

1 Make a single top hem as in step 1 of the basic method, but instead of 6mm (¼in), make it 4–9cm (1½–3½in) deep.

2 If there will be a deep self frill above the heading, you may wish to interface the hem allowance to make it stiffer, or interline it for extra body without stiffness. If so, cut a strip of interfacing or interlining to the width of the upper hem. Either iron it or herringbone stitch it to the hem allowance, stopping at the sewn edges of the hems.

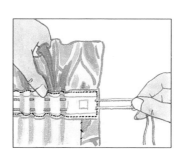

3 Slipstitch the hem allowance to the curtain at the sides. Now proceed as for the basic method, steps 2–6, drawing up the cords as for gathered headings (step 4 of the basic method).

TIP
....

Unlike most curtain tapes, gathered tape allows you to decide its position. Tack the tape in place then hang it up to check the effect.

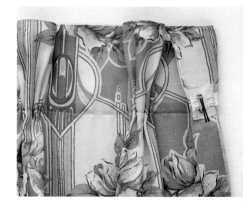

ABOVE ~ *Cluster pleats are more informal than triple pleats and well suited to bedrooms.*

CLUSTER PLEAT TAPE

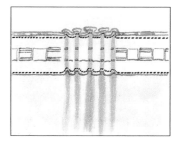

This tape gives you two options – you can draw up either the inner pair of cords for gathers just like gathering tape, or the outer pair for cluster pleats.

1 Knot the ends as for the basic method, step 1. If there is an overlap arm on the curtain track or pole, turn under 4cm (1½in) of tape at this end. Otherwise, turn under 9cm (3½in).

2 Complete the heading following the basic method, drawing up the cords as for pleated headings (step 4 of basic method).

ABOVE ~ *Goblet pleats are shaped like goblets.*

GOBLET PLEAT TAPE

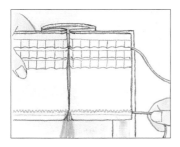

This produces deep pleats very similar to hand-made goblet pleats (see page 93).

1 Make the heading following the basic method but in step 1, turn under 6mm(¼in) of fabric. Pull out the top cord from the first pleat. Knot both cords 4.5cm (1¾in) in from this (or at this point if there is an overlap). Trim cords and tape to 3mm (⅛in) from top. Draw up the cords as for pleated headings with spaces (step 4 of basic method) but pull first the top cord then the bottom cord.

2 If desired, make a small tack in the tape at the top and bottom of the goblet, and also in the front of the curtain just below the tape.

BELOW ~ *Very versatile, pencil pleat headings are suitable for most fabrics.*

PENCIL PLEAT TAPE

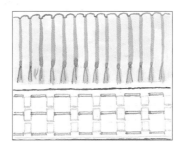

Pencil pleat tape forms even pleats, each about as thick as a pencil. Although it takes a lot of fabric (see chart on page 89), don't be tempted to use less. Not only would the curtains not hang properly, but the pleats in the heading would look flat.

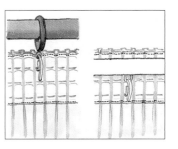

1 Make the heading following the basic method, steps 1–2. For the narrow and the translucent types, position the tape with the single row of pockets at the bottom if you want to cover the track; or, to hang below the track or pole, position them at the top. For the other types, position the tape with the yellow line, if there is one, at the bottom.

2 Stitch the tape to the curtain as for steps 3–4 of the basic method, pulling the cords to draw up the fabric until it is pleated as tightly as possible and then loosening it until it is the desired width. Complete the curtains as for the basic method, steps 5–6.

TRIPLE PLEAT TAPE

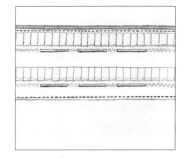

Also known as pinch pleats or French pleats, this heading suits different styles of curtain.

The pleats look similar to hand-made pleats. Although it is the simplest way of making these pleats, the curtain has to be exactly the right width for the track – there is no flexibility. When you buy the tape, check what the manufacturer recommends regarding the fullness.

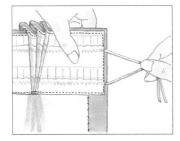

1 Make the heading following the basic method. On the edge of the tape that will be the leading edge, cut in the centre of the first pleat. Knot as for the basic method, then turn under 5cm (2in) if the curtains will butt together, or 2.5cm (1in) if there is an over-lap arm. Draw up the cords as for pleated headings with spaces (step 4 of basic method).

2 Hand sewing a few stitches at the front of the pleats will help keep them neat, but the stitches will have to be removed for cleaning.

VARIATION

Cover buttons in a contrasting fabric, such as the fabric used on the tiebacks, if any and sew one to the front of each pleat, as shown on the left.

ABOVE ~ Covered buttons are a charming way to finish off a triple pleat heading.

FIXED HEADING TAPES

Some headings will not form even pleats when the curtains are opened and so are intended to remain permanently fixed in the closed position at the top. The curtains are draped back with tiebacks or holdbacks, creating attractive curves. Of course, conventional headings can be fixed too, but the following headings can only be used this way (or as valances).

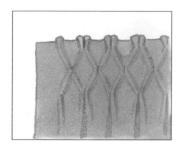

Smock-effect tapes Though not actually smocked, this creates pleats with a similar look. It has three cords.

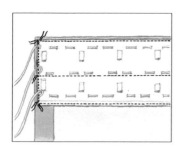

1 Make the heading as for the basic method, steps 1–2. Stitch in the same direction along the inner stitching lines and then the outer ones. Tie the threads at the back, and do not stitch over any of the cords.

2 Pull the three cords to draw up the fabric, pushing the heading along the cords and forming the pleats as you do so. Tie a slip knot, then pinch the pleats on the right side. Complete as for the basic method, step 6.

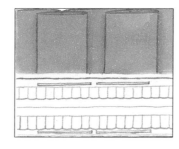

Box pleat tape This tape produces a row of box pleats.

1 On the end of the tape that will be the leading (centre) edge, cut through the centre pleat.

2 Complete as for the basic method, steps 1–6.

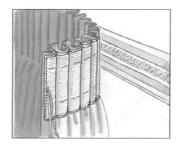

Touch-and-close pencil pleat tape One side of this versatile tape is self-adhesive and is stuck permanently to the wall, window frame or a wooden batten. The other side is stitched to the curtain. When pulled up, it forms pencil pleats. Apply it in the same way as a conventional pencil pleat heading.

CORDLESS TRIPLE PLEAT TAPE

This tape, has deep pockets. Instead of being pulled up with cords, the pleats are formed using four-pronged hooks, with the prongs inserted into four adjacent pockets and then pinched together. They are more fiddly to make, but you can adjust the spacing if desired.

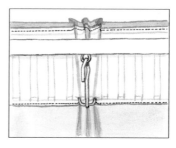

Two types of hook are available. Short-necked hooks (as shown above) are used when the track is to be covered.

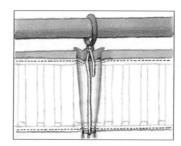

Long-necked hooks (as shown above) are used when the curtains are to hang under the pole or track.

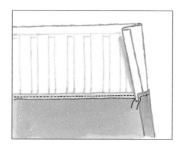

1 Allow for a 1cm (⅜in) upper hem. Position the tape with the wrong side facing the right side of the curtain, and the edges overlapping by 1cm (⅜in). The open ends of the pockets should point away from the curtain. Turn under each end. Pin and stitch along the edge.

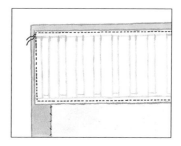

2 Turn the tape to the wrong side of the curtain. Pin, tack and stitch across one turned-under end, then along the lower edge of the tape in the same direction as the first side was stitched, and finally across the other end. Tie the thread ends at the back.

3 Work out where the pleats will be so they will be spaced evenly. Allow for the first pleat on the leading edge to be the same distance from its counterpart on the other side as the spaces between the other pleats. If there is an overlap, you'll need to allow for this too, since pleats should not occur on the "underlap". If there is a return (where the curtain is to go around the ends of the track), position the last pleat at the corner of the return.

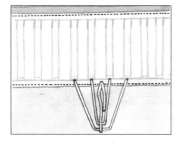

4 Spread out the prongs of the hook slightly and insert them in adjacent pockets. Squeeze the prongs together to close.

RIGHT ~ *This chart summarizes what you'll need to know if you set out to buy a particular heading tape. Study it in the comfort of your own home so that you won't have any unanswered questions when you are buying the tape.*

TYPE OF TAPE	WIDTH	FABRIC FULLNESS	TYPE OF HOOK	NO. OF ROWS OF POCKETS	SUITABILITY
Gathered	2.5cm (1in)	$1\frac{1}{2}$–2	gathered tape hooks	1	Sheers; informal, lightweight short
Narrow gathered	1.5cm ($\frac{5}{8}$in)	2	gathered tape hooks	1	Sheers; informal, lightweight short
Cluster pleat	2.5cm (1in)	2	cartridge tape hooks	1	Sheer, lightweight
Triple pleat	8.5cm ($3\frac{1}{4}$in)	$2\frac{1}{4}$	cartridge tape hooks	2	Traditional, medium to long, medium-weight
Narrow triple pleat	4cm ($1\frac{1}{2}$in)	2	cartridge tape hooks	1	Sheers and short
Deep triple pleat	14cm ($5\frac{1}{2}$in)	$2\frac{1}{4}$	cartridge tape hooks	2	Long
Goblet	14cm ($5\frac{1}{2}$in)	$2\frac{1}{4}$	cartridge tape hooks	3	Long, fairly formal, such as velvet
Pencil pleat	7.5cm (3in)	$2\frac{1}{2}$	pencil pleat tape hooks	3	Any, especially modern; medium
Deep pencil pleat	14cm ($5\frac{1}{2}$in)	$2\frac{1}{2}$–3	pencil pleat tape hooks	3	Long
Narrow pencil pleat	4cm ($1\frac{1}{2}$in)	2–$2\frac{1}{2}$	gathered tape hooks	1	Short; semi-sheers
Lightweight pencil pleat	6.5cm ($2\frac{1}{2}$in)	$2\frac{1}{2}$–3	pencil pleat tape hooks	2	Semi-sheers
Translucent pencil pleat	5cm (2in)	2 or more	gathered tape hooks	1	Sheers
Smocked pleat	7.5cm (3in)	$2\frac{1}{2}$	pencil pleat tape hooks	2	Fixed heading short
Box pleat	7.5cm (3in)	3	cartridge tape hooks	2	Fixed heading
Touch-and-close pencil pleat	7.5cm (3in)	2–$2\frac{1}{2}$	n/a	n/a	Fixed heading
Narrow touch-and-close pencil pleat	5cm (2in)	2–$2\frac{1}{2}$	n/a	n/a	Fixed heading
Translucent touch-and-close pencil pleat	5cm (2in)	2	n/a	n/a	Fixed heading (sheers)
Cordless triple pleat	8.5cm ($3\frac{1}{4}$in)	2	pronged	1	Traditional, medium to long, medium-weight

HAND-PLEATED HEADINGS

These are more time-consuming than using heading tapes, but they give a more professional finish, with invisible stitching and a stiffer heading. They will produce fat, crisp, luxurious pleats on interlined curtains – and if you are going to the trouble of hand pleating the heading, it's false economy not to interline the curtains.

Before the days of heading tapes, all headings were made by hand, and you can, of course, still make, say, pencil pleats by hand if you prefer. Normally, however, hand-made headings are used either for triple pleats or goblet pleats.

The stiffening is inserted after attaching interlining, if used, but before attaching a locked-in lining. The pleating is done at the very end.

The stiffening is generally buckram, which comes in 10cm 12.5cm and 15cm (4in, 5in and 6in) widths and either fusible or non-fusible versions. Make sure you buy heading buckram, not tieback buckram or pelmet buckram, which are too stiff for headings. The 15cm (6in) wide buckram is best for triple pleats (unless you are making short curtains, in which the 10cm (4in) width is better), while the 10cm (4in) wide buckram is the

best one for goblet pleats.

The hooks used for these headings are known as pin hooks, because their sharp prongs allow them to be pushed right into the back of the pleat. Alternatively, special sew-on brass hooks may be used.

STIFFENING THE HEADING

1 Follow the procedure for curtains with a locked-in lining, steps 1–2, or interlined curtains, steps 1–4, allowing for a fullness of 2¼ times. Cut the buckram to the finished width of the curtain (ie, without the side hem allowances). Open out the unstitched tops of the side seams and position the buckram even with the top and side fold lines – ie, 7.5cm (3in) from the top raw edge.

ABOVE ~ *You can recognize hand-pleated headings by the fat pleats and also by the lack of machine stitching across the top.*

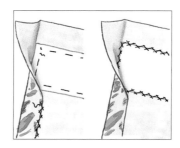

2 If you are using non-fusible buckram, herringbone stitch it in place all around. If you are using fusible buckram, simply tack it in place for now; it does not matter which side is uppermost. Refold the side hems, and slipstitch in place.

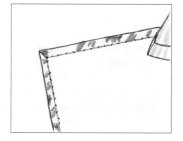

3 Proceed with attaching the lining (page 78, steps 3–6). If using fusible buckram, remove the tacking and iron the heading to fuse it to the fabric, following the manufacturer's instructions.

MARKING OUT PLEATS

1 To work out the number of pleats, their size and the size of the spaces between them, you'll need your calculator unless you want to attempt it by trial and error. Start by measuring the track, including any returns, and halving it. Now add 10cm (4in) for "ease", to cover the space easily – buckram has no give in it. This gives you the pleated width you will require for each curtain.

2 Divide this figure by 14cm (5.5in), which is the optimum size of each space between pleats. Round the result up or down to the nearest whole number, to find out the number of spaces. Divide that number back into the pleated width – the result is the exact width of each space. For the purposes of your calculations, assume that the number of spaces includes half a space between each outside pleat and the edge. The total number of spaces is the same as the number of pleats.

3 Now measure the flat width of the curtain, and deduct the pleated width from it. The resulting figure is the "excess" that can be used for the pleats themselves. Divide the excess by the number of pleats. The result is the width of one pleat.

4 For example, assume your whole curtain track is 178cm (70in) long, and the flat width of one curtain is 200cm (79in). The pleated width of one curtain will be half of 178cm (70in), plus 10cm (4in), or 99cm (39in). Dividing by 14cm (5.5in) and rounding down gives 7 spaces. Dividing this back into 99cm (39in) gives 14.1cm (5.6in) per space.

5 Continuing the example, deduct the pleated width of 99cm (39in) from the flat width of 200cm (79in), which gives an excess of 101cm (40in). Dividing this by 7 pleats gives a width per pleat of 14.4cm (5.7in).

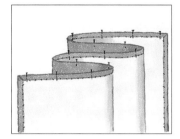

6 Mark out the pleats and spaces with pins or a fabric marker on the wrong side of your curtain. Allow a half-space between each edge and the first pleat, or the length of a return or overlap if there is one; usually a return or overlap is 8.5cm (3¼in). (When there is a return, the pleat goes on the corner, and there is no pleat on an "underlap".)

MAKING TRIPLE PLEATS

1 Working from the wrong side, bring the outer lines or pins marking the pleats together, with wrong sides together, and hold them in place with a clothes peg. Machine stitch for the full length of the pleat – which should be as long as the depth of the buckram – at right angles to the top edge. Start

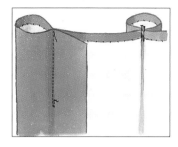

the stitching 6mm (¼in) from the top then backstitch to the top before stitching forward to the bottom of the pleat and backstitching once more. By not starting at the very top, you prevent any ends from sticking up. Repeat for the other pleats.

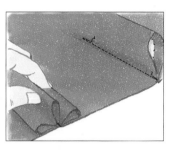

2 Place the curtain flat on the table, right side up. Using both hands (one at the top and one at the bottom of the pleat), push the pleat towards the table so that it forms three equal-sized pleats. Finger press the edges, and hold them together with a clothes peg.

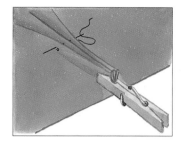

3 Using a double length of strong thread, make a few stitches at the base of each pleat just below the buckram, through all three pleats, about halfway between the top and the stitching line. Do not allow the stitches to come to the top or they will show.

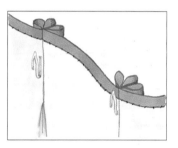

4 Leave the pleats with their clothes pegs holding the tops for a few days before removing them. Finally, insert a pin hook into the back of the pleat, alongside the pleat seam. Alternatively, sew brass hooks to the backs of the pleats. Adjust the height according to the desired height of the curtain on the track or pole. Also attach hooks at each side.

ABOVE ~ *Goblet headings look wonderfully elegant and dramatic on full-length curtains.*

MAKING GOBLET PLEATS

These are made in much the same way as triple pleats, but using 10cm (4in) wide buckram instead of 15cm (6in) wide.

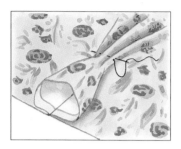

1 Pleat the heading as for triple pleats, step 1, then form each pleat into three pleats, as in step 2, but at the base of the pleat only. Sew through the base of each as for triple pleats, step 3.

VARIATION

Decorate the heading with a swagged cord. Knot the cord into figures-of-eight and sew each knot to the front of a pleat, allowing the cord to hang down in curves between the knots. Or use a double row of cords, with the bottom one a little longer so it hangs over, then sew to only every three goblets or so. The cord(s) can hang down at the sides and centre, with tassels on the ends. (Don't try to do this while the curtains are hanging in position.)

2 Round out each pleat into a goblet shape, and stuff with pieces of wadding, interlining or tissue paper, or a rolled-up piece of stiff paper. Attach hooks as for triple pleats, step 4.

CASED HEADING

This heading is simplicity itself to make, as it requires neither tape nor hooks. It is ideally suited to sheer or lightweight unlined curtains, with a fullness of no more than 1½ times. It isn't easy to open, however, and so is usually treated as a fixed heading, either permanently closed (the usual style for sheers) or tied back at the sides, as in the two examples shown here.

BELOW ~ *A cased heading with a self frill looks fresh and pretty.*

PLAIN CASING

1 Make an unlined curtain (page 74). At the top, turn under and press 1cm (⅜in) and then a deep enough hem to take the wire, rod or pole.

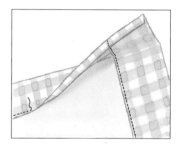

2 Stitch close to the pressed edge, then slot the wire, rod or pole into the casing so that it gathers up.

VARIATION

For a sash curtain, replace the lower edge with another casing, then insert wires or dowels into both casings, and mount on a window in a door. If you increase the length by about 15 per cent, you can pinch in the centre with a fabric tie, creating a waisted effect.

CASING WITH FRILL

1 Make an unlined curtain (page 74). At the top, turn under and press 1cm (⅜in) and then a hem deep enough to take the wire, rod or pole, plus the depth of a self frill.

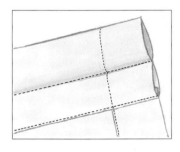

ABOVE ~ *Cased headings are well suited to sheer or very lightweight fabrics.*

2 Stitch close to the pressed edge, and again above it just far enough away to be able to slot the wire, rod or pole easily between the two rows of stitching.

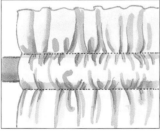

3 Slot the wire, rod or pole into the casing so that the fabric gathers up.

VARIATION

For a puffed heading, make the self frill about 11.5cm (4½in) deep, interlining it first to add body without stiffness. After gathering it onto the wire, rod or pole, bring the heading down over the stitching line at the front. Pull the front and back layers apart, and scrunch the heading into bunches.

TAB HEADINGS

These simple, versatile headings give a crisp, tailored, modern look to curtains hanging from a pole, although they are not as easy to open as headings with hooks. Allow from 1¼ to 2 times fullness, depending on the effect you want. The curtains can be lined or unlined; and the tabs can vary in both width and length, as well as in the actual method of fastening.

BELOW ~ *Buttoned tab headings are ideal for contemporary or informal decor.*

BUTTONED TABS

1 Make tabs with one pointed end (see page 35) or two square ends. They should be long enough to wrap over the pole and overlap the front, with a 1cm (⅜in) seam allowance. Topstitch if desired. Make a buttonhole in the pointed end of each, in exactly the same positions.

2 For an unlined curtain, replace the upper hem allowance with a 1cm (⅜in) seam allowance. Make up the curtain as usual. Cut a 7.5cm (3in) deep facing (see page 25) for the top edge, turning under a narrow hem at each end and on one long edge.

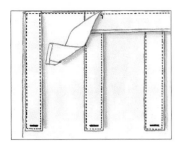

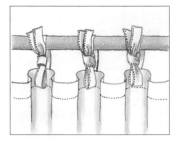

3 Pin the tabs to the right side of the curtain with raw edges even. Stitch 6mm (¼in) from the edge. Lay the facing on top, with right sides together and raw edges even. Stitch a 1cm (⅜in) seam.

3 Tie the pairs of ties around the pole, arranging the ends neatly.

TAB HEADINGS ON LINED CURTAINS

Any of the above headings can be used on lined curtains. Stitch the tabs to the curtain, then cover the raw ends with the lining. Ideally, the lining should come nearly to the top of the curtain.

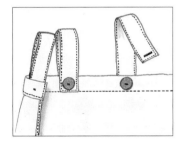

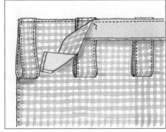

ABOVE ~ *Loops have both ends caught in the seam at the top.*

4 Turn the facing to the wrong side; press. Slipstitch or machine the facing to the curtain along the pressed edge and at the sides. Sew a button onto the front just beneath each tab. Loop each tab over the pole and button it (or button it first and then slot the pole through the loops).

2 Make up the curtain and a facing as for buttoned tabs, step 2. Fold the tab in half crosswise, and pin to the right side of the curtain with the raw edges even. Stitch as for buttoned tabs, step 3.

TIES
1 Make thin ties (see page 35) long enough to fold in half and then tie over the top of the pole, allowing 2cm (¾in) extra for the seam.

BELOW ~ *Ties are less tailored and more frivolous-looking than loop or buttoned-tab headings.*

LOOPS
1 Make tabs with straight, unhemmed ends. They should be long enough to wrap over the pole, with a 1cm (⅜in) seam allowance at each end. Make sure they are exactly the same length.

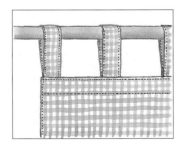

3 Complete the facing as for buttoned tabs, step 4. Slot the pole through the loops.

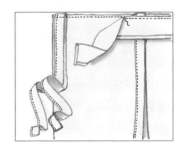

2 Make up the curtain and a facing as for buttoned tabs, step 2. Fold each tie in half crosswise, and pin the folded end even with the raw edge of the curtain. Stitch as for buttoned tabs, step 3, and then complete the facing as for step 4.

SCALLOPED HEADINGS

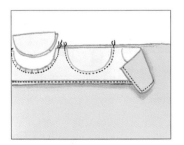

Scallop-headed café curtains are made in much the same way as the scalloped bed hangings on page 143. They are generally hung from curtain rings clipped or sewn on at the top between scallops. The scallops do not therefore need to be as deep as those used for the bed curtains. Extend the straight sides by only 1.5cm (⅝in), rather than 15cm (6in), beyond the top of the semi-circle, and make the facing only 15cm (6in) deep.

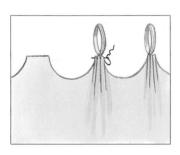

Another idea is to space the scallops further apart – about 8cm (3¼in) instead of 2cm (¾in) apart – then make a triple pleat by hand (see page 91) in each space. For these, allow about 2¼ times fullness rather than 1½ times.

UNUSUAL HEADINGS

Unusual headings have proliferated in the last few years and can look fun and informal.

EYELET HEADINGS

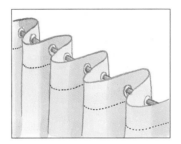

Make lined or unlined curtains, with a fullness of about 1½ times. Interface the heading. Insert jumbo eyelets at 12.5cm (5in) intervals, then fold the heading concertina fashion and slot a rod through the eyelets.

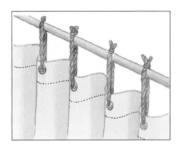

A different idea is to tie the curtain to a pole with individual short lengths of cord through each eyelet.

SEE ALSO

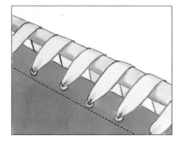

Yet another approach is to lace the curtain to a pole with one long length of cord wound around the pole and through the eyelets. Add separate bows if desired.

CORDED HEADING

1 At the top edge, make a double 1cm (⅜in) hem; machine stitch. Divide the top into equal segments of about 10–15cm (4–6in), marking them with pins.

Take a long length of cord and, at one side, make a loop big enough to slip over a pole. Hand sew firmly in position.

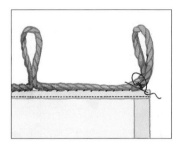

2 Extend the cord along the top of the curtain, sew in place. When you get to the first pin, make another loop of the same size as the original; sew in place. Continue across the top of the curtain, finishing with a loop at the other side. Slot pole through loops.

ABOVE ~ *Strong ribbon can be used instead of cord in an eyelet heading.*

SPECIAL STYLES

With most curtains the principal stylistic difference is their headings but certain styles are distinctive in other ways. These include café, Italian-strung, cross-over, jardinière and shower curtains.

CAFÉ CURTAINS

Café curtains are short, tiered curtains in which the bottom tier usually remains closed, providing privacy but letting in light. Usually, one tier covers the bottom half of the window, and then the top half either has an identical tier, has a valance with a matching heading or is left bare.

RIGHT ~ *A café curtain consisting of a single tier looks pretty with a matching valance.*

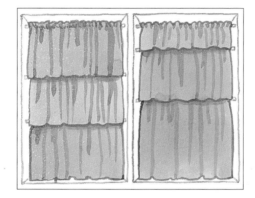

Sometimes, however, three or even four tiers are used, each covering a third or a quarter of the window. These multiple tiers can all be the same length, or they can be graduated, with the shortest on top.

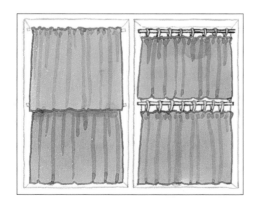

The top of one tier can overlap the one beneath it, or each can finish just above the one below it to expose the headings.

Café curtains are normally unlined. The fullness is determined by the heading, which can be scalloped (with or without pleats between the scallops), cased or tabbed, or made using a conventional heading tape. For the café curtains shown in the photograph below, follow the instructions for a casing with frill (page 93). For a scalloped heading, see page 96.

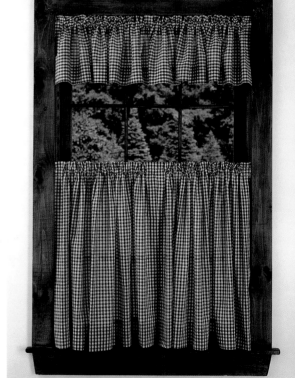

ITALIAN-STRUNG CURTAINS

Also known as reefed curtains, these very elegant curtains have a fixed heading and are drawn up at the sides like puppet-theatre curtains, through the use of diagonally strung cords at the back. Italian stringing looks particularly good with interlined curtains as shown on page 79.

1 Mount a 5 x 2.5cm (2 x 1in) batten flat against the wall just above the window, and fix a pole or track just above that. Insert four screw eyes into the batten, and two into the wall or window frame, as shown. Fix a cleat at chest height into the wall; this will be in line with the pull cord.

2 Make a pair of lined and interlined curtains and hang them from the pole or track. Overlap at the centre, hand sewing the headings together invisibly and dressing them as usual (see page 79).

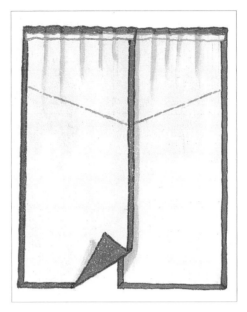

3 On the leading edge of each curtain, mark a point about a third of the way down the curtain. On the outer edge of each curtain, mark a point about one-fifth to one-quarter of the way down the curtain. Draw a diagonal line on the back of each curtain between these two points. Sew brass or plastic rings to the curtains along these lines, sewing through all layers with tiny stitches.

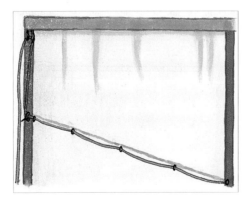

4 Tie a length of cord to the ring on the leading edge of one curtain. Run it

through the rings on the diagonal line, then through the screw eye on the wall next to the last ring, next through the pair of screw eyes in the batten above it, and finally down the side.

5 Tie another length of cord to the ring on the leading edge of the other curtain. Take it up to the batten in the same way, then through the central screw eye and across the length of the batten, and then finally through the pair on the other side and down.

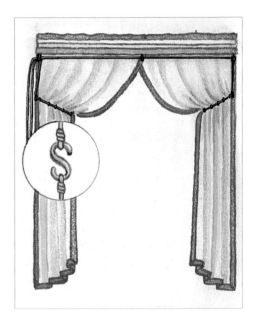

6 Close the curtains and tension the cords evenly. Sew both ends to one S-ring, at about the same height as the ring on the leading edge. Sew a pull-cord with a tassel or acorn to the other half of the S-ring. Cover both sides with coiled cord, sewing it in place. Pull the cord to open or close the curtains.

CROSS-OVER CURTAINS

These consist of two identical sheer curtains layered on top of one another. The tops are stitched together to form one fixed heading, then the curtains are drawn back to opposite sides and held in place with tiebacks.

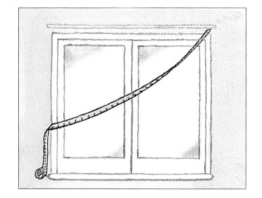

1 Drape a tape measure across the window, following the desired line of one curtain's leading edge, from the top of the window, across in a curve to the tieback point and then straight down to the sill. Add the usual allowances for unlined sheer curtains, and cut out the curtains to this depth. (The width of the curtain is determined by the heading in the usual way.)

2 Mark the depth of the window on the outside edge of each curtain, adding the same allowances as in step 1. Draw a straight line between this point and the lower edge on the opposite side of each curtain. Cut along this line.

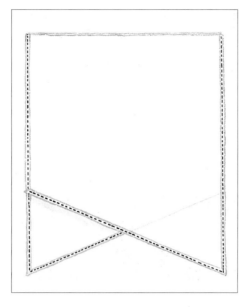

3 Hem the side and lower edges. Place one curtain on top of the other, right sides uppermost.

4 Treating the two layers as one, make the heading of your choice. Hang in the appropriate way for the heading, then pull one curtain back to the right and the other to the left. Secure with tiebacks.

JARDINIÈRE CURTAIN

This sheer curtain is a single panel with a curved bottom edge that is higher in the centre. It is made like the shaped valance on page 108, but with the sides equal to the distance from the covered wire or pole to the sill. A deep frill can be added to the lower edge if desired, in which case take this into account in the length of the curtain.

SHOWER CURTAIN

1 Following the guidelines for PVC and other plastics (page 42), make up an unlined curtain using shower curtain fabric and an eyelet heading with 1cm (⅜in) eyelets.

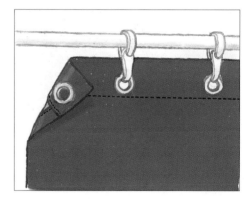

2 Attach the shower curtain to the rail using clip-on shower curtain rings. (Choose the size according to the size of the rail and the eyelets.)

SEE ALSO

UNUSUAL WINDOWS

Choosing the right hardware and accessories means that curtains for awkwardly shaped windows needn't be a problem – you can make a virtue of necessity and turn them into a distinct feature.

ARCHED WINDOW

ABOVE ~ *Touch-and-close curtain tape provides one of the neatest ways to curtain an arched window.*

An arched window looks good with a pair of fixed-headed curtains. These are attached to the window frame or wall, using touch-and-close curtain tape, then held back with tiebacks. This type normally requires 2½ times fullness but in a recess only use 1½–2 times to avoid covering too much of the window.

1 Cut out each curtain to the maximum height of the window (at the centre) plus a 1.2cm (1/2in upper hem allowance and the usual lower hem allowance, joining widths as necessary. Hem the sides and the lower edges.

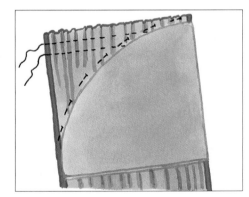

2 Make a template for the arch; fold it in half. Using running stitch, gather up each curtain temporarily to the width of the folded template. Lay the template on the wrong side and mark the outline with pins, leaving an upper hem allowance of 1.2cm (½in) around the curve.

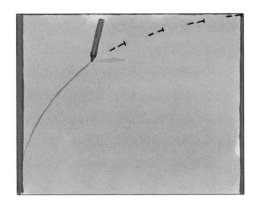

3 Remove the template and pull out the gathering threads. Now, using a fabric marker, connect up the pins to form a curve. Cut out along this line.

4 Turn under the upper hem allowance. Stitch touch-and-close curtain tape around the top of the curtain, easing it to fit the curve, and pull up the cords as for conventional heading tape.

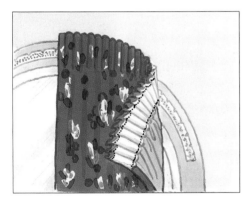

5 Stick the self-adhesive half to the wall or recess, snipping into the top edge to fit around the curve. Fix the curtains in place and hold back with tiebacks.

SEE ALSO

VARIATION

• Rather than tiebacks, use Italian stringing to hold the curtains back.
• Instead of curtains, make an Austrian blind using the touch-and-close curtain tape.
• Instead of using touch-and-close curtain tape, curved track could be fixed around the top of the window. The curtains are made as above, but suspended from the track. Hand sew the leading edges of the heading together to stop it from slipping down the track.
• Make a Roman blind with a flat heading the same size and shape as the arch, and back the arched heading with a thin piece of MDF (medium-density fibreboard). Attach this to the window as for a pelmet board (see page 115).

ROOF WINDOW

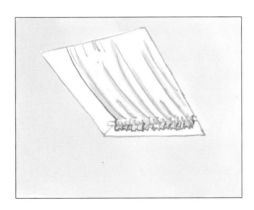

The problem here is the slope of the roof into which the window is set. One way to deal with this is to make a sash curtain; this has casings slotted over a narrow rod or covered wire at both ends of the curtain. It does not open.

Another possibility for a roof window is a Roman or roller blind held against the window by a curtain pole, preferably matching the pole at the top of the window. (Special blinds are also available that fit between the two layers of glass as part of the double-glazed unit and are operated from below the window.)

DORMER WINDOW

To avoid blocking light, make a curtain in reversible fabric, with a cased heading, then slip it over a special dormer rod that swivels back to the reveal (see page 69).

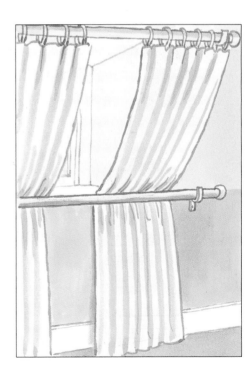

Another idea is to hang floor-length curtains from a pole outside the recess, and use a second pole along the bottom of the window to hold the curtains back against the sloping ceiling.

VALANCES, PELMETS,

SWAGS & TIEBACKS

TIEBACKS

Tiebacks hold curtains open in a graceful, curved shape, allowing more light into the room. They can be made in a wide variety of shapes and styles.

MAKING TIEBACKS

Tiebacks are essential with fixed headings unless you use hold-backs or Italian stringing (see pages 70 and 98 respectively) and can also be used on curtains that open and close. Generous lined and interlined curtains are best for this treatment.

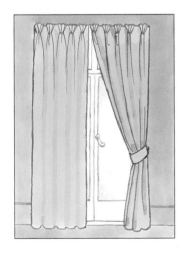

Each tieback is attached to a cup hook on the wall alongside the curtain. Tiebacks may be positioned either two-thirds of the way down, halfway down, or about a third of the way down the curtain, depending on the desired effect. They are traditionally made from thick

cord (with or without tassels) or stiffened fabric that matches, coordinates with or contrasts with the curtain fabric. However, long fabric ties or lengths of natural jute, ribbon, braid, chain or even beads can be used instead of cord, so long as they are appropriate to the curtain style. Rosettes (see page 119) are sometimes used to decorate tiebacks. All instructions are for one tieback. To decide the length, hold a tape measure loosely around the curtain at the desired height.

PADDED TIEBACK

1 Cut a strip of fabric and a strip of heavyweight wadding to the desired tieback length plus 3cm (1¼in), and to twice the desired tieback width plus 3cm (1¼in).

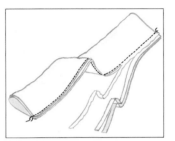

2 Tack the wadding to the wrong side of the fabric strip. Fold the padded strip in half lengthwise, with right sides together and raw edges even, and stitch a 1.5cm (⅝in) seam along the long edge. Trim the seam, cutting away the wadding right up to the seamline.

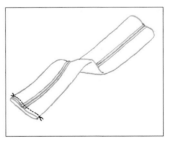

3 Position the seam so that it runs down the centre of the strip, then stitch a 1.5cm (⅝in) seam across one end. Trim the wadding as before, and turn right side out.

4 Turn under 1.5cm (⅝in) on both raw edges at the open end, and slipstitch.

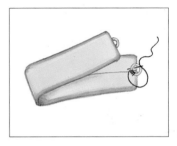

5 Hand sew a ring centrally at each end of the tieback so that it projects slightly beyond the fabric

PLAITED TIEBACK

1 Cut three strips of fabric and three of medium-weight wadding, each 1½ times the tieback length and 12.5–15cm (5–6in) wide.

2 Make up three padded tubes as for the padded tieback, steps 1 and 2, but do not stitch the end. (For a flatter tieback, the fabric tubes can be left unpadded.)

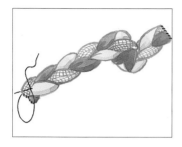

3 Lay the tubes on top of each other with all the seams facing in the same direction, and whipstitch the ends together at one end. Plait the tubes, keeping the seams all on the same side so that they can be hidden when on the curtain. Check the length of the tieback and then whipstitch the remaining ends together.

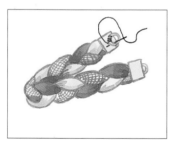

4 Cut two fabric rectangles, each 7.5 x 5cm (3 x 2in) and press under 6mm (¼in) all around. Fold one over each end of the plait and slipstitch in place. Attach rings as for the padded tieback, step 5.

SHAPED TIEBACK

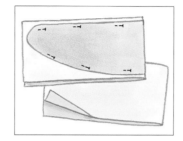

1 Make a crescent-shaped template to the desired length. Cut out two pieces of fabric using the template but adding 1.5cm (⅝in) all round.

2 Cut out a piece of tieback buckram (or stiff interfacing if you cannot get buckram) and two pieces of medium-weight interlining using the template, without adding a seam allowance.

3 Spray the buckram with water, place the interlining on top, and press with a hot iron; the glue sizing in the buckram will make them stick together. Trim off any excess interlining. Repeat this procedure to attach the second piece of interlining to the other side of the buckram.

4 Place the encased buckram on the wrong side of one fabric piece. Turn the seam allowance over the stiffening all around, and press. Clip the curves. Herringbone stitch the seam allowance to the interlining.

5 Attach a ring at each end of the tieback as for the padded tieback, step 5.

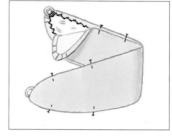

6 Press under a slightly bigger seam allowance all around the second fabric piece, and pin to the stiffened piece, with the wrong side facing the interlined buckram. Slipstitch all around the edge. Fold the tieback so that this piece is on the inside.

TIE-ON TIEBACK

This tieback, which is shown in the photograph below, is a variation of a shaped tieback.

1 Square the end of the template for the shaped tieback (see step 1). Make as for the shaped tieback, steps 1–4 and 6.

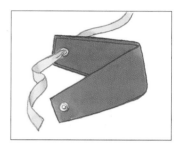

2 Insert a jumbo eyelet at each end, and secure the tieback around the curtain by tying a contrasting ribbon or fabric tie through both of the eyelets. Loop the ribbon or tie over the hook on the wall.

ABOVE ~ *A tie-on tieback is fastened with ribbon instead of rings.*

PIPED TIEBACK

1 Make this in the same way as for the shaped tieback, steps 1–4.

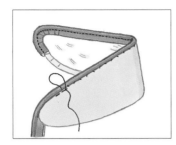

2 Make up piping and, with the right side of the padded fabric piece facing you, position the piping with the covered cord running along the edge and with the raw edges of the piping behind. Slipstitch from the right side along the edge as close to the cord as possible, using tiny stitches.

3 Attach the rings and lining as for the shaped tieback, steps 5–6.

BOUND TIEBACK

1 Make a template and cut out two fabric pieces as for the shaped tieback, step 1, but do not add seam allowances.

RIGHT ~ A frilled tieback, such as this one with a single frill, is perfect for this type of curtain.

2 Cut out the buckram and interlining, and assemble them as for the shaped tieback, steps 2 and 3.

3 Sandwich the interlined buckram between the two fabric pieces, with the right sides of the fabric facing outward. Tack all around.

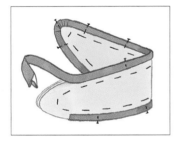

4 Bind the edges using either purchased bias binding or binding made from the tieback fabric or a coordinating or contrasting fabric. Remove the tacking.

5 Attach a ring to each end of the tieback as for the padded tieback, step 5.

TIEBACK WITH SINGLE FRILL

This consists of a band with a frill on the lower edge, as in the photograph above. It is a very suitable style to use with frilled curtains.

1 Decide the depth of the band and the depth of the

frill; usually the frill is about the same depth as the frill on the curtain if there is one. The band is often half the depth of the frill, but in the tieback shown here they are the same depth.

strip of stiff interfacing to the desired finished dimensions, and either herringbone stitch or fuse it to one half of the fabric strip, lining up one edge of the interfacing with the band foldline.

2 For the band, cut one strip of fabric to twice the desired depth of the band plus 3cm (1¼in), by the desired length plus 3cm (1¼in). Cut a

3 Make a single frill for the long edge, gathering it up to the desired finished length of the band. Turn under 1.5cm (⅝in) on all edges of

the band, and fold it in half lengthwise. Insert the frill between the edges, and top-stitch through all thicknesses near the foldline. Attach a ring at each end as for the padded tieback, step 5.

TIEBACK WITH DOUBLE-EDGED FRILL

1 Make a double-edged frill (see page 32) to the desired length and width of the tieback. Cut a strip of fabric to the length of the tieback plus 1.2cm (½in), and 2.5cm (1in) wide.

2 Press under 6mm (¼in) at each end of the strip, then fold it in half lengthwise with right sides together and stitch a 6mm (¼in) seam along the long edge. Turn right side out and press so that the seam is running down the centre back.

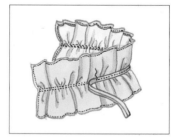

3 Pin the strip down the centre of the frill. Topstitch along the long edges. Attach a ring at each end of the strip as for the padded tieback, step 5.

QUICK AND EASY TIEBACK

This tieback, though very simple to make, is both functional and decorative, as the photograph on page 108 demonstrates.

1 From the fabric, cut two rectangles (or, if you prefer, two crescent shapes, using the template for the shaped tieback) to the desired dimensions plus 3cm (1¼in) each way.

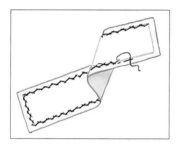

2 Cut a piece of stiff interfacing to the desired size, without the seam allowances. Either fuse or Herringbone stitch the interfacing to one fabric piece.

3 Place the two pieces with right sides together. Stitch around all four edges, leaving an opening. Trim the seam and clip the corners. Turn

right side out, and press. Slipstitch the opening. Attach a ring at each end as for the padded tieback, step 5.

VARIATIONS

• For an easy piped tieback, insert piping between steps 2 and 3, stitching it to the right side of one fabric piece with raw edges even.
• For a scalloped tieback, adapt the crescent-shaped template by drawing around a small glass to create shallow scallops along the lower edge, starting with a full one at the fold.

BOW TIEBACK

1 Cut out two 125 x 22.5cm (49 x 8¾in) strips of fabric. Fold one strip in half lengthwise, with right sides together. Stitch a 1.5cm (⅝in) seam along the long edge, stopping 11cm (4¼in) from the end. Now pivot the fabric and stitch diagonally across to a point on the fold 1.5cm (⅝in) from the end. Trim the seam and turn right side out.

2 Turn in 1.5cm (⅝in) on the raw edges at the unstitched end, press and slipstitch. Repeat for the second strip.

3 Form several small pleats at the square end of the tie and stitch across them 1cm (⅜in) from the end. Hand sew a ring to this end, as for the padded tieback, step 5. Repeat for the other tie.

4 Slip the rings of the two ties over one hook. Arrange the ties in a bow around the curtain.

SEE ALSO

VALANCES

In window treatments, a valance is an unstiffened strip of fabric which covers the top of the window. It can be used with or without curtains.

VALANCE BASICS

A valance is designed to cover a curtain heading and track, but it can also be used on an uncurtained window, with café curtains which have a matching heading, or with a blind.

HANGING VALANCES

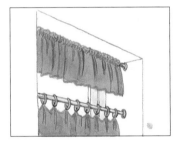

A valance can be hung from a combination track and valance rail, from which the curtain hangs too (see page 67), a separate track, rod, wire or pole, or a pelmet board (see page 115). If you are using two separate rods or tracks, one in front of the other, there should be a distance of at least 5cm (2in) between them.

To attach the valance to a pelmet board, you can use touch-and-close curtain tape, or simply staple or tack it to the board. Curtain hooks are another option – these are attached to a track fixed to the base of the board or to a line of screw eyes screwed into the board.

STYLES

Valances are normally one-eighth to one-fifth the length of curtains. Occasionally they are simple, flat bands of fabric, such as a length of antique lace or toile de Jouy hung from a rod with clip-on hooks. But usually valances are pleated or gathered.

All curtain headings are suitable, including those for fixed headings such as smock-effect and box-pleat heading tapes and also cased headings. The heading determines the fullness required. Valances generally should be fuller than curtains, with 2½–3 times fullness rather than 2–2½. When measuring, don't forget to include the returns.

MAKING VALANCES

Valances are like very short curtains and are made in the same way as the curtains they are accompanying. They may therefore be unlined or lined, and if they are lined, they should also ideally be interlined to make them hang better. Unless the valance is very deep, it will not need to be lockstitched. To make the heading stiff and crisp, you may need to interface it, depending on how soft the fabric you are using is.

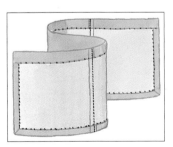

When joining an even number of widths, cut one width in

ABOVE ~ *A valance with a cased heading can be slotted onto a track or pole.*

half lengthwise and stitch one half to each side to avoid a central seam. Use plain seams if you are lining the valance, and flat fell seams if not.

The side hem allowances should be the same as for the curtains, and the lower hem allowance should be half that for curtains (although for some styles a narrow hem may be more appropriate). Alternatively, add a frill to the lower edge instead of hemming it.

BELOW ~ *A straight valance, like tiebacks, may be all that is needed to make a treatment special.*

The unlined valance in the photograph below is the simplest style.

1 This is made as for unlined curtains, allowing 2½–3 times fullness. For the upper hem, allow 1.2cm (½in) when cutting out. Join widths as directed above. Stitch the side and bottom hems.

STRAIGHT VALANCE

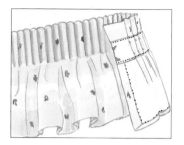

2 Stitch on a heading tape or touch-and-close curtain tape as for curtains, and pull up to form gathers or pleats.

3 Attach the valance to a track with curtain hooks or to a pelmet board using the "gripper" side of the touch-and-close tape.

VARIATIONS

- Instead of using curtain heading tape, make a cased heading and slot the valance onto a pole.
- Bind the lower edge with contrast binding instead of hemming.

SHAPED VALANCE

A lined valance with a shaped lower edge, like the one on page 109 (top left), looks good with or without curtains. The same method can be used to make a jardinière curtain, with a fixed heading (see page 99).

pelmet board or track *including the returns*. For the depth, decide what would look best with your curtains (see above) and add 1.5cm (⅝in) for the lower seam. For the cased heading with frill, add the desired depth of the casing plus the frill, plus 1.5cm (⅝in).

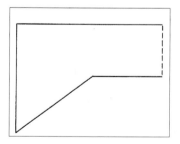

1 Using the shape shown in the illustration above as a guide, make a template for the valance from lining paper. Because it is for half the valance, the template should be 1¼–1½ the width of the

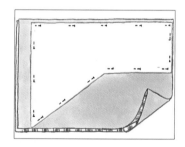

2 Cut out the shape. Fold the main fabric in half, and place the template on the foldline. Cut out and join as many widths as necessary. Repeat for the lining.

ABOVE ~ A shaped valance with a cased heading looks elegant.

3 With right sides together, join the main fabric and lining along the sides and the lower edge, taking a 1.5cm (⅝in) seam. Trim the corners and turn right side out. Press.

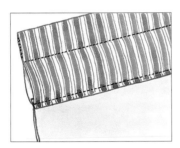

VARIATIONS

- Join the side edges but not the lower edge with right sides together; turn right side out; bind the lower edge with contrast binding.
- When stitching the side and lower edges, insert uncorded piping in the seams.

4 Treating the two layers of fabric as one, press under 1.5cm (⅝in) along the top edge, then press under an amount equal to the casing plus frill. Machine a row of stitches along each side of the casing, making sure that the casing is not too tight for the curtain track or rod. Slipstitch the sides of the heading above the casing. Slot the valance onto the track or pole, gathering it up.

VALANCE WITH BAND

A valance with a traditional buckram-lined band at the top looks very professional. A variety of "skirts" can be used with the band – straight or shaped, gathered or pleated. The valance in the photograph below has a skirt that is ruched up at intervals. Normally the band would be about one-third of the total depth of the valance, but this one is much narrower.

BELOW ~ *This valance has a ruched and frilled skirt set into a narrow band.*

1 From the main band fabric, cut out and join widths to make a band the length of the track or rod, including returns, plus 8cm (3in), and the desired band width plus 3cm (1¼in). Cut out a band of lining the same size, again joining widths if necessary.

2 From the main skirt fabric, cut out a skirt equal to its desired finished depth plus 7cm (2⅝in), and 2½ times the length of the track, plus 3cm (1¼in). Cut the lining to the same size. In both cases, you will probably need to join widths. From the band fabric,

make a double frill twice the length of the skirt, and as wide as you wish.

3 If desired, you can pipe both long edges of the band and the lower edge of the skirt. On the right side of the band, machine tack the piping along the upper and lower seamlines – which are 1.5cm (⅝in) from each edge – leaving 4cm (1½in) unpiped at each end. Tuck in the piping ends.

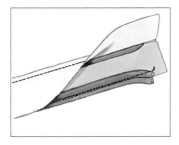

4 With right sides together, stitch the band fabric and lining together along the top edge with a 1.5cm (⅝in) seam.

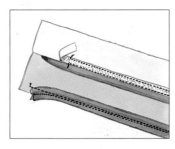

5 Open out the lining and fabric, and stitch touch-and-close curtain tape along the top edge of the lining on the right side, as close to the piping as possible. The tape should finish 4cm (1½in) from each end.

6 On the right side of the skirt fabric, on the lower edge, machine tack the piping along the 1.5cm (⅝in) seamline, stopping 1.5cm (⅝in) short of each edge and tucking in the ends. Lay the frill on top, with its raw edges even with the raw edge of the skirt fabric and again stopping short of each edge; tack in place. With right sides together, join the fabric and the lining together along this edge and the side edges, with 1.5cm (⅝in) seams. Turn right side out and press.

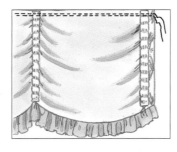

7 Pin the fabric and lining together along the top edge. Stitch several lengths of gathered heading tape vertically, at equal intervals. Knot the cords at the bottom and pull up to gather. Run two rows of gathering stitches within the seam allowance of the top edge, and gather up the top of the skirt until it is the width of the pelmet board plus returns.

8 With right sides together, stitch the skirt to the band main fabric with a 1.5cm (⅝in) seam. The finished edges should be 4cm (1½in) from each end of the band.

9 Turn in 4cm (1½in) at each end of the band and lining; press. Cut a length of interlining and one of fusible buckram to the finished dimensions of the band. (To join widths of interlining, overlap the edges then zigzag or herringbone stitch together.) Lay the interlining on the wrong side of the main fabric, and the buckram on top.

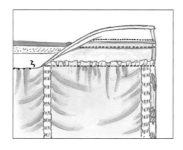

10 Turn under 1.5cm (⅝in) on the lower edge of the lining and pull it tightly over the buckram. Slipstitch it over the skirt seamline. Also slipstitch the sides of the band. Press the back of the band in order to fuse the buckram to the band.

11 Fix the self-adhesive half of the touch-and-close tape to the front of the pelmet board, then stick the valance to it.

VARIATION

Instead of an Austrian blind style of skirt, make a shaped skirt with a gathered top (since you cannot use tape with the band) and bound edges. Use the same fabric for binding the edges as for the piping.

Also known as an integral valance or a self-pelmet, an attached valance gives you the stylish finish of a valance without blocking incoming light when the curtains are open. However, it does not cover the heading or track, so it looks best with a pole.

The curtains and the valance can be either lined or unlined, but avoid using very heavy fabric because there are a lot of layers to stitch through when making the heading. As with other valances one-fifth to one-sixth the length of the curtain will probably look best.

To emphasize the lower edge of the valance, it is common to attach a contrasting band, braid or fringing. The curtains could have a matching double band or trim along the lower edge and leading edge.

UNLINED CURTAINS WITH ATTACHED VALANCES

1 Make the curtains as for unlined curtains (page 74) – allowing for a 1.2cm (½in) seam at the top – but do not make the heading at this stage. Incorporate contrast bands (see Double Bands) if desired.

ATTACHED VALANCES

2 Cut out and join widths as necessary to make a valance the same width as the curtain. Make side hems the same size as the curtain and a lower hem half that of the curtain – or add a double band (page 29) if desired.

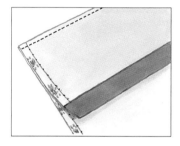

3 Place the right side of the valance against the wrong side of the curtain. Stitch across the top, taking a 1.2cm (½in) seam. Press. Complete as for lined curtains with attached valances, step 5.

RIGHT ~ *This attached valance has a contrast band around the edges to define the shape.*

LINED CURTAINS WITH ATTACHED VALANCES

1 Make the curtain as for lined (or interlined) curtains, allowing for a 1.2cm (½in) seam at the top and making the lining long enough for the top edge to be flush with that of the curtain. Instead of turning in these edges, tack them together along the seamline. Do not make the heading yet. If desired, incorporate a contrast double band.

BELOW ~ *Even without contrasting trim, an attached valance adds interest to curtains.*

2 From the main fabric, cut out a valance to the finished width of the curtain plus 2.5cm (1in), and to the depth plus 2.5cm (1in). If you are having a contrast band, allow for this. Cut out a valance lining of the same size. You will probably have to join widths on both the fabric and lining.

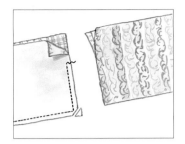

3 Stitch a single band to the lower edge if desired. With right sides together, join the valance fabric and lining around the side and lower edges, leaving 10cm (4in) unstitched at the top of each side seam. Trim off corners and turn right side out. Press the seam and press the unstitched turnings.

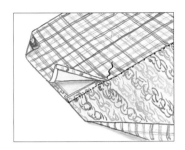

4 Place the right side of the valance against the back of the curtain. Stitch across the top through the valance fabric and the curtain fabric and lining, taking a 1.2cm (½in) seam. Press. Turn under the raw top edge of the valance lining, press and then slipstitch it to the curtain. Slipstitch the open parts of the valance side seams.

5 Turn the valance to the front of the curtain and tack together near the top edge. Make the heading in all layers, using tape or hand-pleating. Remove the tacking.

SEE ALSO

PELMETS

A pelmet is made of stiffened fabric that covers the top of the window, the track and the curtain or blind heading. Whereas valances are usually soft and gathered, pelmets are flat.

TRADITIONAL PELMET

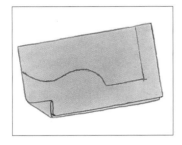

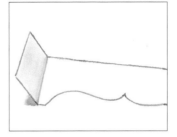

A pelmet board (see page 115) is the basis of the pelmet. If the front and ends are covered in fabric, the fabric can match, contrast or coordinate with the curtains. If you have to join fabric widths, avoid having a central seam (see pages 107-8).

Pelmets are traditionally stiffened with pelmet buckram, but self-adhesive stiffener may be used instead and is quicker.

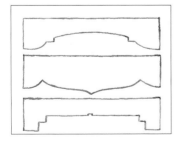

The depth should be as for a valance (page 107). The bottom can be straight or shaped.

1 First make a template that fits around the pelmet board, including the returns. Cut out a rectangle to the desired size, and fold the paper in half crosswise so the template will be symmetrical. Draw the shape of the lower edge. Cut out, then tape it in place to check how it looks.

2 Using the template, cut out the main fabric, joining widths as necessary (with plain seams) to make a piece 2.5cm (1in) larger all around than the template. Cut out a piece of lining 1cm (⅜in) larger than the template all around, joining widths if necessary. Cut out interlining the same size as the template. If you have to join widths of interlining, butt the edges and herring-bone stitch them together.

3 Using a craft knife or heavyduty shears, cut out buckram to the template size. Do not join widths or it will create a ridge. With the blade, score the buckram so it bends easily around the corners.

4 Lockstitch the interlining to the wrong side of the pelmet fabric (see page 78). Lay the buckram on top.

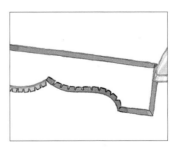

5 Clip into the seam allowances of the fabric on inward corners and curves. Dampen the edges of the buckram and turn in the seam

allowance over it. Iron in place, mitring outward corners. (Even if you are not using fusible buckram, it ought to stick to the fabric. If it doesn't, use fabric glue.) Do not touch the buckram directly with the iron.

6 Press under 1.5cm (⅝in) on all edges of the lining, again clipping into the seam allowances and mitring the corners; tack. Stitch the sew-on side of touch-and-close tape to top edge of the lining.

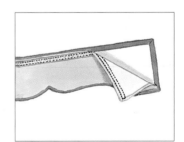

7 With wrong sides together, slipstitch the lining to the seam allowances of the fabric.

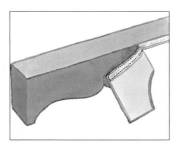

8 Fix the self-adhesive side of the tape to the front and sides of the pelmet board, and stick the pelmet in place.

VARIATIONS

● Add piping at the end of step 5, following the instructions for piped tiebacks, step 2. Or, after attaching the lining (step 7), slipstitch trimming in place using a curved needle, or glue it in place with fabric adhesive.

● Instead of buckram, use double-sided self-adhesive stiffener and omit the interlining. Peel off the backing from one side of the stiffener, press it onto the wrong side of the fabric, then remove the backing from the other side and press the fabric seam allowance onto it. Complete as above, steps 6–8..

QUICK NO-SEW PELMET

1 Make a template as above, step 1, and cut out the fabric 2cm (¾in) larger all around than the template. Cut out a piece of single-sided self-adhesive stiffener the same size as the template. (You can even make the template from the stiffener if you prefer, as the backing is printed with a grid.)

2 Following the manufacturer's instructions, peel off the backing paper from the stiffener, and press the wrong side of the fabric onto it. Work from the centre outwards, carefully smoothing down the fabric as you go.

3 Trim the fabric edges even with the stiffener. If desired, glue braid or fringe over the edges. Fix the self-adhesive side of touch-and-close tape to the front edge of the pelmet board, then stick the velour backing of the stiffener to it.

PADDED BUTTONED PELMET

1 Make a traditional pelmet (see page 113) with a straight lower edge, but replace the interlining with thick wadding, to give the padded effect.

2 When the pelmet is complete, sew covered buttons at regular intervals through all layers (see Button-tufted Cushions, page 171). You'll need to use a strong needle, upholstery thread and a thimble.

LEFT ~ *A padded buttoned pelmet provides a traditional and smart top treatment.*

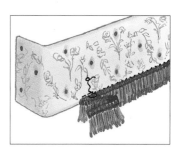

3 Along the lower edge, hand sew fringing or glue it on using fabric adhesive.

SEE ALSO

PELMET BOARDS

Pelmet boards are shelves attached to the wall above curtains, to take valances, pelmets, or swags and tails. Most are straight, but some have curved fronts. The track is bent slightly to follow the curve.

MAKING A PELMET BOARD

If a valance or pelmet and curtains hang from a pelmet board, one or two tracks are fixed to the underside.

CRITICAL DIMENSIONS
A shelf with just one track should be about 13cm (5in) from front to back, and one carrying two tracks should be about 18cm (7in). The distance between the front track and the front of the pelmet board should be at least 7cm (2¾in). The rear track should be at least 5cm (2in) behind the front one and at least 4cm (1½in) from the wall. The track should finish about 2cm (¾in) from each end. A pelmet board can be fitted above a separate curtain track too, in which case it should extend beyond the track by at least 6cm (2¼in) at each end.

The pelmet board is attached to the wall at least 10cm (4in) above the window, using special cast angle-brackets, available from curtain fitting suppliers. There should be a bracket at each end and at 30cm (12in) intervals in between.

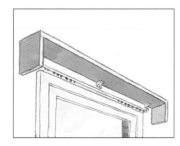

The pelmet board should be made from plywood or MDF (medium-density fibreboard) 1.2–2cm (½–¾in) thick. If a valance is quite wide or deep, the pelmet board can be made more rigid with end pieces.

SPECIAL SITUATIONS

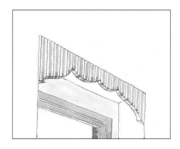

For recessed windows, the pelmet board may be cut to the width of the front of the recess and then mounted on the ceiling of the recess, with the front flush with the wall or architrave.

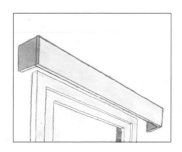

Normally, the front and ends are covered by a stiffened fabric pelmet or a valance, but if the pelmet is to go in a kitchen or bathroom, where the damp atmosphere would warp buckram, it would probably be better to use a

plywood or MDF front and end pieces. If the wood or MDF front is to have a shaped lower edge, you'll need to cut it with a jigsaw or coping saw.

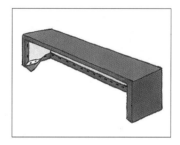

The plywood or MDF is either painted or it is covered with interlining and fabric that are secured in place with a staple gun, hammer and tacks, or fabric glue.

SIMPLE TOP TREATMENTS

Sometimes the simplest ideas for draping or gathering a length of fabric are the most effective. These treatments work well with inexpensive fabrics, which can be used lavishly.

DRAPED POLE

1 Create an effect similar to swags and tails, but less formal, by casually draping fabric over a curtain pole. Variations of this treatment are shown opposite and on page 127. You'll need a full width of muslin or lace that is as long as 1½ times the length of the curtain pole, plus twice the distance from the pole to where the fabric finishes, plus extra for draping. Hem ends.

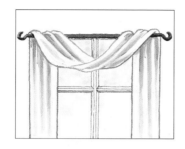

2 On each side, take the fabric up over the top of the pole from the back, draping it across the front.

3 Use touch-and-close dots to hold it in place at each end of the pole, and to catch it up in the centre if desired.

VARIATIONS

- Allow the fabric to pool onto the floor on both sides of the window.
- Cut the ends diagonally and then hem them, to resemble formal tails.
- Arrange the fabric asymmetrically, with one end very short and the other longer, as shown opposite.
- Wind the fabric several times around a pole, fixing it in place with tacks, a staple gun or touch-and-close tape if you wish.

FABRIC FAN FOR ARCHED WINDOW

Also known as a sunburst curtain, a fan-shaped curtain made from sheer fabric filters the light and emphasizes the shape of an arched window. It looks good with a conventional sheer curtain hung from a rod below the arched portion.

SEE ALSO

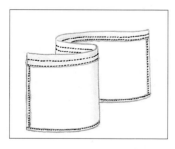

1 Make the fabric fan as for conventional sheer curtains with a cased heading. The length of the curtain should be only 20cm (8in) below the end of the arch, plus a hem allowance. Railroad the fabric (see page 43) to avoid seams, which would show on sheer curtains.

2 Slot a narrow curved track or rod into the casing and mount it at the window. Distribute the gathers evenly across the track or tubing.

3 Gather up the lower edge at the centre with an elastic band, then turn the raw edges back and tuck them into the elastic band. Tie embroidery thread below the elastic band, cut the band and remove it.

ABOVE ~ *An asymmetrically draped pole or window frame is easy to do yet dramatic-looking.*

SWAGS AND TAILS

Supported by a batten or a pelmet board, simple swags drape across the top of the window and down the sides. Classic swags and tails look like one piece of fabric but are usually separate.

There are many different styles of swags and tails. Large windows and high ceilings are best suited to the grander treatments, but there are some relatively simple effects, too.

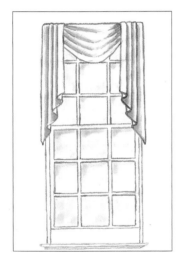

Make sure the scale is right for your curtains, window and room. The depth of the swag should be between one-sixth and one-fifth of the way down the window. The tails should fall about halfway to two-thirds of the way down.

Choose fabrics that drape well, but avoid crisp or heavy fabrics (or, if you do use them, at least do not interface or interline them).

SIMPLE SWAG

Sometimes known as scarf drapery or a swagged pelmet, this consists of just one piece, with no separate tails.

1 Mount a 5cm (2in) square batten over the window, and fix two large hooks just beneath the batten at the corners of the window. Alternatively, mount two U-shaped swag-holders at the corners of the windows.

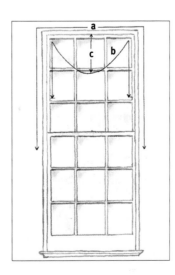

2 Work out the dimensions as shown in the diagram. For the length of the inner edge (a) and outer edge (b), drape a length of cord over

the hooks. For the width, multiply the depth measurement (c) by 2, to allow for the folds.

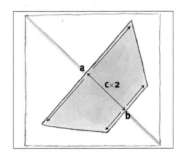

3 Draw up a template to the shape shown, adjusting the proportions to the dimensions calculated in step 2, and adding a 1.5cm (⅝in) seam allowance all around. Cut out this shape from the main fabric and a coordinating or contrasting fabric, placing the centre line on the bias, and joining widths if necessary.

4 With right sides together, join the fabric and lining around all four edges, taking a 1.5cm (⅝in) seam allowance and leaving an opening. Snip off corners, turn right side out and press. Slipstitch the opening closed.

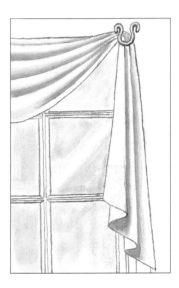

5 Using a hammer and tacks, drawing pins, a staple gun or touch-and-close tape, fix the top of the swag to the top of the batten, if using. Form the fabric into pleats and insert into the hooks. To create a deeper swag, pull gently on the lower folds, towards the brackets or hooks.

VARIATION

On a wide window or a bay window, drape the fabric across several swag-holders or curtain holdbacks, so that it forms a series of swags. Let the fabric hang right down to the floor at the sides.

SIMPLE SWAG WITH ROSETTES

1 For a swag with rosettes like the one in the photograph on the right, follow the instructions for a simple swag, steps 1–5, but make it 120cm (48in) longer. Stitch deep fringing to the outer edge. Hang the swag from U-shaped swag-holders.

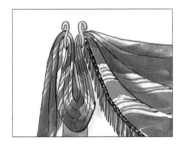

2 For each rosette, measure 60cm (24in) from the swag-holder. Form this part of the fabric into a 30cm (12in) loop, with the short side facing forward. Bring the 60cm (24in) of fabric through the holder, keeping it in its concertina folds.

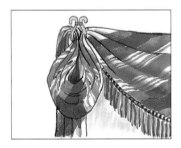

3 Squeeze the swag-holders closed, and loop wire around them. Now pull the innermost fold in the fabric loop, separating the folds. Pull the other folds one by one.

4 Tuck the top and bottom back into the holder, and shape the folds into a rosette.

VARIATION

For separate rosettes, cut a circle of fabric with a diameter twice that of the desired finished rosette plus 2.5cm (1in). Sew gathering stitches around the circle 1.25cm (½in) from the edge, then pull up the thread tightly and fasten off, so that the fabric makes a "pouch" shape. Form the folds into even pleats radiating out from the central hole. Finally, hide the hole by sewing on a covered button.

ABOVE ~ A piece of fabric shaped like a trapezium can be draped into a simple swag, with the corners bunched into rosettes if desired.

CLASSIC SWAG

ABOVE ~ *Window treatments featuring classic swags and tails are suited to rooms with traditional decor.*

This is meant to be combined with tails such as those opposite. It is hung from a pelmet board 10cm (4in) from back to front and 2.5cm (1in) thick.

1 Make a template for the swag to the shape shown in step 2, adjusting the proportions so the inner edge (a) is 40cm (16in) longer than the pelmet board, and the outer edge (b) is 66cm (26in) longer than the board. The width at the sides (c) should be 2½ times the finished depth, and the width at the centre (d) 10cm (4in) more than (c). Add a 1.5cm (⅝in) seam allowance all around.

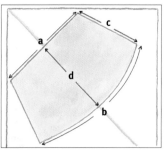

2 With the centre line on the bias, cut out this shape

FORMAL TAILS

from the main fabric and lining. Join the pieces as for the simple swag, step 4 page 118. Mark knife pleats at about 13cm (5in) intervals.

3 Stitch the sew-on half of touch-and-close tape to the lining side of the swag along the top edge. Fix the self-adhesive half of the tape to the front of the pelmet board. Stick the swag in position on the board.

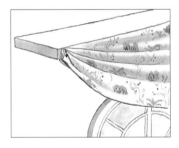

4 Form the pleats and pin together, then remove the swag from the pelmet board. Stitch across the end to hold the pleats in place. Stick back in place on the board.

VARIATION

Round off the inner corner. Do not add a seam allowance all around. Tack the fabric and lining with wrong sides together, and bind the edges with contrast binding, as shown in the photograph.

These are designed to be used with a swag such as the classic swag on page 120.

1 Make a template for the tails to the shape shown, adjusting the proportions so that the width is three times the pleat width, times the number of pleats, plus the unpleated portions, plus the return. For example, for a tail consisting of two 10cm (4in) pleats, 10cm (4in) unpleated areas on each side of the pleated portion, and a 10cm (4in) return, as shown, the width would be 90cm (36in). The inner length should be the distance from the pelmet board to the bottom of the swag. The outer length should be the distance from the pelmet board to a point one-half to two-thirds of the way down the window. Add 1.5cm ((⅝in) for seams.

TIP

Swags and tails use a lot of fabric, so play it safe and make them up first in calico, which is inexpensive. Experiment on this to find the most attractive size for the pleats.

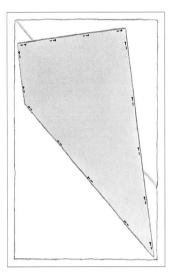

2 Cut out this shape from the main fabric and lining, so that the lower edge is on the bias. Repeat for the other tail. Join fabric and lining as for the simple swag, step 4.

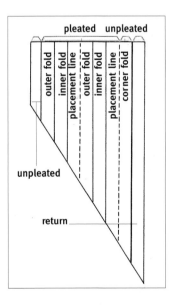

3 Mark the portion of each tail covering the return,

then mark the pleats. Form the pleats, pinning the tail to the shelf to make sure it fits well and looks good.

4 Remove each tail from the pelmet board. Press the pleats and tack across the top. Stitch the sew-on side of touch-and-close tape along the top edge of the wrong side. Remove tacking.

5 Fix the self-adhesive half to the top of the pelmet board front, and to the right side of the swag where the tails will overlap it. Stick the swag and tails in place.

SEE ALSO

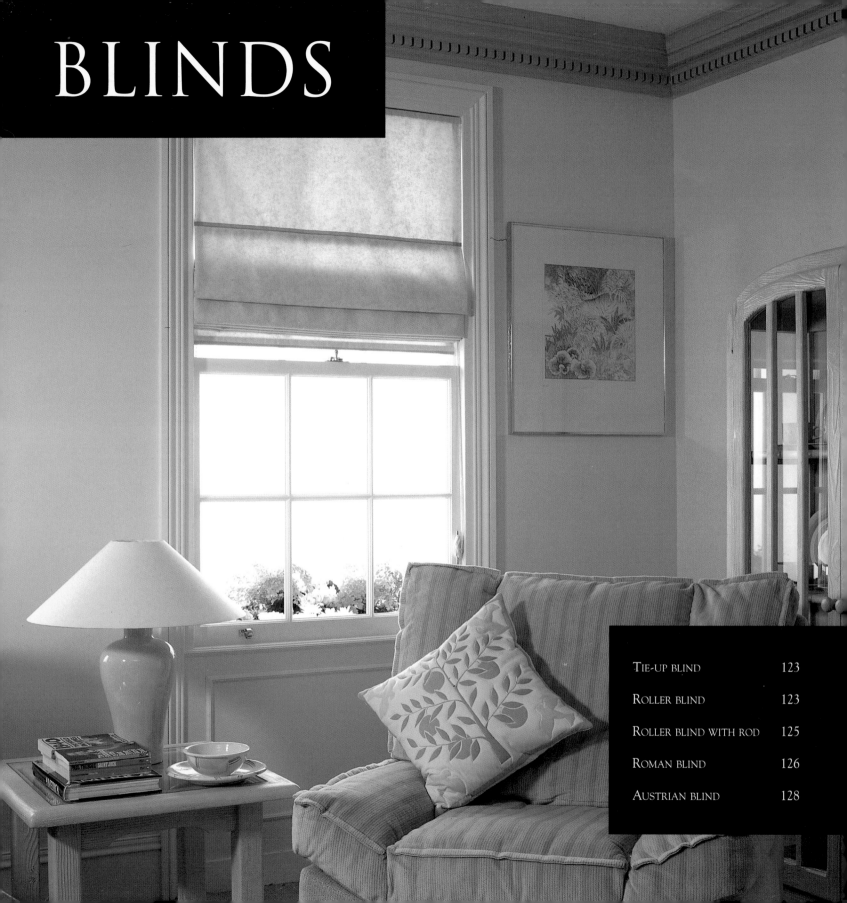

BLINDS

SIMPLE BLINDS

Blinds have more appeal today than ever, as they are both practical and decorative and will suit a variety of decors and styles of window.

TIE-UP BLIND

Tie-up blinds look charming, but they are a little fiddly to tie up, so they tend to be used rather like valances on uncurtained windows. They couldn't be easier to make.

1 Cut out a piece of main fabric and a piece of lining fabric, each about 1¼ times the width of the window (including surround), plus 3cm (1¼in), and the depth of the window plus 3cm (1¼in).

2 Cut two very long ribbons, and fold them in half. Tack to the right side of the main fabric, with the fold even with the top edge of the fabric, and the same distance from each edge.

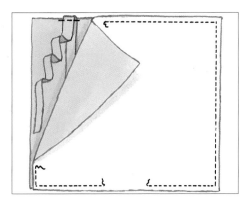

3 Join the lining to the main fabric with right sides together, stitching around all four edges with a 1.5cm (⅝in) seam, and leaving an opening. Turn right side out, press and slipstitch the opening.

4 Stitch touch-and-close curtain tape to the top edge, and gather it up. Fix the self-adhesive side to the top of the window, and stick the blind to it. Hold it up with the ribbons tied in bows.

ROLLER BLIND

Among the simplest of all blinds, these can nevertheless have enormous impact with an interesting lower edge fabric or trimming.

The simplicity and lack of fussiness of roller blinds is part of their charm. In addition, they require very little fabric – and are an excellent solution for sloping windows such as skylights.

Pre-stiffened roller blind fabric is available, or you can stiffen the fabric yourself. Choose a medium-weight, closely woven fabric that is neither too thin (which would crease) nor too thick (which wouldn't roll up properly).

BASIC ROLLER BLIND
1 Buy a roller blind kit that is exactly the size of the window recess. (However, do check whether the size specified on the kit allows for the size of the blind mechanism.) If it is going to hang outside the recess, allow for it to overlap the wall each side by at least 3cm (1¼in). If necessary, buy a slightly larger roller than you need, and cut it down to size after fixing the brackets in place.

2 Unless you are using PVC or pre stiffened fabric, you will need to stiffen the fabric (before cutting it out, since it may shrink a little). Following the manufacturer's instructions, test a sample piece of fabric (glazed fabrics, for example, may lose their sheen as a result of stiffening). Spray both sides with an aerosol, or paint a liquid onto both sides, or dip it in the liquid. The stiffener will make it easy to sponge clean. It also prevents fraying, so side hems are probably not necessary. After stiffening, press well.

5 Lay the fabric on a cutting mat. Using a set square, check that the fabric is completely square. Cut out the blind to the required dimensions, using a sharp craft knife or scalpel and a straightedge. If the fabric has a tendency to fray despite being stiffened, zigzag stitch the edges.

6 If you will have to join widths, do so with a plain seam. After pressing open the seam, either stitch it down again on both sides, or use iron-on hem webbing to bond each seam allowance to the blind.

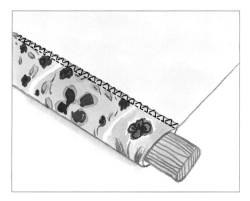

7 Trim the batten supplied in the kit so that it is 1.2cm (½in) shorter than the width of the blind. Turn in a single fold of fabric on the lower edge for the casing – it will need to be wide enough for the batten once the casing is stitched. Stitch then zigzag stitch over the raw edge through all layers. Insert the batten into the casing and sew up the ends.

TIP
....

The blind normally comes down from behind the roller, with the wrong side of the fabric showing on the roller. If your fabric is not reversible, and you'd prefer not to see the roller, place it on the wrong side of the fabric in step 9, with the spring on the right. Also mount the brackets on opposite sides.

ABOVE ~ *A roller blind can be used on its own, behind curtains or with either a valance or pelmet.*

3 Mark the fixing positions of the brackets, then measure where the roller blind will be fitted. The fabric width should be the length of the roller, excluding the protruding pins, plus a little extra for squaring the fabric. The length should be the distance from the roller to the windowsill plus 30cm (12in) for covering the batten and to ensure the roller is covered when the blind is down. If the blind will not be hanging in a recess, add a further 5cm (2in) to the length.

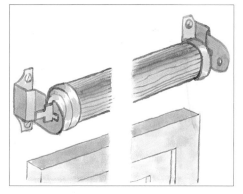

4 Fix the brackets to the wall, 3cm (1¼in) from the top if in a recess, or 5cm (2in) above the window and 3cm (1¼in) to each side if not in a recess. Now cut the bare end of the roller to size if it is too large. Cover the bare end with the cap, and hammer the pin into the hole in the cap.

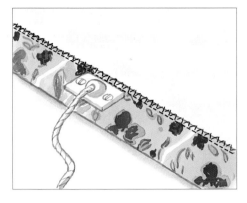

8 Push the cord through the hole in the cord-holder, adjust the cord length and knot the cord behind it. Trim off the excess. Screw the cord-holder through the fabric into the centre of the batten.

9 Place the roller at the top of the fabric on the right side, with the spring mechanism on the left. Use the marked guideline to position it straight. (If there isn't a guideline on the roller, pencil one in). Tape the edge of the fabric to the roller, then secure it with the tacks or self-adhesive strip in the kit. Remove the tape.

10 Roll the blind around the roller by hand, and insert the roller into the brackets. Pull the blind down to cover the window, then remove it from the brackets and roll it up again by hand, to increase the tension. Pull it down again, and test it with a soft tug – it should roll up. Repeat until the tension is tight enough – but avoid making it too tight.

1 To make a roller blind like the one in the photograph below, follow the instructions for the basic roller blind, steps 1–6. Now cut a separate facing strip. Glue the bottom half to the lower edge of the blind, leaving the top half unglued. Make two rows of stitching parallel to the lower edge, in the unglued portion, to form a casing for a batten. Insert the batten and sew up the ends.

BELOW ~ *The castellated lower edge of this roller blind is accentuated by the decorative rod; a cord would spoil the clean lines. To avoid too many straight lines, the valance has a shaped lower edge.*

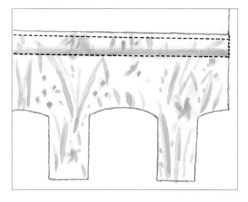

2 Using a template, draw a castellated edge in the same way as for a scalloped heading (see page 143). Cut out the faced edge along the outline.

3 Turn half of each tab to the wrong side without creasing, to form a slot for a decorative rod. Stitch.

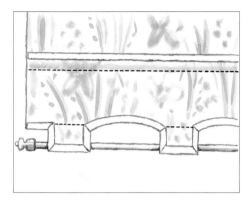

4 Stitch or glue braid around the castellated edge, mitring the corners. Slot a decorative rod through the tabs, adding finials to the ends of the rod if desired. Complete the blind as for steps 9 and 10 of the basic roller blind.

VARIATIONS

• A scalloped, pointed, wavy or curved lower edge could be used instead of the castellations.
• Glue the entire facing to the blind and omit the casing and batten, relying on the rod to keep the blind flat and straight.
• Choose a striped fabric for the blind and align the castellations with the stripes.
• Make a shaped lower edge, with a batten in a casing above the shaped portion, as here, but omit the decorative rod and attach a cord and cord-holder to the batten as for the basic roller blind, step 8.

RIGHT *Plain fabrics with simple decorative detail such as topstitching in a contrasting colour are well suited to Roman blinds.*

ROMAN BLIND

Use simple checked, striped or geometric patterns. Plain fabrics look good, when decorated with contrast bands or bold trimmings. Large patterns or florals do not suit the style. Dowels inside the folds are essential, so the fabric needs to be sturdy. Roman blinds use very little fabric and can be lined easily.

Straight lines are essential. The window and your fabric need to have square corners, and your seams must be absolutely straight.

1 Cut a piece of fabric the size of the finished blind plus 5cm (2in) all around. Cut a piece of lining to the finished width, and to the finished length plus 3cm (1¼in), plus 5cm (2in)per channel (see step 2). Turn under 5cm (2in) all around the main fabric, and 3cm (1¼in) all around the lining, mitring the corners.

2 On the wrong side of the lining, mark a line 10cm (4in) from the lower edge, and another 5cm (2in) above. Divide the

remaining area into pairs of lines parallel to them and 5cm (2in) apart, with equal spaces of about 20cm (8in) between them. With wrong sides together, stitch the pairs of lines as you would for tucks, keeping the side hems turned under.

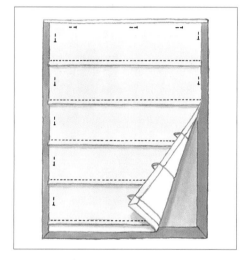

3 Stitch the sew-on side of touch-and-close tape along the lining top edge, leaving 3cm(1¼in) projecting at each end. With wrong sides together, pin fabric to the lining around the edges, so they are even at the top, and 3cm (1¼in) fabric shows all around on the other sides. Pin along the channel seams, keeping them straight. Slipstitch the top and side edges, leaving the ends of the channels free.

4 Tuck a 6mm x 3cm (¼in x 1¼in) batten that is 6mm (¼in) shorter than the blind under the lower hem of the main fabric. Slipstitch the lining to the fabric at the lower edge. Hand sew the ends of the tape in place. Machine along each channel seam from the back of the blind. Insert 1.2 cm (½in) dowels that are 6mm (¼in) shorter than the width of the lining, into the channels. Slipstitch the ends.

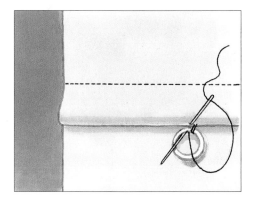

5 Sew a small curtain ring to the edge of each channel, 8cm (3¼in) from the side, so that they are all in a vertical line. Repeat 8cm (3¼in) from the other side. Sew more vertical lines of rings between these, spacing them equally, about 30–60cm (12–24in) apart.

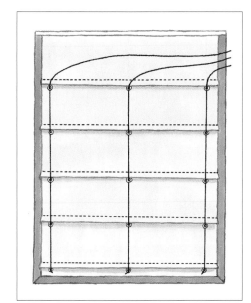

6 Cut a length of nylon cord for each vertical line of rings. The lengths will vary, as they will run up the blind, across the top and down one side. Tie each cord to the bottom ring in its line, then thread them through the rings as shown. (These will hang to the left of the blind, but do it in reverse to hang on the right.)

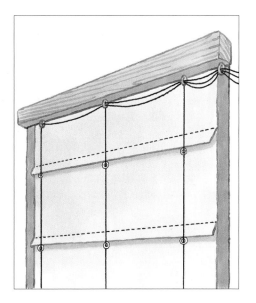

7 Fix the self-adhesive side of the tape to a 5 x 2.5cm (2 x 1in) batten, along the top of a 5cm (2in) deep side. Insert screw eyes in the underside of the batten in line with the rings, and one on the outside; thread cords through. Plait the cords and slide an acorn onto the ends, knotting them together. Mount the batten on the recess ceiling or the wall above the window.

8 Draw the blind up, forming horizontal pleats along each dowel.

ABOVE ~ Narrow Roman blinds are ideal for French doors that open inwards. Notice how the stripes add to the graphic look of the blinds.

9 Secure the blind in the raised position by winding the plaited cords around the cleat in a figure-of-eight.

AUSTRIAN BLIND

Austrian blinds have extra fullness in the width, which is gathered up in a pencil pleat Austrian blind heading. They also have extra fullness in the length, so that even when they are fully let down, they are not quite flat – the base is still ruched. As they are drawn up, the ruching increases over the whole length. They differ from festoon blinds, which are permanently ruched over the entire length.

Austrian blinds often have frills around the lower edge and side edges, but this is by no means obligatory. Similarly, the fussiness depends upon the number of cords.

Most fabrics are suitable for this treatment, but understated ones like cotton and damask often have more impact. Pencil pleat heading tape is most often used, but gathered tape or a cased heading could be used instead.

The blind is constructed much like a curtain. Allow an extra 50cm (20in) or so on the length to create the ruched effect. A generous amount of fabric is essential to the look, so allow for a fullness of about 2–2½ times. (The lighter the fabric, the more fullness is needed.)

ABOVE AND LEFT ~ *Austrian blinds can be either lavish or simple – examples of both are shown here.*

1 Mount an Austrian blind track on the ceiling of the window recess or on the wall above the window if not in the recess. For an unlined blind, make as for unlined curtains, but trim the seam allowances to 6mm (¼in) and make double 2cm (¾in) hems on the side and bottom edges. Or stitch double frills to the edges. For a lined blind, make as for tube-lined curtains, with top edges of the fabric and lining even. Tack edges with wrong sides together.

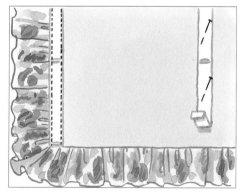

2 Pin a length of Austrian blind tape along the side frill, or side hem if there is no frill, from top to bottom, turning

under the ends. Stitch along both edges of the tape, in the same direction. Stitch another length of tape to the other side edge, lining up the loops across the blind. Divide up the area between them into equal spaces 30–50cm (12–20in) wide, and mark the lines with a fabric marker. Stitch lengths of tape along these lines, still aligning the loops across the blind.

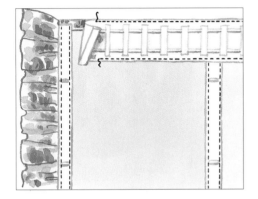

4 On the top edge, turn down 2cm (¾in) of both the main fabric and the lining (if used), and also the tapes. Stitch heading tape over the raw edges.

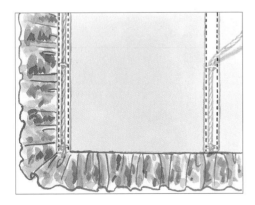

5 For each tape, cut a length of nylon cord as long as two lengths of the blind plus one width. Tie each length of cord to the bottom loop and run it up through the other loops in the line.

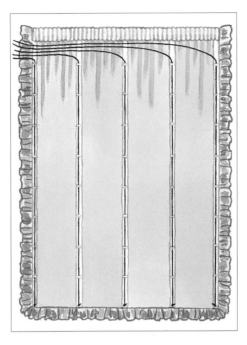

6 Gather up the heading tape, and insert curtain hooks. Hang blind on the track. Lock the cord-holders in position above the tapes, then thread the cords through them towards one side of the blind. Mount the cleat on the wall, knot the cords together and trim off excess. Pull up the blind and wind the cord around the cleat.

VARIATION

For a tailed Austrian blind, omit tape down each side. The blind shown in the photograph here has just two rows of tape, which have been covered with ties inserted in the heading, as for a tie-up blind (see page 123). The blind is folded into horizontal pleats and held in the raised position by the ties.

SEE ALSO

ABOVE ~ This tailed Austrian blind is rather like a cross between an Austrian blind and a tie-up blind.

BEDSPREADS

A bedspread can be either a simple throw-over type or a fitted style. If fitted, it can be tailored (with pleats) or flounced (with gathers), and many variations of these styles are possible.

THROW-OVER BEDSPREAD

This is the quickest type of bed cover to make. If the bed is a single bed or if you are using very wide fabric, you may not have to join widths. Otherwise, join them so that a central panel runs the length of the bed, with a narrower panel on each side. This will look better than joining two panels with a centre seam.

1 The finished width of the bedspread will need to be the width of the bed plus twice the drop (the distance from the top of the mattress to the point where you want the bedspread to finish – eg, at the floor, or just below the top of a valance). To the finished width add 10cm (4in) for the hems, plus a further 6cm (2½in) if the bedspread will consist of three panels stitched together. The finished length will need to be the length of the bed plus the drop plus about 15–30cm (6–12in) to allow it to wrap over pillows. To the finished length, add 10cm (4in) for the hems.

2 Cut out the fabric to these dimensions. Join the three panels, if necessary, with 1.5cm (⅝in) seams.

RIGHT ~ *It may be simple, but when combined with a valance and cushions, a throw-over bedspread can look very good.*

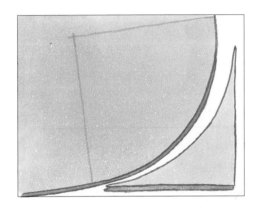

3 If you wish to prevent the corners from trailing on the floor at the foot of the bed, you can round off the corners. To do this, fold the bedspread in half lengthwise, right sides together. At the corner, measure in from each side and mark a distance equal to the drop measurement plus the 5cm (2in) hem allowance. Draw a quarter-circle (page 149) with the centre at that point. Cut along this line through both layers. Staystitch each curve and then notch it within the seam allowance.

4 Stitch a double 2.5cm (1in) hem all around the edge of the bedspread, mitring the square corners (see Mitring Wide Double Hems, page 24).

VARIATIONS

● Stitch insertion lace into the two lengthwise seams. To do this, pin the lace and one fabric panel with right sides together and raw edges even; stitch. Repeat for the other edge of the lace and the other fabric panel. Stitch matching lace edging along the lower edge.

● Line the bedspread to make it hang better and last longer. To the finished length and width, add only 3cm (1¼in), and add a further 6cm (2½in) if the bedspread consists of three panels stitched together. Cut out and prepare the top as for the unlined bedspread, but don't hem the edges. Make an identical piece from the lining fabric. If desired, tack piping or a frill around the edge of one piece on the right side. With right sides together, join the two pieces around all four edges, leaving an opening at the top edge. Turn right side out and press. Slipstitch the opening.

TAILORED FITTED BEDSPREAD

A fitted bedspread is made in two sections –
the top and the skirt. The design included here
will not fit over pillows, so they can have
matching pillow covers if desired.

A tailored fitted bedspread for a bed with an
attached headboard, like the one in the photograph on the right, has a skirt on the sides and
foot only, with only two corner pleats.

A single bed placed lengthwise against the
wall, with no headboard, generally has a
cover with a skirt on all four sides, and four
corner pleats. Combined with box cushions
and perhaps bolsters, it can be made to look
like a sofa by day.

ABOVE ~ A fitted bedspread with corner pleats suits children's and adults' rooms alike.

1 The top should be the same dimensions
as the bed plus 3cm (1¼in) each way
for seams. Also allow an extra 2cm (¾in)
or so each way so that it is not too tight.
Cut out the fabric, if necessary joining
widths as for a throw-over bedspread (steps
1–2). Tack piping all around the seamline
on the right side (omitting the bedhead
end if the skirt is to be three-sided).

2 The depth of the skirt should equal the
drop – in this case, the distance from
the top of the mattress to the floor – plus
6.5cm (2⅝in). The length of a skirt to
cover all four sides should equal the outside measurement of the bed plus 163cm
(65¼in). The length of a skirt to cover
only three sides should equal twice the bed
length plus one width plus 83cm (33¼in).
If you wish to avoid having seams in the
skirt, cut it on the lengthwise grain. If the
pattern needs to run from top to bottom,
however, you will have to join pieces to
make the strip long enough. If possible,
plan it so that the seams will be either
hidden inside the pleats or will be positioned centrally. Cut out the skirt, joining
pieces if necessary.

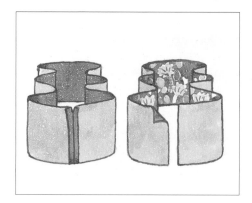

3 If the skirt will cover all four sides, join
the ends, right sides together, with a
1.5cm (⅝in) seam, leaving 1.5cm (⅝in)
unstitched at the top. If the skirt will
cover only three sides, do not join the ends.

4 Stitch a double 2.5cm (1in) hem at
the lower edge of the skirt.

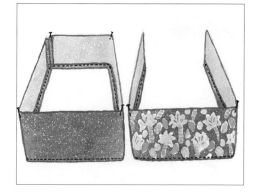

5 For the four-sided skirt, starting with
the seam, measure a distance equal to
the bed length plus 40cm (16in). Mark
this point. Mark a further distance equal
to the width plus 40cm (16in), and then
the length plus 40cm (16in). For the
three-sided skirt, measure from each end a
distance equal to the bed length plus
21.5cm (8⅝in); mark these points.

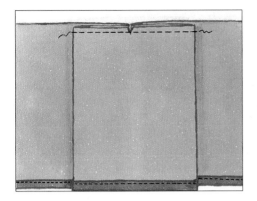

6 Mark points 20cm (8in) each side of these corner marks. At each corner, use the three marks to form an inverted pleat, making the folds at the outer lines and bringing them in to meet at the centre line. Stitch across the top 1.5cm (⅝in) from the edge, and clip into the seam allowance at the centre mark.

7 With right sides together and raw edges even, pin the skirt to the top panel, matching the clips in the pleats to the corners. With the zip foot on the machine, stitch, taking a 1.5cm (⅝in) seam and pivoting at the corners. Turn the bedspread right side out and press the seam.

8 For the three-sided version only, turn under 5mm (¼in) and then 1cm (⅜in) along the raw edges of the skirt ends and top; press and stitch.

VARIATIONS

● Make box pleats all along the skirt instead of inverted pleats at the corners. For 10cm (4in) wide pleats, make the strip six times the length of the bed plus three times the width, plus a further 10cm (4in).
● Use contrasting fabric for the pleat underlays (see page 20).
● Make a scalloped lower edge (see page 150).

● Add a contrast band (see Double Band, page 29).
● Divide the skirt into two sections: the upper skirt, which is the same depth as the mattress, and the lower skirt. Cut the upper skirt on the lengthwise grain, like the top panel, and cut the lower skirt on the crosswise grain. Pleat the lower skirt, join it to the upper skirt, then join this to the top panel, piping both seams.

FLOUNCED FITTED BEDSPREAD

Like the tailored fitted bedspread, the skirt of this bedspread can go around three sides or four sides. Instead of being pleated, the skirt is gathered onto the top.

1 Make the top in the same way as the tailored fitted bedspread, step 1, omitting the piping.

2 The skirt will need to have two to three times fullness, depending on the weight of the fabric. The length of the skirt should therefore equal two to three times the outside measurement of the bed. The depth of the skirt should equal the drop – in this case, the distance from the top of the mattress to the floor – plus 6.5cm (2⅝in). Cut out the skirt and join the seams as necessary.

VARIATIONS

● Add lace edging to the lower edge.
● Stitch contrasting braid trim near the bottom edge.
● Bind the edges instead of hemming them. Allow 4cm (1½in) less on both dimensions, and use binding made from the same fabric or a contrasting one.

3 Make up the skirt as for the tailored fitted bedspread, steps 3 and 4. Gather the fabric and join it to the top panel (see Gathering, page 22). Complete the three-sided version as for the tailored fitted bedspread, step 8.

SEE ALSO

VALANCES

Valances conceal the bed base and space underneath, extending the soft furnishings right to the floor. They are made in much the same way as bedspreads.

PLEATED VALANCE

With valances, the top panel goes between the mattress and the divan. The only other difference between valances and bedspreads is that the drop is shorter on valances.

Like bedspreads, valances can go around all four sides, or only around two sides and the foot, depending on whether there is an attached headboard.

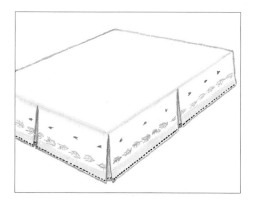

For a pleated valance like the one shown on the right, follow the instructions for the fitted bedspread, but make inverted pleats at the centre of each side as well as at the corners. For each extra pleat, add 40cm (16in) to the length of the skirt.

TIP

Because the top of the valance cannot be seen, you can use a cheaper fabric or a sheet for it. Do not be tempted to use an old, worn-out sheet, however, or it will quickly tear.

ABOVE ~ *Like a tailored bedspread, a pleated valance has a crisp, fresh look that is just right in the bedroom.*

GATHERED VALANCE

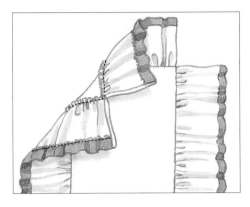

For a gathered valance like the one shown on the right, follow the instructions for the flounced fitted bedspread (page 133), adding a contrasting band along the bottom edge (see Double Band, page 29). Each side of a four-poster bed will probably need to have a separate valance, so do not join the strips together; hem both ends of each strip instead. When attaching them to the top, line up the hemmed edge with the seamline of the top.

RIGHT ~ *A simple calico flounce with a blue contrast band along the lower edge echoes the curtains with their matching contrast band and tiebacks.*

SEE ALSO

QUILTS AND COMFORTERS

A quilt consists of two layers of fabric, with wadding sandwiched between. All three layers are held together by stitching or hand tying. A comforter is a large, lightweight quilt.

BASIC QUILT OR COMFORTER

ABOVE ~ *Extending down to just below the mattress, or all the way to the floor, a comforter can be used like a bedspread, covering the pillows too if you prefer. Quilts and comforters are made in the same way, apart from the dimensions and the weight of the wadding. This photograph shows a comforter that reaches right to the floor.*

1 For a quilt, measure the width and length of the bed, and add 5–10cm (2–4in) extra each way for "take up" (shrinkage caused by the quilting). For a comforter, find the width by measuring from where it will finish (just above the floor or just below the top of the divan) on one side to the same point on the other side, then add the allowance for take-up. Find the length of the comforter by measuring from where it will finish at the foot of the bed to the bedhead, then adding the allowance for take-up, plus 15–30cm (6–12in) if you want the comforter to wrap over pillows.

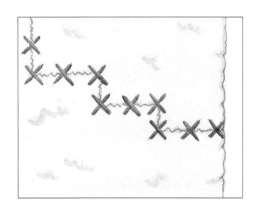

2 Cut the top and wadding to these measurements, joining pieces if necessary but avoiding a centre seam. Cut the backing 3cm (1¼in) larger all around if you wish to incorporate self binding, as for the comforter in the photograph. Tack (or glue) the layers together (see Quilting, page 54). To join wadding, stagger the join as shown, using large cross stitches.

3 The comforter in the photo has been quilted with a shell pattern. Using a water-erasable fabric marker and a semi-circular template, draw a row of adjacent semi-circles. Draw the next row, staggering the circles in relation to the first row. Continue in this way till the entire top is marked. Now quilt the layers (see Quilting Patterns, page 54).

4 Trim and bind the edges, either with self binding or with separate binding.

DUVET COVERS

Duvet covers are quick and easy to make, and if you use sheeting you can avoid having to join widths. Because a duvet is reversible, using a coordinating fabric for the back adds interest.

BASIC DUVET COVER

1 Cut two rectangles of fabric, as long as the duvet plus 9cm (3½in), and as wide as the duvet plus 3cm (1¼in).

2 Stitch a double 2.5cm (1in) hem along the bottom edge of the front piece. Repeat for the back piece.

3 Cut a length of press stud tape about 50cm (20in) less than the width of the duvet. Separate the two strips. Pin one strip centrally along the hemmed edge of one fabric piece, on the right side. Stitch along both long edges of the tape. Stitch the other strip onto the remaining fabric piece in the same way, checking that the press studs are directly opposite each other on the opening edges.

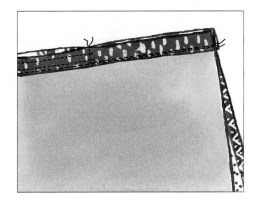

4 Place the two fabric pieces with right sides together, and fasten the tape. Join the hemmed edges, stitching alongside the

hem to a point just beyond the end of the tape. Pivot the needle and stitch across the tape to the edge (being careful not to stitch into a press stud). Do the same on the other side.

5 Join the sides and top edge of the cover with French seams. Turn right side out and press the seams.

BELOW ~ *Make the most of the reversible nature of a duvet cover with interesting patterns and colours.*

Duvet Cover with Appliquéd Decoration

An attractive idea is to use the same fabric for the front and back, but add a wide band in a contrast fabric (preferably the same fibre as the rest of the cover, to reduce shrinkage problems when washing), as in the photograph below. Decorating the band with machine appliquéd decoration like this adds interest, though appliquéing narrow pieces is quite tricky. Stitching braid to the band gives a similar effect. Make sure the fabric you use for the decoration is washable and will not

shrink more or less than the duvet cover itself. For example, if you are using coloured sheeting for the cover, white sheeting could be used for the appliqué.

1 Cut the back as for the basic duvet cover, step 1. Cut the two pieces for the front (ie the main piece and the contrast band) to the same width as the basic duvet cover but with their combined length adding up to the desired length plus 3cm (1¼in) for the seam that will join them.

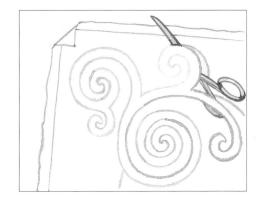

2 If you are decorating the band, iron fusible web to the back of the fabric to be appliquéd. Draw the scroll pattern on the backing, and cut it out. Remove the backing, position the pattern on the band and iron it in position, being very careful not to get adhesive on the iron. Now using a straight machine stitch, machine around each edge and, if you wish, down the middle. To make the decoration more durable, zigzag the edge instead of straight stitching.

3 Join the contrast band to the main fabric with a 1.5cm (⅝in) French seam. Now proceed in the same way as for the basic duvet cover, steps 2–5.

LEFT ~ *Applied scroll decoration adds interest to this duvet cover and matching pillowcases.*

DUVET COVER WITH BANNER EDGING

Another idea is to insert a "banner" edging consisting of triangles of different fabrics into the top seam, fold it over and button it to the duvet cover, as in the photograph below.

ABOVE ~ *A charming banner edging finishes off a child's duvet cover.*

1 Cut out and make up the duvet cover as for the basic duvet cover, steps 1–4.

2 For the edging, cut two 23cm (9in) deep strips of contrast fabric, each as wide as the duvet cover plus 3cm (1¼in).

3 Make a window template as shown – choose a size that will allow the triangles to fit exactly across the top of the duvet cover between the seamlines. Add a seam allowance of 1.5cm (⅝in) around each shape. Cut out around both outlines. Draw around the template onto different-coloured fabrics.

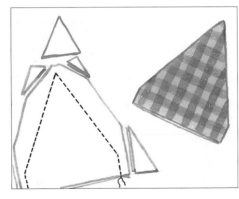

4 Cut out twice as many shapes as there will be triangles across the duvet cover. Interface half of them using fusible interfacing. With right sides together, stitch them together in pairs (interfaced triangles with uninterfaced ones), as shown above, leaving the bottom edges unstitched. Trim the seams and corners, turn the cover right side out and press.

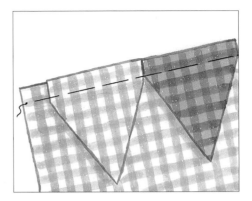

5 With raw edges even, tack the triangles side by side to the right side of the contrast strip along one long edge, making sure that the triangles do not extend into the seam allowances at each side. Now, with right sides together, stitch this strip to the other one along the edge with the triangles, sandwiching them in between and taking a 1.5cm (⅝in) seam. Turn right side out and press. Make machine buttonholes in the edging, following your machine instruction manual, or bound buttonholes if you have some experience of making them.

6 Complete the duvet as for the basic duvet cover, step 5, but using a plain seam rather than a French seam for the top edge. Cover some buttons (see page 33) in the fabric used for the triangles and sew these to the front of the duvet cover to correspond to the buttonholes on the edging.

SEE ALSO

PILLOWCASES AND COVERS

The difference between pillowcases and pillow covers is that the former are meant to be slept on, while the latter are only decorative and have a lapped opening at the back.

PLAIN PILLOWCASE WITH FOLD-OVER FLAP

Sometimes known as a "housewife" pillow-case, this has a flap inside to stop the pillow from slipping out.

1 Cut out one piece of fabric twice the length of the pillow plus 21cm (8¼in), and the width of the pillow plus 3cm (1¼in).

2 Stitch a double 5mm (¼in) hem on one short edge. Turn under a further 15cm (6in), press and pin.

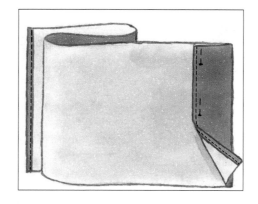

3 On the other short edge, turn under and press 1cm (⅜in) then a further 4cm (1½in); press and stitch.

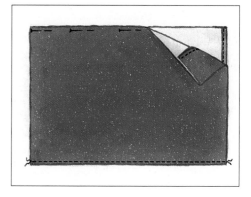

4 Fold the fabric in half crosswise, aligning the ends, and stitch 1.5cm (⅝in) French seams. Press.

FRILLED PILLOW COVER

This is easy to make yet very decorative. It can coordinate with the bed cover, or be made in a luxurious fabric such as lace.

1 Cut out a piece of fabric for the front to the same dimensions as the pillow plus 3cm (1¼in) each way. Cut out two pieces for the back, each as wide as the pillow plus 3cm (1¼in), and half the length plus 7cm (2¾in).

2 Cut out and make up a double frill (see page 32). With right sides together and raw edges even, stitch it to all four edges of the front, taking a 1.5cm (⅝in) seam.

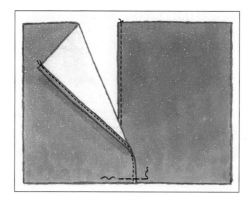

3 Turn under a double 5mm (¼in) hem on one short edge of each back piece. Overlap the hemmed edges of the two back pieces to make a back the same size as the front. Tack at the top and bottom.

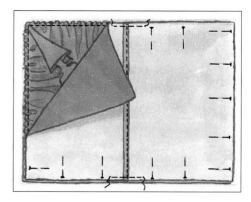

4 With right sides together and raw edges even, stitch the front to the back, taking a 1.5cm (⅝in) seam. Trim the seam and corners, turn right side out through the back opening, and press.

FLANGED PILLOW COVER

This technique is simplicity itself, but the flange cannot be made in a contrasting colour.

1 Cut out a front piece 16cm (6¼in) wider and 16cm (6¼in) longer than the pillow. Cut out two back pieces 16cm (6¼in) wider than the pillow and half the length plus 13.5cm (5¼in).

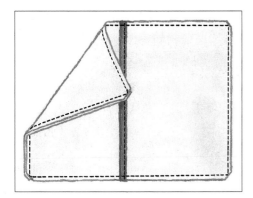

2 Make up the back and stitch it to the front as for the frilled pillow cover (steps 3 and 4).

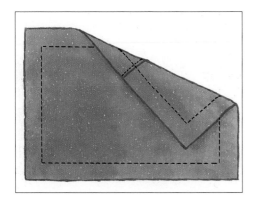

3 Topstitch 6.5cm (2½in) from the edges all around, forming the flange. The flange is formed between the topstitching and the outer edge.

PILLOW COVER WITH CONTRASTING FLANGE

This method allows you to use a different fabric for the flange.

1 Cut out the front and two back pieces as for the frilled pillow cover (step 1). Cut out back as for frilled cover (step 3).

2 Cut out eight 9.5cm (3¾in) wide strips of contrast fabric, four the width of the pillow plus 15.5cm (6¼in), and four the length of the pillow plus 15.5cm (6¼in).

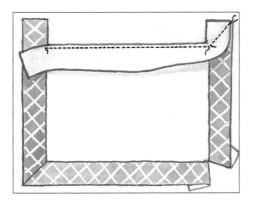

3 Stitch two short strips and two long strips to the front with 1.5cm (⅝in) seams, mitring the corners, as for a single band (page 29). Do the same for the back.

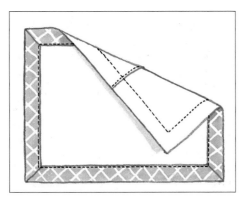

ABOVE ~ *Pillow covers with contrasting flanges are too pretty to cover up.*

SEE ALSO

Frills 32
Knife-edge cushions 164

4 Join the front and back as for the frilled pillow cover (step 4). After turning the cover right side out and pressing it, topstitch through the front and back along the inner edge of the flange.

5 If desired, add tassels at the corners (see Tassels, page 64).

BED HANGINGS

Whether you have a four-poster bed or not, bed curtains make a dramatic focal point for a bedroom. There are lots of ways to make bed curtains, depending on where and how they will hang.

FOUR-POSTER BEDS

Traditional hangings for a four-poster bed consist of a curtain between the bedhead and wall, and curtains that open and close at each corner, surmounted by a wood or fabric canopy. If the canopy is wood, it might have a fabric valance. Sometimes a canopy (with or without a valance) is used without curtains, or with curtains only at the bedhead end. The construction of these will vary according to the bed. Note that if you do not line the curtains and canopies, you will need to use a fabric that looks good from the wrong side (unless you are making just one curtain to hang against the wall).

A popular modern alternative is the simple wooden or iron frame, which consists of four uprights attached to the bed, with horizontal rails around the top. Tie curtains (see page 95), or tab curtains with button or touch-and-close tape closures (see page 94), work well on this type of frame. You could make eight curtains to hang in pairs at each corner, or just one to hang behind the bedhead. When hung in pairs, the finished width of each should be about three-quarters the distance between posts. Hung singly, the finished width should be one and a half times the distance between posts.

RIGHT ~ This simple wrought iron four-poster bed is complemented by the soft but equally simple tie-top bed curtains.

SCALLOPED BED HANGING

An attractive heading for a bed curtain hanging from a rail is one with very deep scallops, as shown in the photograph on the right. Because the scallops have a facing, the curtain is designed to be seen from only one side, hanging behind the bedhead. (If, however, you wanted scalloped curtains all around the bed, you could simply use a separate full-length lining instead of a facing. In that case, add a seam allowance at the top edge and stitch between scallops.)

1 Cut out and join widths of fabric using flat fell seams, to create a single panel. The width should be one and a half times the width of the rail plus 10cm (4in) for the 2.5cm (1in) double hem at each side. The length should be the distance from the top of the rail to the floor plus 15cm (6in) for the hem at the lower edge and 30cm (12in) for the self facing at the top.

ABOVE~ A deeply scalloped heading is ideal for this wooden four-poster frame.

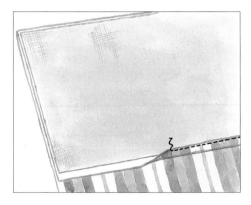

2 Turn back 30cm (12in) to the right side at the top of the curtain to form the self facing; press the fold. Interface it and stitch a narrow hem along the raw edge of the facing.

3 The scallops should be 2.5cm (1in) apart and 10–15cm (4–6in) across. The number of scallops and their exact width will depend on the width of your fabric. You can work out the exact size either by trial and error or by doing the following calculation. First subtract 12.5cm (5in) from the fabric width, then divide by 15cm (6in), rounding the answer up or down to the nearest whole number. This is the number of scallops. Now divide this number back into the figure you got by subtracting 12.5cm (5in) from the fabric width. This gives you the exact width of one scallop and one gap. Deduct 2.5cm (1in), the width of one gap, and you have the exact scallop width.

4 For example, for a 229cm (90in) wide panel, subtracting 12.5cm (5in) gives 216.5cm (85in). Dividing by 15cm (6in) and rounding down equals 14 – so 14 scallops will fit onto the hypothetical panel. And 216.5cm (85in) divided by 14 equals 15.5cm (6.07in), the width of one scallop and one gap. Deducting 2.5cm (1in), the width of one gap, from that gives a scallop width of 13cm (5.07in).

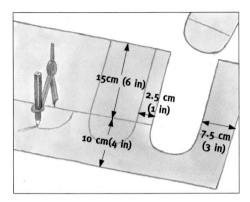

5 Make a paper template 25cm (10in) deep and as wide as your fabric panel. Draw a line 15cm (6in) from the top edge. Using compasses, draw semicircles with diameters on this line. The diameter of each should be the width calculated in step 3, and the semicircles should be 2.5cm (1in) apart and 7.5cm (3in) from the ends of the template. Extend both sides of each semicircle to the top of the template with parallel straight lines. Cut out the resulting "U" shapes and use the remainder as the template for the scallops.

6 Lay the template on the facing, lining up the top and side edges. Draw around the template with a fabric marker.

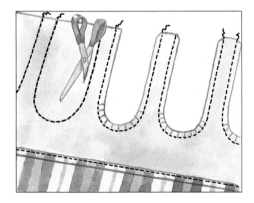

7 Pin and stitch along the marked lines. Trim above the stitching to 6mm (¼in). Trim the interfacing seam allowances back to the seamline if you haven't fused it. Clip curves and corners.

8 Stitch a 5cm (2in) seam at each side edge, starting at the fold at the top and stopping at the lower edge of the facing. Trim these seams to 6mm (¼in). Clip into the curtain seam allowance at the bottom of the facing.

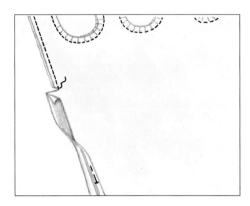

9 Press a double 2.5cm (1in) hem at each side, and a double 7.5cm (3in) hem at the lower edge, mitring the corners. Slipstitch in place.

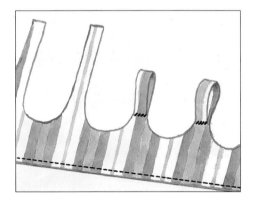

10 Turn the heading right side out and press. If the rails of the four-poster frame can be removed easily, make the "tabs" between scallops into loops and slipstitch into place at the back. Otherwise, stitch touch-and-close dots to the tabs to hold the loops in place. Be sure to make the loops exactly the same size so the curtain will hang evenly.

CANOPIES FOR WOODEN FRAMES

An alternative treatment for a simple wooden frame is a canopy over the top and no curtains. The canopy can be made as a rectangle large enough (after hemming the sides) to cover the top and hang down a short distance over the edges. To keep it in place but allow it to be removed for cleaning, use sew-and-stick touch-and-close tape on the underside of the canopy and the top of the rails. An antique linen sheet could also be used in this way.

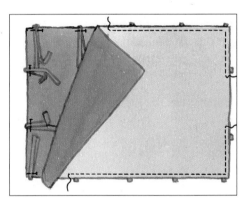

A different form of canopy could be made from two fabric rectangles, each the size of the frame plus a seam allowance all around. Join them with right sides together, inserting ties (see page 35) in the seam on all four edges at 30cm (12in) intervals, and leaving an opening for turning right side out. Tie the canopy to the underside of the rails.

MOCK FOUR-POSTER

This creates a very convincing four-poster effect without the four posts.

1 Fix four 5 x 7.5cm (2 x 3in) timber battens securely to the ceiling above the perimeter of the bed, with the one above the bedhead not quite flush with the wall. Stick the self-adhesive side of sew-and-stick touch-and-close tape around the outside of the battens.

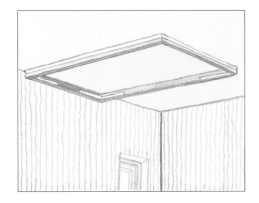

2 If you don't want the curtains to close, mount 40cm (16in) strips of sew-and-stick curtain tape along the lower edge of the corners of the battens, on the inside. If you do want them to close, mount curtain track along the lower edge of each batten, on the inside, for the entire length.

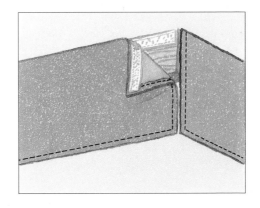

3 Cut four rectangles of fabric for the pelmet, adding 5cm (2in) to the desired depth and 2.5cm (1in) to the desired length. Turn up double 6mm (¼in) hems on each edge. Stitch the sew-on side of the touch-and-close tape to the right side along the top edges, then fold to the wrong side. Attach the pelmet pieces to the frame.

4 For each corner, make a pair of lined or unlined curtains long enough to extend from the lower edge of the battens to the floor. If the curtains are to close, the finished width should be three-quarters of the length or width of the wooden frame, depending on the position. (This will give one and a half times fullness when they are closed.) If they are not to close, the finished width can be less than that.

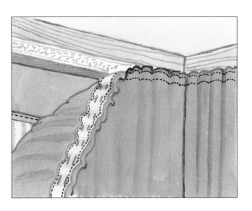

5 Sew the heading tape to the right side of the curtains, not the wrong side. Pull up the cords and hang the curtains.

CORONAS AND CORONETS

Mounted on the ceiling above the centre of a conventional bed, a corona creates an effect similar to that of a four-poster. Coronas are about 80–100cm (30–40in) across and circular. There is also a type that can be mounted above the bedhead, and these generally have a flat side cut out of the circle so they will fit flush against the wall. Curtains are hung from track or touch-and-close tape and draped around the bed.

A coronet is shaped like a short, thick shelf and is mounted on the wall near the ceiling. The curtains hanging from it drape on either side of the bedhead (sometimes with bosses holding them back), and occasionally also behind the bedhead.

BEDHEAD HANGINGS

Another way of creating the sumptuous effect of draped fabric without actually having a four-poster bed is simply to hang a curtain on the wall above the bedhead. Either hang it from a pole in the conventional way, or make narrow ties and form them into small loops,

inserting both ends into the curtain seam. Hang the loops from hooks or a Shaker-style peg rail. The curtain can hang more or less flat (in which case the loops should be only slightly further apart than the hooks or pegs) or in soft folds (with the loops further apart).

WALL-MOUNTED CANOPIES

A simple canopy can be created by draping fabric over short poles mounted on the wall above the bed. Position the bed either with the bedhead against the wall or, if it is a single bed, lengthwise along the wall.

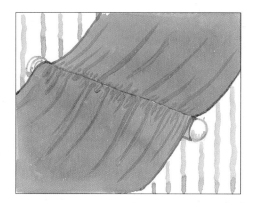

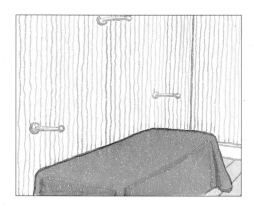

1 Mount two short poles on the wall at the same height, or three arranged in a triangular shape. The poles should be only about 30cm (12in) long because they project at right angles from the wall. You could, in fact, use just one pole in the centre, with a holdback (see page 70) on each side.

2 Cut a length of lined or unlined fabric long enough to drape over the poles with the ends hanging down to the floor on each side of the bed. Allow 2.5cm (1in) extra for the hems and an extra amount to encase each pole – probably about 15cm (6in) per pole, depending on the thickness of the poles.

3 Stitch a double 6mm (¼in) hem across each end and along the sides. (However, if you use a full width of fabric, and if the selvedge is not noticeable, the side hems will not be necessary).

4 Mark the positions of the poles on the fabric. Make a casing for each pole by folding the fabric in half crosswise, right sides together and stitching a seam wide enough to slot the pole through. Turn over the canopy so that the right side is on top and the casings underneath. Slot the casings over the poles, allowing the fabric to hang down.

SEE ALSO

An overhead canopy, as shown in the photograph opposite, is another way of creating a dramatic effect without actually having a four-poster bed.

1 Hang two dowels, each as long as the width of the bed, from the ceiling using cords and screw hooks, so that they are parallel (and very secure). The first dowel should be next to the wall above the bedhead, and the other one should be above the foot of the bed.

2 Join fabric widths using flat fell seams, to make a rectangle as wide as the bed (or 1½ times the width, to look gathered). It should be long enough to drape over the poles and hang down below the bed at the bedhead end and as far down at the other end as desired. (For example, it could stop short of the bed, as here, or it could be knotted and drape on the floor.) Add an allowance for two dowel casings, if using, and two hems.

3 Hem the side edges, or use the selvedges if suitable, and make a narrow hem at each end. Make a casing (see Wall-mounted Canopies, step 4) for each dowel if desired. Slip the dowels through the casings, hang from the cords and drape the fabric over the ends of the bed. Or simply tack the fabric to the dowels.

SUSPENDED CANOPIES

ABOVE ~ *This handsome canopy draped over two thick dowels hung from the ceiling looks almost regal.*

TABLE LINEN

TABLECLOTHS

Almost any table will benefit from a custom-made tablecloth. As well as dining tables, they are suitable for dressing tables, bedside tables and occasional tables.

Sewing a tablecloth yourself enables you to make it in a particular fabric, perhaps to coordinate with dining chair seats or curtains. You can give it any of a variety of edgings, or design it to fit your table.

Unless you are making a fitted tablecloth, try to use a fabric that is wide enough not to require seams. If this is not possible, at least avoid having a central seam – instead, sew a strip of fabric to each side of a wider central panel. This applies to circular tablecloths as well as square, rectangular and oval ones.

Cloths for occasional, bedside and dressing tables are often layered, with the underneath one floor-length, or even a little longer so that it pools onto the floor. Cloths for dining tables, however, should have a drop (overhang) of no more than 15–30cm (6–12in), so that the cloth does not get in the way of the diners.

BASIC SQUARE OR RECTANGULAR TABLECLOTH

1 Cut out the fabric to the desired dimensions, plus 5cm (2in) each way for the hem allowances.

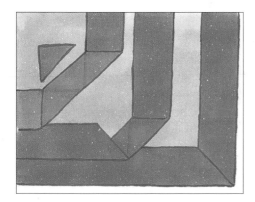

2 Press under a double 1.5cm (⅝in) hem on each edge, mitring the corners. (Or, if the fabric is bulky, just neaten the edges and press under a single hem, adjusting the dimensions accordingly.) Stitch.

VARIATIONS

● Add a contrast band to the lower edge (see Double Band, page 29). This is useful for emphasizing the shape when a square tablecloth is used on a round table, as in the photograph opposite.
● Press 1.5cm (⅝in) to the right rather than the wrong side. Do not turn under the raw edge – instead, stitch braid, ribbon, fringing or tassel trimming around the hem, covering the raw edge.
● Bind the edge with bias binding instead of hemming it.
● Line the tablecloth. Cut out identical pieces of main fabric and lining fabric (and, if desired, interlining). Lockstitch the main fabric to the lining, and interlining if using (see Lined Curtains, page 78). Press under a single 1.5cm (⅝in) hem on the main fabric and on the lining, trimming away the hem allowance on any interlining. Slipstitch the folded edges of the hems together.

BASIC CIRCULAR TABLECLOTH

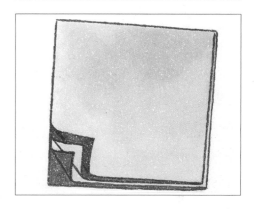

1 Cut out a square of fabric equal to the desired diameter of the tablecloth, plus 3cm (1¼in). Fold it into quarters.

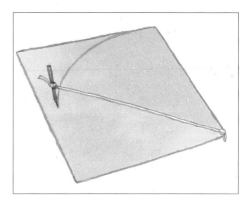

2 To make a paper pattern, cut out a piece of paper the size of the folded fabric square. Tie a piece of string to a pencil and use this like a pair of compasses, to draw a quarter-circle from one corner of the square to the diagonally opposite one. Cut out the pattern.

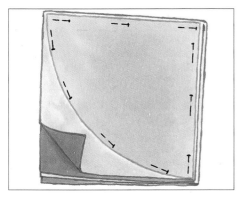

3 Pin the pattern to the folded fabric, with the centres matching. Cut along the marked line through all four layers.

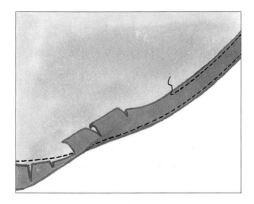

4 Stitch 1.5cm (⅝in) from the raw edge, all around. Press the seam allowance to the wrong side so that the stitching falls just inside the fold. Make 6mm (¼in) clips in the seam allowance at 2.5cm (1in) intervals all around. Press under the raw edge so that it meets the stitching, forming a narrow double hem. (Or, if the fabric is very bulky, just neaten the edge and leave it as a single hem.) Machine or hand stitch close to the inner edge.

VARIATIONS

- Try any of the variations given for a square or rectangular tablecloth, apart from the band.
- Rather than hemming the lower edge, add a deep frill to it, inserting piping in the seam.

CIRCULAR TABLECLOTH WITH A SCALLOPED EDGE

1 Cut out the tablecloth as for the basic circular tablecloth (steps 1–3). Using the edge of the cloth as a guide, make a template for a 20cm (8in) deep facing that extends one-quarter of the way around the circle. Add 1.5cm (⅝in) seam allowances at each end. Use the template to cut out four facings.

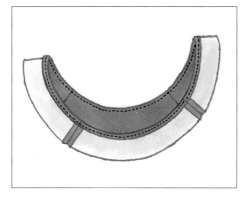

2 With right sides together, join the ends of the facings with 1.5cm (⅝in) seams to make a complete ring. Stitch a single narrow hem along the inner edge of the facing.

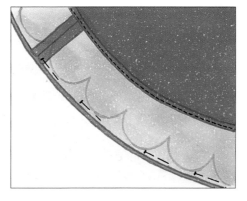

3 Pin the facing to the edge of the tablecloth with right sides together. Work out the size and number of scallops so that they will fit evenly around the

facing. Use a pair of compasses to draw a semicircular paper template of the correct size. Cut it out and draw around it onto the facing, with the scallops beginning 6mm (¼in) from the outer edge. (To make them fit exactly, you can if necessary make a few scallops slightly large or smaller.)

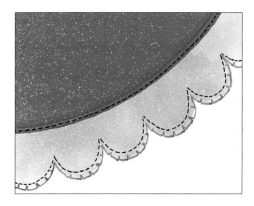

4 Stitch along the marked line, then cut 6mm (¼in) outside the seamline. Grade the seam allowance. Clip the curves within the seam allowance, and clip into the "valleys" between scallops. Turn the facing to the inside; press. Slipstitch the hem edge of the facing to the cloth.

VARIATION

Use the same basic technique to make a zigzag-shaped edge or a castellated edge.

CIRCULAR TABLECLOTH WITH CONTRAST BORDER

Because part of a circular tablecloth is cut on the bias, it is difficult to attach a wide contrast band in the same way as you would on a straight edge. The easiest way to get a similar effect is with a visible shaped facing.

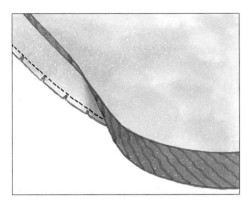

1 Prepare a shaped facing of the desired depth, as for the circular tablecloth with a scalloped edge (steps 1–2), but press under the narrow hem on the inside edge without actually stitching it.

2 With the right side of the facing to the wrong side of the cloth, stitch the raw edge of the facing to the lower edge of the cloth with a 6mm (¼in) seam. Clip into the seam allowance at 2.5cm (1in) intervals.

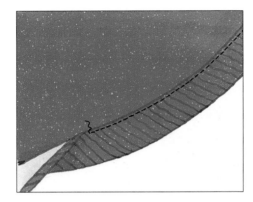

3 Turn the facing to the right side and press. Topstitch it to the cloth along the turned-under inner edge of the facing.

BASIC OVAL TABLECLOTH

1 Measure the length and width of the table at the widest points, and decide what drop you will need. Cut a rectangle from the fabric as long as the table length plus two drops plus 3cm (1¼in), and as wide as the table width plus two drops plus 3cm (1¼in). Mark the centre of the fabric.

2 Place the fabric rectangle on the table so the centre is exactly at the centre of the table. Place weights on the fabric to stop it from slipping. Cut and fold a piece of card so that the distance from the fold to one edge equals the desired drop plus 1.5cm (⅝in).

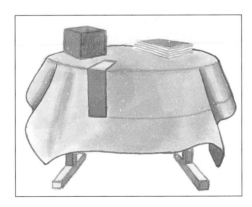

3 Place the card so the fold is on the table edge, as shown. Mark the drop, then move it around the table, marking the drop at intervals. Join up the marks, and cut along this line. Hem the edge of the cloth as for a circular table.

FITTED TABLECLOTH WITH SKIRT

This method can be used for a square, rectangular, circular or oval table. Either the skirt can be gathered or it can have inverted pleats at the corners.

1 Cut out a piece of fabric the same dimensions as the table top plus 3cm (1¼in) each way.

2 Make a pleated or gathered floor-length skirt in exactly the same way as a fitted bedspread with pleats or a flounce (see pages 132–133).

SEE ALSO

PLACEMATS

Placemats can be any shape, and the size is up to you. They can be round and as small as a plate, or they can be oval or rectangular and large enough to hold cutlery too.

QUILTED BOUND PLACEMATS

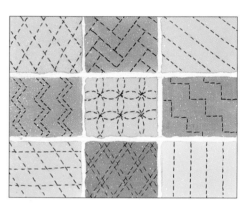

ABOVE ~ *These placemats are quick and easy to make, and the wadding between the layers of fabric helps protect the table from heat. Provided you use suitable fabric, they are fully washable.*

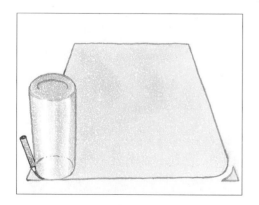

1 Cut out the main fabric, backing and wadding to the desired size. For a circular mat, either draw around a tray or plate, or use a pair of compasses. For an oval placemat, cut out a rectangle, then round off one corner by drawing around a plate and cutting out; use the cut-away portion as a template for the other three corners. Do the same for a rectangular mat with rounded corners, but draw around a glass so that less of the corner is rounded off.

2 For each mat make a "quilt sandwich" (see page 54). Hand or machine quilt the layers using a background quilting pattern (see page 55) such as diamonds, diagonal lines, shells, stepped lines, overlapping circles, herringbones or zigzags. Diamonds have been used on the placemats in the photograph.

3 Bind the edges with ready-made or home-made bias binding to either match or contrast with the fabric.

VARIATIONS

- Make small, round mats in the same way to use as coasters under drinks.
- Use pre-quilted fabric, omitting step 2.

LINED PLACEMATS WITH CONTRAST BORDERS

1 From the main fabric and wadding, cut out a 30 x 46cm (12 x 18in) rectangle. From the contrast fabric, cut out a 44 x 60cm (17½ x 23½in) rectangle. Press under 6mm (¼in) on all four edges of the contrast fabric piece.

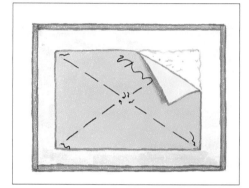

2 Centre the wadding on the wrong side of the contrast fabric piece, and place the main fabric piece on top, right side up. Pin or tack together.

3 On each edge, bring the contrast fabric over to the front, pressing it along the edge of the main fabric. Leaving the raw edges turned under, mitre the corners as for wide plain hems of the same width (page 24). Topstitch all around the folded edge.

UNLINED PLACEMATS WITH RIBBON OR BRAID TRIM

1 Cut out a 33 x 48cm (13 x 19in) rectangle from the fabric. Press 1.5cm (⅝in) to the *right* side all around the edge.

2 On one edge, pin the trimming to the right side of the fabric, with the outer edge of the trimming even with the fold, and the end of the trimming extending 1.5cm (⅝in) beyond the folded edge of the fabric.

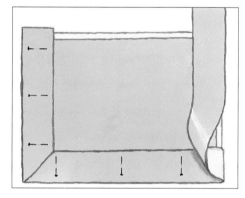

3 Pin the trimming around the mat, so that it covers the raw edges of the fabric. Pin mitres at the corners but do not stitch them yet. (To form a mitre in the trimming, fold it back on itself so the fold is even with the fabric edge, then fold it diagonally and press.)

SEE ALSO

Edgings   23
Quilting   54

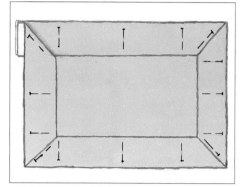

4 At the last corner, fold the first end under diagonally, on top of the other end, leaving the turned-under end projecting beyond it at this stage.

5 Adjust the mitres if necessary so the border fits smoothly, then stitch along the diagonal corner folds on the wrong side, beginning at the inner edge and backstitching at each end. Trim the seam allowances to 6mm (¼in); press open. Press under the seam allowance that is still extending beyond the final corner.

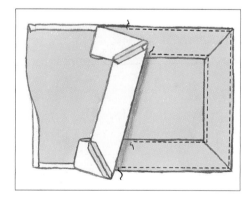

6 Stitch the trimming to the fabric first along the outer edge and then along the inner edge of the placemat.

NAPKINS AND ACCESSORIES

Though small and simple, table napkins and accessories can add to the impact of your dining table, so it is worthwhile devoting a little thought to their design.

NAPKINS WITH A NARROW, UNMITRED BORDER

Plain napkins can be made by making narrow or rolled hems on fabric squares. A contrast border in the same type of fabric adds interest without affecting washability. This technique for attaching a border with unmitred corners can be used for other items too, such as cushions, but it is rather wasteful of fabric. These instructions are for one napkin measuring 44.5cm (17½in) square.

1 From the main fabric and the border fabric, cut out a 46cm (18in) square. From the border piece, cut out and discard a 38cm (15in) "window", leaving a 4cm (1½in) wide border all around. Turn 6mm (¼in) under around the inner edge of the border, clipping into the seam allowance at the corners.

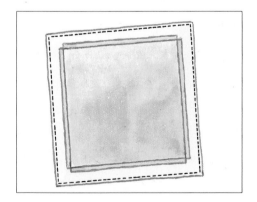

2 Join the right side of the border to the wrong side of the main fabric with a

5mm (¼in) seam around the outer edge. Grade the seam and clip corners. Turn the border to the front.

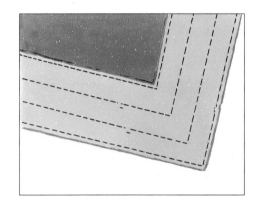

3 Topstitch along the inner edge all around, then along the outer edge. Now topstitch one or more evenly spaced rows between these, all around the border.

TABLE RUNNER WITH SELF FRINGE

This looks best on a rectangular or oval table or a sideboard. Placemats and napkins coordinating with it could be made with narrower, unknotted self fringes.

1 Cut a strip of loosely woven fabric at least 30cm (12in) wide and at least 30cm (12in) longer than your table. Cut it out precisely on the straight grain (see pages 11–12). Finish the long edges with a narrow hem.

2 Make a 10cm (4in) deep fringe at each end (see Self-fringed hem page 25).

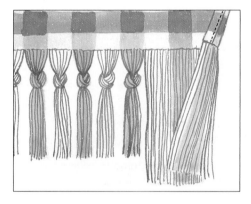

3 Divide the fringe into equal sections, possibly using the pattern as a guide. Tie each section in a knot about 1.2cm (½in) from the edge.

FABRIC BREAD BASKET

RIGHT ~ *This charming fabric basket for bread will add colour to your table (and is also great for picnics). Make it to match your table linen, using pre-quilted fabric.*

1 For a basket measuring 20 x 20 x 5cm (8 x 8 x 2in), cut a 30cm (12in) square of pre-quilted fabric. Prepare bias binding if you are not using ready-made binding.

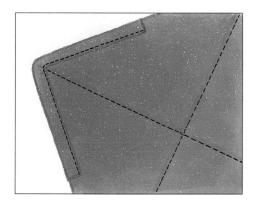

2 At each corner, bind the edges for 5cm (2in) on each side of the corner, turning under the ends.

3 Cut four 60cm (24in) lengths of binding. Use one of these to bind the raw edge between two bound corners, leaving ties of equal length at either end of the stitching. Repeat for the other three sides.

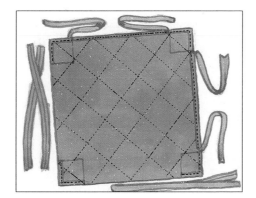

4 With a water-erasable fabric marker, draw 5cm (2in) squares at each corner on the top of the fabric.

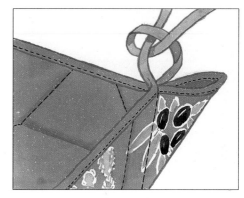

5 Bring the marked lines together at each corner, making a diagonal fold in the fabric on the outside. Stitch along the marked lines, as though you were making a dart. Tie pairs of ties in bows at the corners. Turn in each edge by 5cm (2in) and press.

SEE ALSO

Edgings   23

OPTIONS

Whatever style of cushion you plan to make, you need to decide what fabric, trimmings, filling and type of opening you will want to use. There is a wide range of options.

CUSHION FABRICS

Cushion covers can be made in virtually any fabric, so decide what look you want, and what will suit your style of decor.

SUITING THE STYLE
Here is a list of fabrics that suit a particular effect (though many are just as appropriate for other styles too).

Classic/traditional: Crewelwork, cotton damask, wool, union, tartan
Opulent: Damask, brocade, silk, tapestry fabric, fragments of old kelims, velvet, paisley
Natural/rustic: Linen, hessian, ticking, Madras, teatowel fabric
Fresh: Gingham, chintz, Provençal print, antique linen
Romantic: lace, toile de Jouy, sprig print
Modern: primary coloured cotton, graphic patterns, plain glazed chintz, stone-washed silk, canvas

Classic/traditional

Opulent

Romantic

Natural/rustic

Modern

Fresh

PRACTICAL ASPECTS
Take the amount of use and laundry requirements of cushions into account when choosing the fabric. Medium to heavy, firmly woven fabrics such as chintz, heavy cotton, sateen, wool, linen, union, silk and sheeting are excellent for cushions.

Interfacing a soft or lightweight fabric will make it crisper and firmer. If possible, avoid using a very delicate fabric like fine muslin or lace on its own – to prevent it from pulling apart at the seams, back it with another fabric such as cotton.

If the fabric you are using has a large motif, think carefully about how you cut it out. The motif will probably look best centred – and the cushion may be too small for it.

CUSHION TRIMMINGS

As well as the trimmings that can be sewn, such as frills and piping, there is a vast choice of ready-made trimmings you can use to decorate cushions.

MAKING A CHOICE

Suitable trimmings include bobble, bullion, tasselled and chenille fringe, fan edging, gimp, twisted rope, ribbon, braid, cotton lace edging and tassels. All are available in an enormous range of styles.

When choosing a braid or edging, make sure it isn't too heavy for the fabric. Also, take care when stitching braid to a cushion that the sewing machine isn't flattening it at all; if in doubt, sew it on by hand.

BELOW ~ All sorts of tassel trim and individual tassels look great on cushions.

LEFT ~ Use trimmings to unify cushions that have been made in a variety of fabrics.

APPLYING TRIMMINGS

While braid has two decorative edges, edgings have one plain edge and one decorative one. The plain edge can be inserted into a seam like piping prior to stitching the front and back of the cushion cover together.

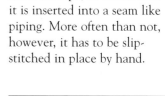

Alternatively, the plain edge can be tucked under a finished edge of the cushion and stitched in place, or sewn to the top of the finished edge.

Jumbo ricrac, a type of braid, can be stitched to the top of the cover or tacked along the seamline before the front and back are joined, so that one side extends beyond the edge, creating a saw-toothed effect. Two contrasting colours, positioned with the zigzags staggered, can look good too.

Twisted rope, also known as cording or corded rope, is sometimes available with an attached tape, in which case it is inserted into a seam like piping. More often than not, however, it has to be slip-stitched in place by hand.

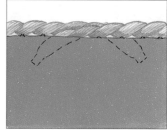

Leave an opening in the seam into which the ends can be inserted; oversew the ends of the rope to stop them from fraying, and slipstitch the opening. To make looped corners, simply wrap the cord around a pencil, and oversew it in place.

CUSHION FILLINGS

Cushion covers go over either cushion pads (purchased or home-made, and in a choice of fillings) or foam blocks.

READY-MADE CUSHION PADS

Ready-made cushion pads come in standard sizes – ranging from about 25cm (10in) to 75cm (30in) – and shapes (such as square, rectangular, round or cylindrical). You also have a choice of whether or not it has a gusset (see page 168) and the type of filling.

The choice of filling includes goose down (the quill-less feathers of geese or ducks, and the most luxurious),

feather-and-down or feather; synthetic wadding; and foam chips. If you use a cushion pad, you may still wish to pad out the corners or edges with synthetic wadding.

If you want a plump effect, cut the cushion fabric so that the cover will be the size of the pad (i.e. do not add on the seam allowance).

HOME-MADE CUSHION PADS

If you can't find a ready-made pad in the shape or size you are looking for, simply make your own. Make a casing out of downproof cambric or ticking (if using feathers or down,

which tend to "migrate" through a looser weave), lining fabric or calico. Follow the instructions for the cushion cover, and fill the casing with synthetic wadding or with down and/or feathers. (For the latter, it's best to work outdoors, as it's a messy job.)

Making your own cushion pad enables you to make cushions in unusual shapes – see Knife-Edge Cushions (page 164) for some ideas.

BELOW ~ *Ready-made cushion pads come in all the shapes shown here, a choice of fillings and a range of sizes.*

TIP

To transfer feathers from an old cushion casing to a new one, leave a 15cm (6in) opening in the new one and unpick 15cm (6in) of one seam in the old one. Tack the two openings together. Now ease the filling from one casing to the other. Remove the tacking and slipstitch the opening in the new casing.

FOAM

Another alternative for a cushion filling is foam, which is used for seating or for unusual cushion shapes. It comes in blocks of different thicknesses and can be cut to shape by the supplier, who has specialist tools. It is not easy to cut yourself, but if you do attempt it, use an electric or serrated knife – spraying silicone lubricant on the blade – or sharp dressmaker's shears. And take care!

Foam will eventually crumble, so cover it with a casing, or wrap it in wadding, to extend its life. Once you have inserted the foam in the cover, you may wish to smooth out the corners and edges with wadding.

Foam chips (shredded foam) are inexpensive and useful for cushions that will be used outdoors, as they are non-absorbent. However, they are uncomfortable, look lumpy (unless wrapped in wadding) and will crumble so are not recommended for cushions used indoors.

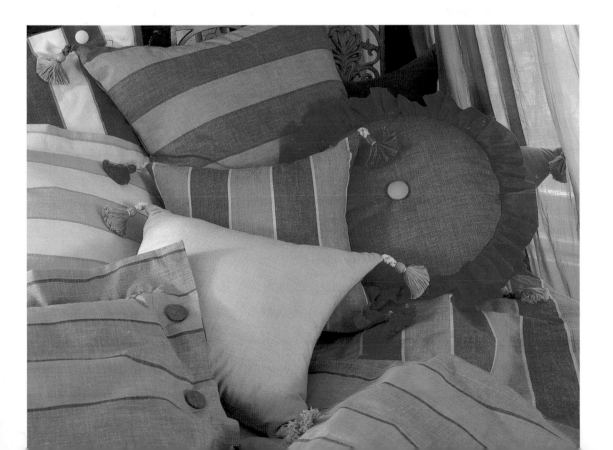

CUSHION OPENINGS

The openings in a cushion can be highly inconspicuous or so decorative that they are design elements in themselves.

Conventional openings in scatter cushions generally go either in a seam across the back or in a side seam. For cushions with a gusset, the opening goes in the centre of the gusset or in the seam. If a seam in a cushion is piped, a zip can go alongside the piping.

On a straight-edged cushion, the opening should be about 10cm (4in) shorter than the finished edge. On a round one, it should be one-third of the outside measurement.

SLIPSTITCHING

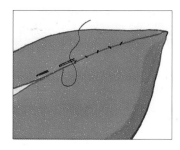

The simplest and least noticeable method is to insert the cushion pad in an opening in a seam, then slipstitch the opening closed. This can be used on cushion pad casings (although machine stitching is also suitable here). On covers that need to be removed for cleaning, however, it will mean unpicking the slipstitching and resewing it each time.

LAPPED OPENING

Another quick and easy closure, this has an overlap rather than an actual fastening. The main disadvantage of this method is that it tends to gape open, especially on large cushions, preventing the front of the cover from staying taut and smooth.

1 Cut out two pieces for the back. Each piece should be the desired depth plus outer seam allowances, and half the desired width plus the outer seam allowance plus 3cm (1¼in) for hemming the edge plus 4–6.5cm (1½–2½in) for the overlap. (The smaller overlap is suitable for smaller cushions, and the larger one for larger pillows.)

2 Turn under 5mm (¼in) then 2.5cm (1in) on the opening edge of each back piece; stitch. Overlap the edges by the amount allowed, so that the back is the same size as the front. Tack the lapped back pieces together at the top and bottom, then treat as one piece.

ZIP OPENING

The zip should be inserted in either a side seam or a back seam, preferably with a 2.5cm (1in) seam allowance. The zip should be 5cm (2in) shorter than the finished length of the seam. Insert the zip (see Zips, page 33) before stitching other seams.

TAPE

Touch-and-close tape and press stud tape are particularly good fastenings for cushion covers in heavy fabrics. They must be set into a lapped seam. To set tape into a side seam, follow steps 2–4 for duvet covers (page 137). To set it into a seam in the centre of the back of the cushion, follow the steps given here.

1 Cut two back pieces for the cover, each the desired depth plus outer seam allowances, and half the desired width plus outer seam allowances plus 2cm (¾in).

2 Place the two back pieces with right sides together. On one edge, mark the opening to begin and end 6.5cm (2½in) from the edges. Stitch a 2cm (¾in) seam at each end of the opening, backstitching at the marks. Press the seam open, pressing under the 2cm (¾in) seam allowances in between the stitching. Trim one seam allowance to 1.2cm (½in).

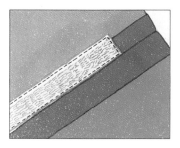

3 Cut a length of 1.5cm (⅝in) wide tape 2.5cm (1in) longer than the opening. Separate two halves of the tape, and tack the hook (or ball) strip along the fold of the trimmed seam allowance, with 1.2cm (½in) extending beyond the opening at each end. Stitch along both long edges and both ends, through the seam allowance and the main fabric.

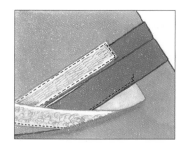

4 Lap the loop (or socket) strip over the *wrong* side of the other seam allowance by 3mm (⅛in). Once again, the tape should extend 1.2cm (½in) beyond the opening at each end. (If using press stud tape, make sure the sockets will be aligned with the balls). Stitch along the long edge through the tape and seam allowances only.

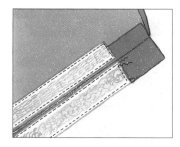

5 Fold the loop (or socket) strip to the right side of the seam allowance. Stitch along the long edge and both ends through the tape and seam allowance only.

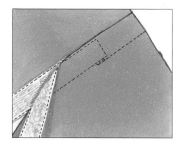

6 Place the hook (or ball) side over the loop (or socket) side. Now complete the cover in the usual way.

BUTTON OPENING

Buttons can look very smart, whether they are fabric-covered or not.

1 Make a knife-edge cushion (see page 164), piping it if desired, but make a lapped opening at the front rather than at the back. The opening can be positioned either centrally or off-centre.

RIGHT ~ *The lines of the button openings echo those of the tucks on these cushions.*

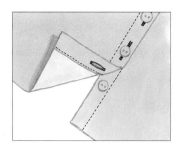

2 Make buttonholes in the overlap, and sew buttons to the underlap before joining the front and back.

BUTTON-AND-LOOP OPENING

The red cushion in the photograph on the right makes a feature of the elongated button loops.

1 Cut out two front pieces to the desired width plus outer seam allowances, and half the desired depth plus the outer seam allowance plus 7cm (2¾in).

2 Turn under 5mm (¼in) and then 2.5cm (1in) along the top edge of the lower front piece; stitch. Do the same for the bottom edge of the upper piece but slipstitch the hem. Lap the upper piece over the lower one by 8cm (3in); tack at the sides.

3 From contrasting fabric, cut two 2.5cm (1in) wide strips, each about 5cm (2in) longer than the depth of the unstitched cushion cover. Fold the long raw edges in to meet at the centre, wrong sides together. Now fold each strip in half lengthwise and stitch along the long edge.

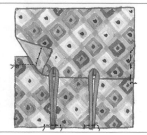

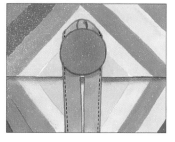

4 Divide the bottom edge of the front piece into thirds, marking the points. Fold each strip in half, and position the two halves of the loop side by side on the right side of the lower front piece. The ends should be at the marked points and approximately even with the lower edge. Adjust the position of each so the looped end overlaps the lower edge of the upper front piece by slightly more than the diameter of the button. Tack.

5 Cover the buttons in the same fabric as the loops, and sew them to the lower edge of the upper front piece. Check that their positions will allow the loops, when buttoned, to be straight.

6 Make up the cover as for knife-edge cushions (page 164), piping the edges in the same fabric as that used for the loops and buttons.

ABOVE ~ *A decorative button-and-loop opening is the focal point of this cushion.*

TIE OPENING

This tie opening can be used on two opposite sides of a cushion, as in the instructions here, or on just one side. Two pairs of ties are used on each opening edge, but if the cushion is large, three pairs may be preferable.

1 Cut out one front and one back, to the desired finished size plus 1.5cm (⅝in) all around. Also, for each opening, cut out two 6.5cm (2½in) wide facings as long as the side edge of the front and back pieces.

2 For each opening, make four 33cm (13in) long ties (see Ties, page 35); their width can be between 1.2cm (½in) and about 5cm (2in), depending on the effect that you want.

3 With right sides together and raw edges even, tack two of the ties to the opening edge of the front piece, and the other two to the opening edge of the back piece in the same positions. Repeat for the opposite opening edge.

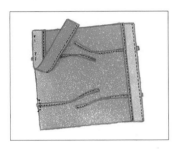

4 Turn under 6mm (¼in) on one long edge of each facing; press and stitch. With right sides together, join one facing to the opening edge of the front piece, and the other to the opening edge of the back piece, sandwiching the ties between the two layers and taking a 1.5cm (⅝in) seam. Press the facings away from the front and back pieces, and the seams towards the facings. Repeat for the other opening edge.

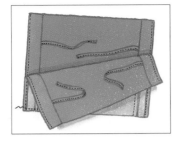

5 With right sides together, join the front and back along the top and bottom, taking 1.5cm (⅝in) seams, and stitching across the facings.

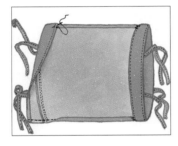

6 Fold the facings to the wrong side, and press. Understitch each facing close to the seamline. Hand stitch the facings to the top and bottom seam allowances. Turn the cover right side out; press.

VARIATION

Omit the ties, and stitch button loops into the opening edges on the back piece. (Make these as short versions of the button loops in the button-and-loop opening on page 162, step 3.) Sew buttons onto the opening edges of the front piece. The fastening should not be too tight, since the aim is to see some of the inner cover.

7 For the inner cover, cut out one piece of contrasting fabric as deep as the finished cushion cover plus 3cm (1¼in) and as wide as twice the finished width plus 3cm (1¼in). Fold this in half crosswise. With right sides together, stitch a 1.5cm (⅝in) seam along the side opposite the fold. Press the seam open and refold the piece so the seam is central. Stitch the top and bottom, leaving an opening. Trim the corners, turn right side out and press. Insert the cushion pad and slipstitch the opening.

8 Now insert this into the outer cover so that the seamless sides are at the openings. Tie two bows at each side.

TASSEL OPENING
This is similar to the tie-on opening, but the ties are replaced with tassels and the facings are omitted.

1 Cut out a front and back, each to the desired finished depth plus 3cm (1¼in), and the desired finished width plus 15cm (6in). On the two side edges of each piece, stitch double 4cm (1½in) hems.

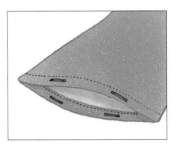

2 For each opening, make two buttonholes in the front piece and two in the back piece.

3 Complete the outer cover and make the inner cover as for the tie-on opening, see steps 5 and 7.

4 Tie or sew cord loops to two tassels. Insert each looped cord through one pair of buttonholes, then take the tassel through the loop.

SEE ALSO

KNIFE-EDGE CUSHIONS

At their most basic, knife-edge cushions – which are fat in the middle, with sharp edges – can look simple and elegant, but they may be embellished in any number of ways.

BASIC KNIFE-EDGE CUSHION

All cushions, whatever their shape, are either "knife-edge" or "box-edge" (usually called simply box cushions – see page 168). While box cushions are of uniform thickness because of a gusset between the panels, knife-edge cushions are made from two panels sewn together, so they are plump in the middle, tapering to sharp edges.

Knife-edge cushions can be any shape. Round, square and rectangular are the most common, but the same technique can be used for other simple shapes – such as a heart, triangle, crescent moon, star, oval, diamond, initial, number, Christmas tree, flower or fish.

1 Cut out the front to the desired shape and size, adding 1.5cm (⅝in) all around for seam allowances.

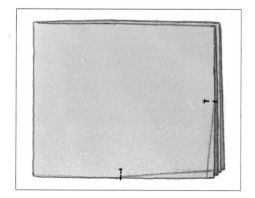

2 To prevent the corners from looking too sharp, you can taper them if you

wish. Fold the front into quarters, and mark points halfway along the sides. Draw lines from these to a point 1.2cm (½in) from each side at the corner, tapering the lines gradually. Trim along these lines.

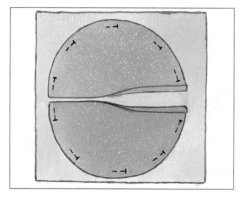

3 Decide what type of opening you will use (see Cushion Openings, page 160). If it will be a side closure, cut out the back to the same dimensions as the front. If the closure will be in the back, cut the back as two pieces, adding the specified allowance for the type of closure. (If you are making a round pillow, make a pattern for the back. Cut a paper circle to the desired size, then cut it in two and insert a strip of paper on the opening edge equal to the width of two seam or hem allowances. Use this as a template when cutting out the two back pieces.) If you have tapered the corners on the front, use them as a template for the corners on the back.

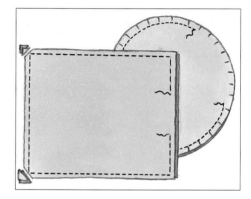

4 Join the front and back pieces with right sides together, taking a 1.5cm (⅝in) seam. Trim the seams and either clip curves or trim off corners, depending on the shape. Turn right side out and press. Insert a cushion pad then close the opening.

VARIATIONS

● Decorate with ready-made trimmings (see Cushion Trimmings, page 158) or a decorative technique such as appliqué, embroidery, smocking or quilting.

● Insert a frill or piping into the seam, as in the photographs on page 165 (top left and bottom left).

● Add a pleated frill. Cut a double frill that is three times the outside measurement of the cushion, then make continuous knife pleats or box pleats all round, inserting the frill into the seam as for a gathered frill.

● Make tucks across the front (see Tucks, page 21) before joining the front and back, as shown in the photograph on page 161.

FLANGED CUSHION

Flanged cushion covers like those in the photograph on the right are made in the same way as for the flanged pillow cover (see page 141). Ribbon trimming can be stitched over the inner edge of the flange. Cushions with a contrast band, as in the photograph below right, are made as the pillow cover with contrasting flange, page 141.

LEFT AND BELOW LEFT ~ Piping is a classic way of embellishing knife-edge cushions. RIGHT AND BELOW RIGHT ~ Flanged cushions are a type of knife-edge cushion, but the techniques are different for self-flanges and contrasting flanges.

SEE ALSO

BOLSTERS

Bolsters – which technically are round box cushions with very deep gussets – are often used on divans as arm or back rests, providing comfort as well as looking good. They may have flat or gathered ends.

BOLSTER WITH FLAT ENDS

1 Measure the end of the bolster cushion pad and make a paper pattern for a circle of this diameter plus 3cm (1¼in). To make the pattern, cut a square piece of paper at least as large as the diameter of the circle. Fold it in quarters, and draw a quarter-circle with a radius of half the desired diameter, using a piece of string tied to a pencil as a pair of compasses. Cut out along the line through all four layers, then open out the pattern. Use the pattern to cut out two fabric circles.

2 Measure the length of the cushion pad, and add 3cm (1¼in). Measure the distance around the cushion, adding 5cm (2in) if you will be having a zip or 3cm (1¼in) if the opening will be slipstitched instead. Cut one rectangle of fabric to these dimensions.

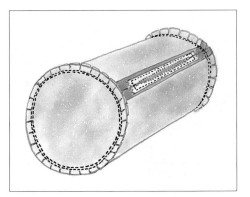

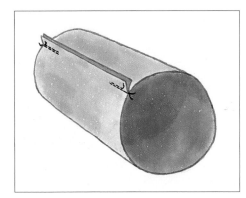

3 Fold the rectangle in half, right sides together and raw edges even, along the length. Pin a 2.5cm (1in) seam along the edge. Stitch the seam at each end for at least 5cm (2in), backstitching the ends. Either tack the rest of the seam, then insert a zip and remove the tacking, or leave it open for now.

4 Staystitch just inside the 1.5cm (⅝in) seamline at both ends of the tube and also around both circles. Now clip into the seam allowance at 2.5cm (1in) intervals on the circles and at the ends of the tube. Avoid cutting through the staystitching.

5 With the zip open (if using), and working with the circle on top, stitch a circle to one end of the tube. Repeat for the other end. Turn right side out, press and insert the cushion pad. Close the zip or slipstitch the opening.

VARIATIONS

- Tack piping around the seamline of the circles before joining them to the tube, as for the bolster in the photograph on page 171.
- Attach braid parallel to the ends before joining the rectangle into a ring.
- Hand stitch cording around the seamlines at the ends of the bolster.

TIPS

- If you can't find a cushion pad the right size, make your own by rolling up a sheet of wadding to the desired dimensions. Slipstitch the end of the sheet to hold the roll in place, and make a casing if you wish.
- If you want to use a zip closure along the length, the zip should be as long as at least half the distance around the bolster. Note that if the bolster is too long and thin, it won't fit onto your machine; in that case, you will either have to use a tiny hand backstitch or omit the zip and slipstitch the opening instead.

BOLSTER WITH GATHERED ENDS

1 Cut out a rectangle as long as the distance around the cushion pad plus 3cm (1¼in) and as wide as the length of the pad plus the distance across one end plus 3cm (1¼in).

2 Make up the rectangle as for the bolster with flat ends, step 3. (If you do not use a zip, there is no need to leave an opening in the seam, as the cushion pad can be inserted through the end.)

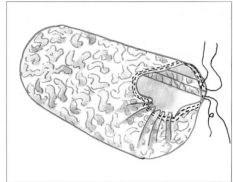

3 Turn under 1.5cm (⅝in) at each end of the tube. Gather up one end (see Gathers, page 22), fastening the ends of the gathering securely.

4 Put the cushion pad inside the cover. Gather up the remaining end and fasten off. Cover two buttons and sew one to each end at the centre.

VARIATION

For piped gathered ends, as on the bolsters in the photograph above, add 6cm (2½in) to the length and cut a strip from each side of the rectangle 1.5cm (⅝in) outside of where the ends of the cushion pad will begin. Join these edges with 1.5cm (⅝in) seams, inserting piping in the seams.

ABOVE ~ Bolsters nestle in nicely to any collection of cushions, as this pair with piped gathered ends do.

SEE ALSO

BOX CUSHIONS

A box cushion is a firm, tailored cushion used for seating. The gusset strip, or welt, inserted between the front and back panels gives the box-like effect.

BASIC BOX CUSHION

Box cushions can be any simple shape but are most often round, square or rectangular. They are used in window seats, on benches, chairs and stools and sometimes as scatter cushions.

A row of box cushions makes a perfect backrest for a divan bed with a tailored fitted bedspread (see page 132). Either lean the cushions against the wall or mount a batten on the wall, screw cuphooks into it then sew loops to the cushions that can be slipped over the hooks.

This basic box cushion has crisp, clearly defined edges and a neat, tailored look. If you are using patterned fabric, remember to match the pattern all the way around, including on the gusset (unless you are cutting it on the crosswise grain, with the top and bottom on the lengthwise grain). A round cushion will be easier to make up if the gusset is cut on the bias.

1 From the fabric, cut out a top and bottom to the desired dimensions plus 3cm (1¼in) each way.

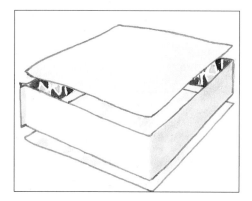

2 Now cut out the gusset strip. If you are not using a zip closure, it can be cut as one strip, as long as the outside measurement of the pad/foam plus 3cm (1¼in), and as deep as the depth of the pad/foam plus 3cm (1¼in). Alternatively, for a *square* or *rectangular* cushion, use a strip of this depth for each side, cutting two strips to the length of the pad/foam plus 3cm (1¼in) and two to the width plus 3cm (1¼in).

TIP

To make a foam block easier to insert into the cushion cover, wrap it in a thin polythene bag, removing the bag once the foam is inside.

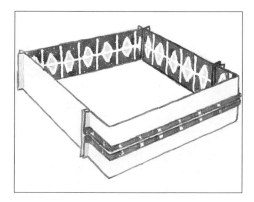

3 If you are using a zip closure, the gusset will have a zip section at the back. The zip section of the gusset is cut as a top and bottom half, each of which is half the depth of the pad/foam plus 4cm (1⅝in). On a *square* or *rectangular* cushion, the zip should ideally extend about 5cm (2in) around each corner, but if the sides of the cushion will be visible, the zip will have to cover only the back part. On a *round* cushion it should go at least one-third of the way around the cushion. The length of the zip section of the gusset should be the length of the zip plus 8cm (3¼in). The depth of the remaining gusset section should be the depth of the pad/foam plus 3cm (1¼in). Its length will be the outside measurement of the cushion minus the length of the zip section plus 6cm (2½in). On a *square* or *rectangular* cushion where the zip doesn't extend around the sides, you can if you wish use separate strips for the front and each side; each should be as long as the front or side plus 3cm (1¼in).

4 For a zip closure, pin the two back gusset strips with right sides together along one long edge, and stitch a 2.5cm (1in) seam for 2.5cm (1in) at each end, machine tacking in between. Insert the zip and remove the tacking. Open the zip.

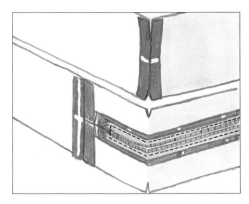

5 Join the ends of the gusset strip(s) into a ring with 1.5cm (⅝in) seams, leaving any seams that will be at corners unstitched for 1.5cm (⅝in) at each end. If there are no seams at the corners, clip into the seam allowances for 1.2cm (½in) at these points. Check that the gusset fits closely around the pad/foam.

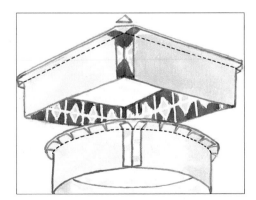

6 With right sides together, join the gusset to the top. At corners, instead of pivoting sharply, shorten the stitches and take one or two stitches diagonally across. On a *round* cushion, clip into the gusset seam allowance at 2.5cm (1in) intervals.

7 Join the gusset to the bottom in the same way. If you haven't used a zip, leave an opening in the centre of the back edge.

8 Trim the seams and corners, turn right side out and press. Insert the pad/foam. Slipstitch the opening if there is no zip.

ABOVE AND LEFT ~ *Fat box cushions with piped seams make these seats look more inviting and interesting than plain chairs.*

VARIATIONS

• Tack piping to the top and bottom before joining them to the gusset, as for the cushions in the photographs above and left.
• Make the gusset twice as long as usual, then ruche it (eg, gather both edges) before inserting it. Use a slipstitched opening rather than a zip for this type of gusset, and machine stitch along the seamline of the gusset at the opening to hold the gathers in place there.

Mock Box Cushion

Use this technique to make a knife-edge cushion resemble a box cushion.

1 Cut out a top and bottom as long as the length of the pad/foam plus the depth plus 3cm (1¼in), and as wide as the width plus the depth plus 3cm (1¼in).

2 Insert a zip, if desired, and join the front and back as for a basic knife-edge cushion (page 164), pressing the seams open.

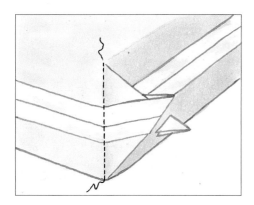

3 At each corner, pull the top and bottom apart and centre the seams, one over the other. Mark a point on the seamline a distance of half the pad/foam depth from the corner. Draw a line at right angles to the seamline through this point. Stitch along the line. Trim the original seam allowance but do not cut off the excess fabric. Turn right side out and insert the cushion pad/foam. Slipstitch the opening if used.

Soft-edged Box Pillow

Although this cover is for a box cushion pad or foam, the front edge is smooth rather than crisply defined, giving a contemporary look that is also very durable.

1 Cut the front and back in one piece. To calculate the length, measure the cushion pad/foam from the back edge of the top across the top, down the front and to the back edge of the bottom, then add 3cm (1¼in). To calculate the width, add 3cm (1¼in) to the width of the pad/foam.

2 Make the gusset (with or without a zip) as for the basic box cushion, but so that it goes around the sides and back only. Do not stitch the gusset into a ring. At each end, fold the gusset in half lengthwise and mark the centre point; unfold. Fold the main fabric piece in half crosswise and mark the foldline on both side edges. Unfold.

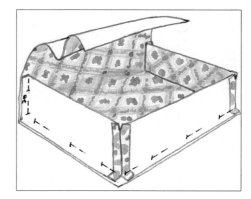

3 Pin one end of the gusset to one side of the main piece, with right sides together and raw edges even. Match the marked centre point on the gusset to the marked foldline on the edge of the main piece. Clip into the gusset seam allowance at the corners. Repeat for the other end of the gusset, then pin the remainder of the gusset in place.

4 Stitch all around, stitching the corners as for the basic box cushion (step 6, page 168) and leaving an opening if you haven't used a zip. Trim seams and corners. Turn right side out; press. Wrap wadding around the pad/foam, insert and slipstitch the opening if there is no zip.

ABOVE ~ *A soft-edged box cushion has a rounded front and sometimes a rounded back.*

Variation

Make the back edge like the front edge, inserting a separate gusset on each side. Both sides of each gusset are stitched in the same way as the ends of the gusset above (steps 3–4).

See Also

BUTTON-TUFTED CUSHIONS

Both knife-edge and box cushions can be button-tufted. For scatter cushions, one central button looks good, while overall button-tufting looks especially nice on squabs.

1 Make up a knife-edge or box cushion cover and insert the cushion pad. Because the cover cannot be removed, a slipstitched opening is all that is necessary for the closure.

2 Use covered flat buttons with shanks. Thread a long upholstery needle with cotton. Insert the needle from the bottom. While holding the thread, take the needle up through the cushion, through the button shank and then back down again through the cushion.

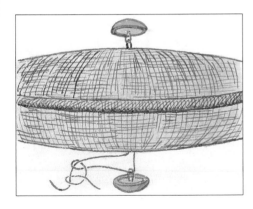

3 Now thread it through a second button shank at the bottom of the cushion. Tie the ends in a slip knot as shown, pulling the thread tight. Fasten off the ends securely.

VARIATION

For a stylish miniature mattress, make a rectangular cushion in ticking, stuffing it with wadding. Pinch some of the wadding along the edges at the top and work a line of small stitches all around, about 1cm (³/₈in) from the edge, to create an effect similar to thick piping. Repeat around the edge of the bottom piece. Now make button tufts at regular intervals.

ABOVE ~ *Use a button-tufted cushion in a group to add further variety.*

SEE ALSO

BEANBAGS AND CUBE CUSHIONS

Great fun in children's bedrooms and playrooms, big squashy beanbags and lightweight cube cushions are made in much the same way. Choose colourful, strong fabric for both types.

ABOVE ~ *Children prefer beanbags and cube cushions to conventional seating any day.*

BEANBAG

The filling most often used for beanbags is polystyrene granules. The filling must be enclosed in a casing so that the outer cover can be removed for washing. Use the same fabric as you would for the casing of a cushion pad or wadding (see page 159).

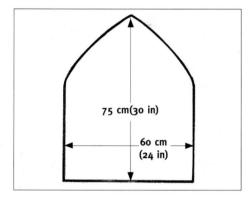

1 On paper, draw the shape in the diagram to the dimensions indicated, and cut out. Use it to cut out four sides from your fabric(s). Following the instructions on page 149–150 for making a fabric circle using a template (steps 1–3), make a pattern for a 72cm (28 in) diameter circle. Use it to cut out a base from your fabric.

TIPS

- For extra strength, either press the seams of the beanbag and cube cushion to one side, or make flat fell seams.
- To pour the granules into the beanbag casing, use an improvised paper funnel.

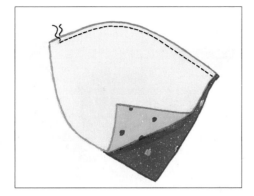

2 With right sides together and raw edges even, join the side pieces to each other along the side edges. Take 1.5cm (⅝in) seams and stop the stitching 1.5cm (⅝in) from the top. Leave a large gap in one seam.

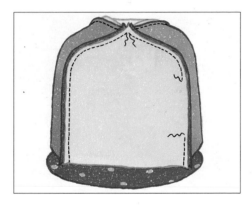

3 With right sides together and raw edges even, stitch the bottom edge of the sides to the circular base, clipping into the seam allowances on curves. Turn right side out and press.

4 Make an inner casing in the same way, but stitch alongside each seamline a second time within the seam allowance. Pour the granules into the casing until it is half to three-quarters full. Machine stitch the opening with two rows of stitching. Insert the inner beanbag into the outer cover, and slipstitch the opening.

CUBE CUSHION

Because these cushions are multi-sided, they are tailormade for the colourful treatment children love, using different brightly coloured fabrics as in the photograph opposite. Make sure the fabrics you choose are washable and hard-wearing. You can use inexpensive foam chips or wadding for the filling.

1 Cut out six squares of fabric to the desired dimensions. With right sides together, join four of them at the sides, taking 1.5cm (⅝in) seams and leaving 1.5cm (⅝in) unstitched at the top and bottom of each seam.

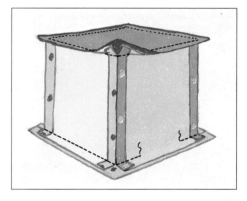

2 With right sides together, join the top to the sides around all four edges. Do the same for the base, leaving an opening in one seam. Trim the corners, turn right side out and press. Stuff with wadding or foam chips, and slipstitch the opening.

SEE ALSO

Cushion fillings   159

SQUAB CUSHIONS

These cushions for chair seats are cut to the exact shape of the seat and are usually tied to the chair back. Squabs can be either knife-edge (as in the photograph below) or box cushions.

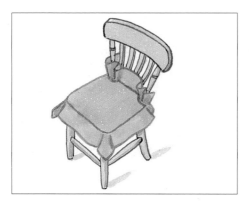

4 Complete the cover as for a knife-edge or box cushion. When stitching the seam, clip into the seam allowances on curves. If you are adding a frill, make separate frills for the front/sides and the back, because the struts would be in the way of a continuous one.

1 First make a template for the cushion. Place a large piece of paper on the chair seat, folding it back around the struts so that it creases along the seat line. Fold it down over the seat to crease the outline. Go over the creases with a pencil, marking the positions of the ties. Fold the pattern in half and cut it out, adjusting the outline slightly if necessary.

2 Use the template to cut out two fabric pieces, adding 1.5cm (⅝in) all around. If you are making a box cushion, you'll need a pad or foam 2.5–4cm (1–1½in) thick, or possibly 5cm (2in) thick. Cut a gusset strip(s) to the desired depth plus 3cm (1¼in) and as long as the outside measurement of the template plus 3cm (1¼in). (A separate segment of the gusset can have a zip if desired – see Basic Box Cushion, page 168, steps 3–4.) Tack piping to the front piece if desired.

RIGHT ~ *Make knife-edge squabs to the exact shape of the chair seats they will be tied to. (For the little covers on the backs, see the variation on page 181.)*

3 For the four ties, cut out two 30 × 9cm (12 × 3½in) fabric strips. Press under 6mm (¼in) on each long edge and one end, then fold in half lengthwise. Stitch. Tack the unfinished end of each tie to the marked point on the cover, with right sides together and raw edges even. (If the design of your chair allows, the two ties can be made as one long tie, folded in half.

VARIATION

Replace the ties with longer, wider ones tied in big floppy bows, or with short, narrow ties which can either be knotted or have touch-and-close tape stitched on.

SEE ALSO

LOOSE COVERS

Many attractive styles of loose cover can be made for chairs and stools without the need for upholstery skills. Tailored designs generally look right for angular chairs, and flouncy styles for curvy chairs.

FABRICS FOR LOOSE COVERS

Choose a firm, closely woven fabric, avoiding very thick or heavily textured fabrics. Linen union, ticking, medium-weight cotton and cotton/polyester mixes are ideal. Chintz, though not suitable for upholstery, can sometimes be used for loose covers. However, it is not tough enough for covers that will take a lot of wear.

If you choose a fabric with a large pattern, don't forget that it will have to be matched carefully and any large motifs placed centrally. Like patterned fabric, fabric with a nap must run in the same direction over the entire cover.

Other considerations include whether the fabric will fade in sunlight, how well it will drape and whether it can be washed. Fabrics that are used to cover furniture must be flame-resistant.

DECORATING LOOSE COVERS

Ready-made fringings can look wonderful on loose covers, and many styles will benefit from a contrast band along the lower edge. Gathered frills are often added, but pleated frills can also look very smart. Tucks can be used to great effect over an otherwise flat, plain expanse of fabric. Piping is used a lot on loose covers, as it emphasizes the outline and strengthens seams. Contrast piping is useful for picking out a colour.

PIN-FITTING

If the chair has an old cover that can be removed and the seams unpicked, this can be used as a pattern (unless it has stretched). Otherwise, the best way to make a loose cover for a chair is pin-fitting – draping the fabric over the chair and then cutting out and pinning together the fabric pieces on the chair.

TIP

. . . .

The easiest fabric to use for loose covers is one with a small, all-over pattern. Not only does it not need to be matched, but it will camouflage any sewing imperfections.

A very simple cover in a fabric that doesn't require pattern matching or have a nap can be cut out on a flat surface; otherwise, deal with it in situ.

If you are using expensive fabric, you may prefer to make up the cover in calico or old sheeting first, and then use these pieces as a pattern.

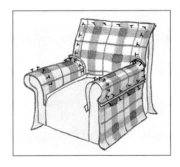

Think of the cover as an arrangement of rectangles. You start by measuring each part of the chair at the widest points (using the seams on the existing cover as a guide where possible). Then rectangles are cut to these dimensions from fabric and positioned right side up on the chair. First they are pinned to the chair, and the excess fabric cut away, then they are pinned to each other. Finally, the pinned cover is removed, each piece turned over and repinned, and the cover stitched together.

The fabric is pinned onto the chair right side up because it is easier to match the pattern and because chairs are not necessarily symmetrical. Similarly, chairs in a set are not always identical, so for tight-fitting covers the process is repeated for each chair.

PRACTICAL CONSIDERATIONS

Tight-fitting covers often need a fastening. The usual place to put this is along the right-hand side seam of the outer back. A zip, touch-and-close or hook-and-eye tape or decorative ties are all suitable.

If two widths have to be joined to gain the required width, it should not be done with the seam running down the middle of the chair. Instead, cut one width in half lengthwise and stitch the halves on either side of the full width. Joining widths almost certainly will be necessary for a sofa.

Any pattern or nap should always be vertical, so never cut the outside arm and the inner arm, or the outside back and the inside back, as one piece on patterned or one-way fabric. Similarly, the horizontal pattern should be level with the floor, not with the seat.

PLEATED FITTED COVER

1 Measure each part of the chair at the widest points. Note that the fabric will extend around the sides and top of the inside back, and around the sides and front of the seat, so allow for this in your measurements.

2 Now draw a plan of the cover on paper, indicating the straight grain of the fabric, and adding seam allowances of at least 2.5cm (1in). They will be trimmed to 1.5cm (⅝in) later but this gives you room for adjustment. Use scale drawings of the fabric pieces and of the fabric to plan a cutting layout that will suit the width and pattern of the fabric.

3 Drape the fabric over the chair to work out the best position for each rectangle. Cut out rectangles to the correct dimensions from your fabric.

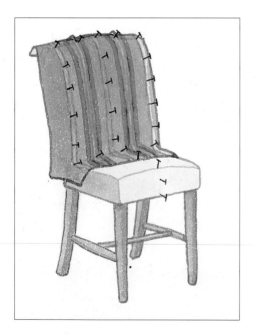

4 Mark the middle of the inside back, outside back, front and seat of the chair with lines of pins stuck into it at

right angles. The extra-long pins known as T-pins are easiest to work with. Fold the inside back rectangle in half and pin the centre along the marked chair centre. Check that the straight grain of the fabric is vertical. Smooth out the fabric, working from the centre out to the edge. Pin the fabric to the chair at 12.5cm (5in) intervals. Cut off excess fabric, leaving seam allowances of at least 2.5cm (1in), except on the lower edge (see step 5).

5 On the lower edge of the inside back piece, allow an extra 15cm (6in) at the centre, tapering to the edges, for a semicircular "tuck-in" – the fabric that will tuck into the crevice around the seat, to allow some movement in use. (Chairs with arms also may need to have a tuck-in at the base or back edge of the inside arms, and wing chairs need it between the wings and the back.)

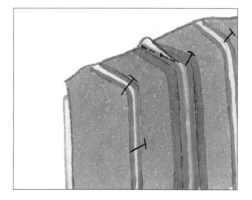

6 Make a small dart at each top corner of the inside back piece. Curved areas can also be shaped using gathers or tucks.

7 Mark the height of the skirt all the way around the chair with pins. Measure from the floor up, to make sure that the line is level.

RIGHT ~ *The techniques involved in making this versatile, classic style of loose cover apply to most loose covers.*

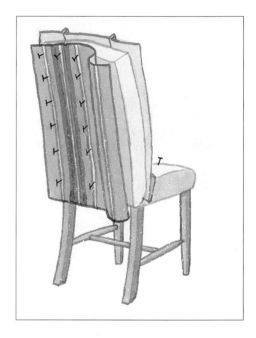

8 Pin the centre of the outside back rectangle to the centre line of pins, then pin-fit and cut as for the inside back piece (step 4), pinning from the back. The outside back piece will extend as far down as the beginning of the skirt, plus a seam allowance.

9 Where the outside back piece will be seamed to the inside back piece, around the top and sides, pin the two edges with wrong sides together. Use ordinary pins and, as you go, remove the T-pins anchoring it to the chair. Place the pins at 12.5cm (5in) intervals, then fill in the gaps with more pins so that the pins are nose-to-tail along the seamline.

12 Also cut out four pleat underlays to the same depth. Three of the underlays should be 18cm (7¼in) wide; if you are having an opening at one edge of the outside back (see step 19), the fourth underlay should be 23cm (9¼in) wide; if you are not having an opening, the underlay should be the same width as the others.

13 If you are having an opening at the outside back, cut the wider underlay in half from top to bottom, then pin the cut edges back together with a 2.5cm (1in) seam allowance (do not stitch them). Using 1.5cm (⅝in) seams, stitch the other side edge of one underlay half to the side piece adjacent to the planned opening, and the remaining side edge of the other underlay half to the back.

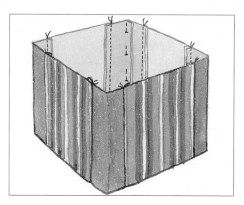

14 Join all the skirt pieces and pleat underlays along their side edges, taking 1.5cm (⅝in) seams, to form a ring. Press the seams towards the skirt pieces.

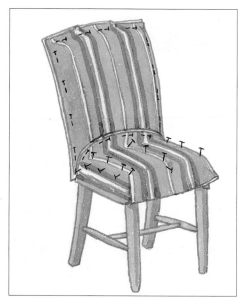

10 Position, pin-fit and cut the seat piece, pinning the back edge to the edge of the tuck-in on the inside back. Make darts or mitres at the front corners.

11 The skirt is made in much the same way as skirts for bedspreads and fitted tablecloths, but with a separate piece for each side, and pleat underlays in between. Measure the widest part of the portion that each skirt piece will cover on the front, back and sides of the chair. Add 18cm (7¼in) to that measurement – this is the width of the corresponding fabric piece. The depth of each should be the measurement from the marked line where the skirt begins, to just above the floor, plus 6.5cm (2⅝in). Cut out the four rectangles to these dimensions.

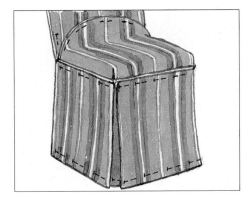

15 Mark the foldlines and placement lines for 15cm (6in) wide inverted pleats at each corner. Pin the skirt to the rest of the cover on the chair, and form the pleats at the corners, adjusting the size if necessary to make the skirt fit exactly. Tack and press the pleats (see Making Pleats, page 19), then remove the tacking. Clip into the seam allowance in the centre of the pleat at the top. Turn up a double 2.5cm (1in) hem along the bottom of the skirt.

16 Once the cover fits perfectly, mark the stitching line of each seam on the wrong side of the fabric by opening the seam out and running tailor's chalk along the crease. Make marks across both seam allowances, to use for matching up the seams when repinning later.

17 Remove the cover from the chair. Unpin a small area, and repin those pieces with right sides together, inserting piping in the seams if desired. Turn the pinned cover right side out and put it on the chair to check the fit. Adjust the pins if necessary. Remove the cover from the chair and turn it wrong side out again. Trim the seam allowances to 1.5cm (⅝in), apart from the tuck-in and hems. For the zip, if using, allow for a 2.5cm (1in) seam at the back, on the side with the tacked pleat underlay.

18 Stitch the seams (apart from the zip seam, if using – see step 19). Clip into the seam allowance on curves, and snip off corners within the seam allowance. For the darts on the front corners of the seat, stop the stitching 1.5cm (⅝in) from the front seamline. Hand stitch the hem, following step 5 of Inverted Pleats with Separate Underlays (page 20) when hemming the pleat underlays.

VARIATIONS

● Instead of a skirt with inverted pleats at the corners, make a gathered skirt or a skirt with box pleats all around. Allow twice the fullness for gathers and three times for continuous pleating.
● Omit the skirt entirely. Cut out a small square on the lower edge of the seat piece for the top of each leg, facing the edges (see Attaching a Hem Facing, page 27). Finish the remainder of each lower edge with a facing, which is then stapled, tacked or fastened with touch-and-close tape, to the underside of the chair.
● Cover a footstool in the same way as the chair seat is covered – ie, wrapping the fabric around all four sides and making darts at the corners. Stitch a pleated or gathered skirt to the lower edge, piping the seam.

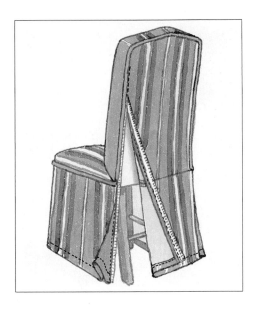

19 If you are having an opening at the back, it does not need to go all the way to the top; start 5–10cm (2–4in) below the top. Stitch the seam above this point, and press under the seam allowances below this point. Insert a zip which will run alongside any piping and down the inside of the pleat. When closed, the zip tab will be at the bottom. To insert the zip, open it and tack it to the piped side of the seam, with the piping just covering the teeth. Using the zip foot, stitch in the ditch of the piped seam, breaking the stitching at the skirt seam (because the zip is stitched to the pleat underlay). Close the zip and lap the other seam allowance over it to meet the piped seam allowance. Tack and stitch across the top and 1cm (⅜in) from the edge, once again breaking the stitching when you reach the skirt seamline.

TIE-ON CHAIR COVER

The sections of this informal chair cover are tied together rather than being stitched. Because the arms are cut as one piece, however, they are not suitable for one-way fabric. The pin-fitting techniques are the same as those explained in detail in the instructions for the pleated fitted cover (page 176).

1 Measure the chair and work out the dimensions of the five rectangles that form the basis of the cover – the inside back, outside back, left arm, right arm, and seat/front. Be sure to measure across the widest part of each section, and to continue the measurement around areas where the fabric will wrap over an edge, such as the front of the arms and the top of the outside back.

2 Add seam/hem allowances of 7.5cm (3in) all around; these will be trimmed later. Cut out the rectangles.

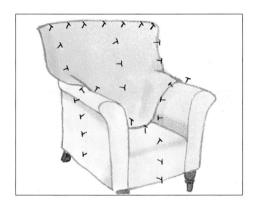

3 Mark the centre of the chair inside back, outside back, seat and front with T-pins. Fold in half and position the fabric rectangles for the inside back, then the outside back, next the arms and finally the seat. Pin-fit using the T-pins, and cut away the excess fabric, leaving the 7.5cm (3in) seam/hem allowances.

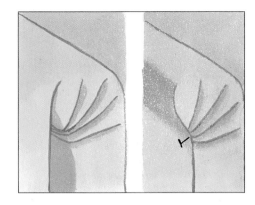

4 After pinning the inside and outside parts of each arm to the chair, form the top of each arm into radiating pleats at the front as shown above, pinning them in place along the edge.

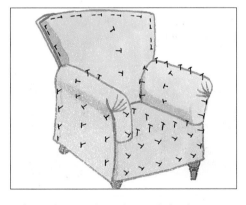

5 Pin the inside and outside back pieces together across the top and down the sides as far as the arms, making darts at the top corners.

6 Instead of pinning the other pieces together, turn under a double 2cm (¾in) hem on each raw edge. Remove the T-pins anchoring the fabric to the chair.

7 Once the cover pieces are fitting smoothly and neatly and have all been cut and the hems pinned, remove the cover. Unpin each piece and turn it wrong side out, repinning as you go.

8 Stitch the pleats on the arms along the edge, the darts at the top of the back, the seam joining the inside and outside back, and all the hems.

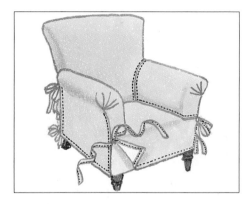

9 Make 12 long, narrow ties (see Ties, page 35). Stitch them to the edges on the wrong side in the positions shown. Stitch one half of a touch-and-close dot on the wrong side of the outer back corner of each arm, and the corresponding half on the side of the back piece.

10 From the same fabric, make a box cushion (see Box Cushions, page 168). Assemble and tie the bows.

SEE ALSO

TWO-PIECE CHAIR COVER

A simple padded seat cover combined with a matching cover for the chair back can transform a dull chair into something elegant and frivolous, as shown below.

CHAIR SKIRT

1 Make a paper template for the top of the skirt (see Squab Cushions, page 174, step 1). Use this to cut out two fabric pieces, adding 1.5cm (⅝in) all around. Mark the position of the struts on the wrong side of the fabric.

2 For the front skirt, measure from one strut around the front of the chair to the other strut. Cut out a strip of fabric to this length plus 6cm (2½in), and a width of about 20cm (8in). (This is for a skirt 15cm (6in) deep, but you can alter the depth if desired.)

3 For the back of the skirt, measure between the struts and cut a piece to this length plus 10cm (4in) and the desired depth (ours is about half the depth of the main skirt).

4 Stitch double 1.5cm (⅝in) hems on the side and lower edges of both skirts. Stitch fringing to the lower edges.

LEFT ~ An exotic fabric and stylish design enable chairs to make a major contribution to a dining room's decor.

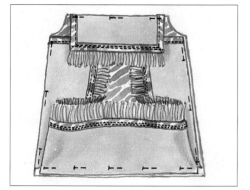

5 With right sides together and raw edges even, pin the main skirt to one top piece, with a 1.5cm (⅝in) seam allowance. Start and finish the pinned seam at the marks for the struts. Clip into the skirt seam allowance at the corners. Pin the back skirt to the back edge in the same way.

6 Turn right side out and place the pinned cover on the chair to check for fit, adjusting the pinned seams if necessary. Turn wrong side out again and stitch.

7 Place the other cover piece over the top, right side down, sandwiching the skirt between the two pieces. Stitch a 1.5cm (⅝in) seam all around, leaving an opening in one side edge. Trim seam and snip off corners. Turn the cover right side out and press.

8 Use the template to cut out a piece of wadding, omitting the seam allowance. Insert the wadding into the cover and slip-stitch the opening.

CHAIR BACK COVER

1 Tape paper to the chair back and make a pattern of the back (see Squab Cushions, page 174, step 1). Use this to cut out two fabric pieces, adding 1.5cm (⅝in) all around.

2 Cut a gusset strip 3.5cm (1⅜in) wider than the thickness of the struts, and 3cm (1¼in) longer than the distance around the part of the back that the fabric will cover.

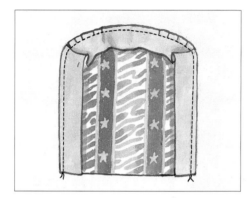

3 With right sides together, pin the gusset to one back piece around the sides and top. Clip into the seam allowance of the gusset at 2.5cm (1in) intervals all around the curve. Put it on the chair to check for fit, then stitch a 1.5cm (⅝in) seam.

4 Join the other edge of the gusset to the other back piece in the same way, checking for fit again before stitching. (A small amount has been allowed for ease – so the cover can be slipped on and off easily – but you may have to adjust the seam allowance slightly, as it needs to be taut.) Trim the seams, turn the cover right side out and press.

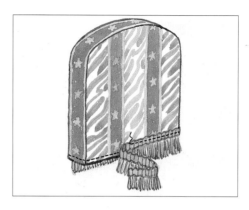

5 Stitch a double 1.5cm (⅝in) hem around the lower edge. Attach fringing to the hemmed edge.

VARIATION

An even simpler chair back cover, like the one in the photograph on page 174, can be made by making the main fabric pieces only long enough to cover the wooden top of the chair back, and omitting the gusset. Add interest by piping the top and side edges. To hold it in place, stitch ties to the wrong side of the outer hem edge of the front and back. These can be like the ties used on the matching cushions, as in the photograph.

SEE ALSO

LLOYD LOOM CHAIR COVER

Soften the look and feel of a Lloyd Loom or wicker chair with a simple cover and cushion. Front and back pleats decorated with bows add interesting detail.

MAKING THE COVER

ABOVE ~ *A Lloyd Loom or wicker chair takes on a new look with a fabric cover and cushion.*

1 First cut out a rectangle for the outside back piece. To work out the width, measure around the widest part of the chair, from one front edge around the back to the other front edge. Add 5cm (2in) for seams, 76cm (30in) for pleats, and a further 3cm (1¼in) for ease, as the cover is loose. For the depth, measure the chair height at the centre back; add 5cm (2in) for the hem and 2.5cm (1in) for a seam.

2 Next, cut out a rectangle for the inside back piece. It should be the same width as the outside back piece, excluding the 75cm (30 in) pleat allowance. For the depth, measure the chair height at centre back, from the seat to the top, and add 5cm (2in) for seams.

3 Now cut out the front piece. For the width, measure the width of the chair and add 5cm (2in) for seams, 25cm (10in) for the pleats and 3cm (1¼in) for ease. For the height, measure the height from the seat to the floor and add 2.5cm (1in) for a seam and 5cm (2in) for the hem.

4 Cut out the seat. For this make a template (see Squab Cushion, page 174, step 1) and add 2.5cm (1in) all around.

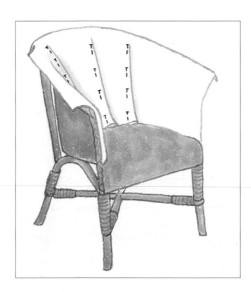

5 Tape the inside back piece to the chair, wrong side up, and trim off some of the

excess fabric at the top of the sides, to make fitting easier. If necessary, pin darts around the inside back (starting with the wide part at the bottom and tapering to the top) to make the cover fit smoothly.

6 Put the seat piece on the seat, wrong side up, and pin its back/side edge to the lower edge of the inside back piece, allowing for a 2.5cm (1in) seam.

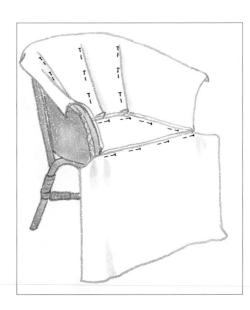

7 Take the front piece and pin its top edge to the front edge of the seat piece, right sides together again, and with a 2.5cm (1in) seam allowance. About 15cm (6in) of the front piece should extend at each side; this will be used in making each front pleat.

other seam and parallel to it – ie, just below the edge of the seat. Repeat for the other side. These will become the front pleats.

10 From these points, begin pinning the outside back piece to the inner back piece, still using the 2.5cm (1in) seam allowance. Cut away some of the excess fabric at the top to make it easier.

11 When you reach the point above each back leg where you stopped pinning in step 8, form the remaining outside back fabric into a 12.5cm (5in) wide inverted pleat above each back leg.

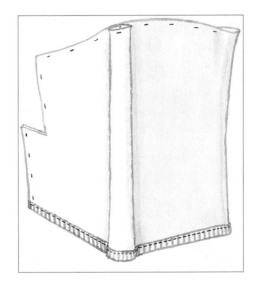

12 Adjust the pins over the whole cover till it fits smoothly and snugly but can be slipped off easily. Trim the seam allowances to 1.5cm (⅝in). Turn up and pin a double 2.5cm (1in) hem around the lower edge of the front and outside back.

13 Remove the cover. At each front corner, unpin the temporary row of pins holding the pleat together. Stitch the 1.5cm (⅝in) pinned seam for each pleat, and press it open. Form the fabric into 12.5cm (5in) wide inverted pleats, with the seam centred inside (see Making Pleats, page19). Tack across the top.

14 Stitch the darts in the inside front piece. Stitch all the seams. Clip into the seam allowance on curves, and snip off corners within the seam allowance. Hand or machine stitch the hem. From the right side, topstitch the back pleats so that the release point of each is at the top of the leg.

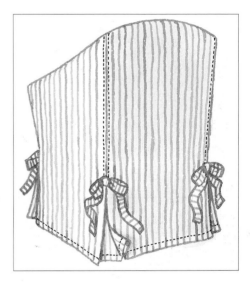

15 Make four 4cm (1½in) wide ties about 1m (39in) long (see Ties, page 35). Tie them in bows, and hand sew to the release points of the pleats. From the same fabric, make a piped box cushion (see Box Cushions, page 168).

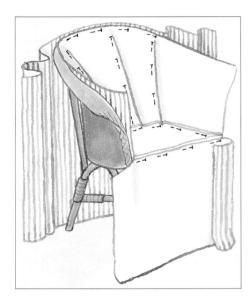

8 Find the centre of the outside back piece on the top edge, and pin it to the centre of the top edge of the inside back. Pin the top edges together as far as a point immediately above each back leg, allowing for a 2.5cm (1in) seam.

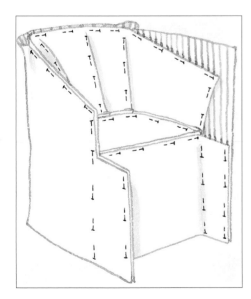

9 Pin the lower part of one side edge of the outside back to one side edge of the front with a 2.5cm (1in) seam. To help in fitting the covers, pin the two layers together again, 12.5cm (5in) from the

See Also

DIRECTOR'S AND DECK CHAIRS

The classic design of a director's chair or deck chair lends itself well to a new cover in a stylish fabric. Choose strong fabric such as upholstery fabric or, if the chair will sometimes be left outdoors, canvas.

ABOVE ~ *New covers have spruced up this director's chair and deck chair.*

DIRECTOR'S CHAIR COVER

1 Remove the old back and seat, cutting them away if necessary. Hammer any nails used on them into the wood.

2 Measure the old back and seat, excluding hem allowances and casings, allowing for any stretching that may have occurred. (If they are badly stretched, it will probably be easier to measure the chair frame.) For the back, add 7.5cm (3in) to the depth and 24cm (9½in) to the width. This will give 10cm (4in) wide casings for the rails holding the back cover; you may need only 6.5cm (2½in) or so, in which case adjust the width. For the seat, add 7.5cm (3in) to the depth and 4cm (1½in) to the width. From the fabric, cut out one back and one seat to these dimensions.

3 Neaten the long edges of both pieces, then turn under 4cm (1½in) on each long edge and stitch.

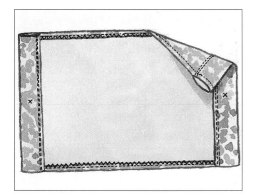

4 Turn under 2cm (¾in) then 10cm (4in) on each short edge of the back, and pin in place. Slide the cover onto the chair rails to check for fit. At the same time, mark the positions of any screw holes. Remove the back and stitch from top to bottom along each turned-under edge, forming a casing on each side. Stitch again close to the first stitching.

5 Make holes in the fabric at the marked points, using an eyelet kit. Put the cover back on the chair; fasten the screws.

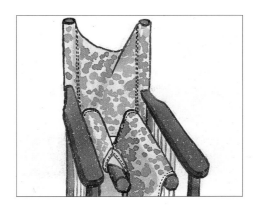

6 Turn under 2cm (¾in) on each short edge of the seat; press. With the chair folded, lay one short edge over a seat rail. Using a heavy-duty stapler, staple one short folded edge to a rail; alternatively, hammer in upholstery tacks. Holding the other side in place, check that the seat will be taut with the frame fully open. Adjust the size of the hem if necessary, then staple (or tack) the other side.

SEE ALSO

DECK CHAIR COVER

1 Remove the old tacks from each end and take off the old cover. Use it as a pattern for the new one, adding 4cm (1½in) to the width.

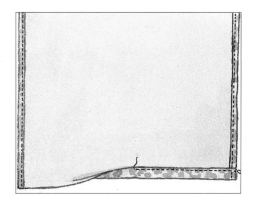

2 Press under a double 1cm (⅜in) hem on each long edge; stitch. Press under 2.5cm (1in) on each short edge.

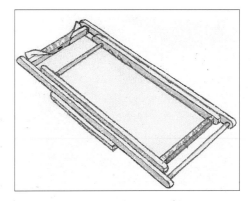

3 Lay the cover wrong side up on the floor, and place the deckchair frame on top. Wrap one short edge of the cover up over the chair bar. Using a heavy-duty stapler (or a hammer and upholstery tacks), staple the centre of the cover to the bar. Continue stapling out to each edge. Repeat at the other end, but before attaching, check whether the fabric is the correct length.

GLOSSARY

The terms included here are covered more fully in the book (see Index). Words shown in roman, rather than italic, type have their own entries in the Glossary.

ATTACHED VALANCE

See Valance.

BAND

An extension of fabric, generally in a contrasting colour when it is sometimes known as a contrast band. A band is also sometimes known as a border.

BIAS

Any diagonal direction on the fabric (as opposed to the true bias, which is exactly on the diagonal). The fabric is stretchier than on the lengthwise or crosswise grain.

BIAS BINDING

See Binding.

BINDING

Narrow strips of fabric used to wrap around raw edges to neaten them. Bias binding (cut on the bias and therefore stretchy) is used on curved edges; seam binding (cut on the lengthwise or crosswise grain and therefore not stretchy) is used on straight edges. Bias binding is wrapped around cord to create corded piping.

BOLSTER

A cylindrical cushion.

BOX CUSHION

A cushion made from two layers of fabric with a gusset between them; the cushion is therefore of uniform thickness.

CAFÉ CURTAINS

Short, tiered curtains in which the bottom tier usually remains closed.

CASING

A channel in fabric through which a curtain rod, wire, batten, elastic, etc, may be threaded.

CLEAT

A double-pronged hook mounted on the wall or window frame, around which the cords of a blind or Italian-strung curtain are wound.

CONTRAST BAND

See Band.

CORDED PIPING

An edging created by wrapping bias binding around piping cord, and then inserting it into a seam. Usually referred to simply as piping.

CROSSWISE GRAIN

See Grain.

CURTAIN CUT LENGTH/WIDTH

The length/width of a curtain after cutting out but prior to hemming. The adjusted cut length is the length after allowing for a pattern repeat.

CURTAIN FINISHED LENGTH/WIDTH

The length/width of a flat, unpleated curtain after all edges have been hemmed.

CURTAIN PLEATED WIDTH

The width of a curtain after it has been hemmed and pleated.

CURTAIN USABLE WIDTH

The width of fabric that can be used after the crosswise pattern on a curtain has been matched.

DARTS

Stitched wedges of fabric that taper to a point. Used for shaping.

DRESSING CURTAINS

Training curtains that have just been hung to fall into even pleats each time they are opened.

EDGESTITCHING

Topstitching close to a finished edge or seamline, as on a pleat.

FACING

A separate piece of fabric that is the same shape as an edge, and is stitched to the edge to neaten it. Used where a hem would not be suitable, for example on a scalloped edge.

FIXED HEADING

Curtains that remain permanently closed at the top. They are held back with tiebacks or holdbacks (or Italian stringing).

FLANGE

A flat, double-thickness fabric trim extending beyond the edges of a cushion, like an ungathered frill.

FRILL

Strip of gathered fabric. A single frill consists of one layer of fabric, while a double frill consists of two layers. A double-edged frill has two finished edges, with gathers between them.

FUSING

Bonding two layers together using the heat of an iron to melt the adhesive on the fusible material.

GATHERS

Tiny folds of fabric into which fabric is drawn up.

GRADING

Trimming seam allowances by different amounts to reduce bulk when seams consist of several layers. Also known as layering.

GRAIN

The lengthwise (warp) or crosswise (weft) threads of a woven fabric. The lengthwise grain consists of the threads that run parallel to the selvedges; it is also known as the straight grain. The crosswise grain consists of the threads at right angles to the selvedges.

GUSSET

A fabric strip inserted between two parallel layers of fabric, such as a box cushion or a loose cover. Also known as a boxing strip.

HEADING

The finish used at the top of a curtain, incorporating a casing, heading tape or hand pleating.

HEADING TAPE

Tape stitched to a curtain to form a heading.

HEM

A method of finishing a raw edge, whereby the edge is folded to the wrong side. A single hem is folded once, and a double hem twice.

HOLDBACKS

Hardware mounted on the wall or window frame which functions like tiebacks to hold curtains back.

INTERLINING

A fabric placed between a curtain and its lining. Bump is used on curtains, and domette, which is lighter, on swags and tails, blinds and lightweight curtains.

ITALIAN STRINGING

Curtains with a fixed heading which are drawn up at the sides by means of diagonally strung cords attached to the back. Also known as reefed curtains.

JARDINIÈRE CURTAIN

A sheer curtain consisting of a single panel with a curved bottom edge that is higher in the centre.

KNIFE-EDGE CUSHION

A cushion made from two layers of fabric sewn together at the edges; the cushion is therefore plump in the middle and sharp at the edges. It can be any shape.

LAPPED EDGES

Edges that are overlapped. Hemmed edges are lapped to create a lapped opening (used for cushion covers), and raw edges lapped and then stitched to create a lapped seam (used for PVC fabric).

LAYERING

See Grading.

LEADING EDGES

The inner edges of a pair of curtains; they meet when the curtains are closed.

LENGTHWISE GRAIN

See Grain.

LOOSE COVERS

Fabric covers that can be slipped on and off chairs. Also called slipcovers.

MITRE

A method of finishing a corner, involving a diagonal fold. Mitres are formed in many different ways.

MOIRÉ

A watermark effect applied to fabric as a finish. Also known as watered silk.

NAP FABRIC

A fabric in which the pile or a finishing process makes it look different depending on which way up it is. Also known as pile fabric.

PATTERN REPEAT

See Repeat.

PELMET

Stiffened fabric that covers the top of a window, the track and the heading of the curtain or blind.

PELMET BOARD

A shelf attached to the wall above curtains, to take a valance, pelmet or swag and tails.

PILE FABRIC

See Nap fabric.

PIN-FITTING

Pinning fabric pieces directly onto a chair in order to fit them together like a jigsaw to make a loose cover.

PIN TUCKS

Very narrow tucks.

PIPING

An edging consisting of folded bias binding inserted into a seam. Corded piping has cord inside the binding, although this is usually just called piping and is more common than uncorded piping.

PLEATS

Folds of fabric held in place at the top. The three main types are knife, box and inverted pleats.

PORTIÈRE

A curtain over a door, hung from a portière rod.

RAILROADING

Cutting fabric so that the lengthwise grain runs horizontally.

REEFED CURTAINS

See Italian stringing.

RELEASE POINT

The point at which a topstitched pleat begins.

REPEAT

The vertical distance between each complete part of the pattern.

RETURN

The distance between the front of a curtain track or pole and the wall or window frame. Also, the continuation of a window treatment around the corner to cover this area.

REVEAL

The side walls of a window recess.

RUCHE

Gather both edges. The term is also used more loosely for blinds, to mean gathering up in soft folds.

SEAM BINDING

See Binding.

SELF BINDING

Binding created by folding over the edges of a back layer to encase the raw edges of a front layer.

SELF FRILL

A frill formed by gathering fabric near the edge; the self frill is between the gathers and the edge.

SELF FRINGE

A fringe formed on the edge of fabric by pulling out threads parallel to the edge.

SELF PELMET

See Valances.

SELF PIPING

Piping made from the same fabric as the item being piped.

SELVEDGES

The finished edges, running the length of the fabric.

SHEERS

Curtains made from thin, translucent fabric such as muslin, lawn or voile.

SQUAB

A cushion cut to the shape of a chair seat. Can be either a knife-edge cushion or a box cushion.

STACKBACK

The distance by which the track or pole extends along the wall on each side of a window.

STAYSTITCHING

Straight stitching that is done through a single thickness of fabric just inside the seamline, to prevent the fabric from stretching when handled or tearing when the seam allowance is clipped.

STITCH IN THE DITCH

Topstitching just alongside (virtually in) the groove of a previously stitched seamline.

STRAIGHT GRAIN

See Lengthwise grain.

SWAG

Fabric draped across the top of a window. When not used with tails, it is sometimes known as scarf drapery or a swagged pelmet.

TACKING

A long running stitch used for temporarily holding fabric layers together. Can be worked by hand or machine.

TAILS

Fabric arranged into pleats that drape down the sides of a window. Always used with a swag.

TIEBACKS

Cord, fabric or chain that holds curtains open. They are often used with a fixed heading.

TOPSTITCHING

A straight stitch that is stitched from the right side.

TOUCH-AND-CLOSE TAPE

A fastening tape such as Velcro consisting of two interlocking strips, one with tiny hooks and the other with tiny, soft loops. Also available as touch-and-close dots and touch-and-close curtain tape.

TRUE BIAS

A line at an angle of 45 degrees to the selvedges. The fabric is stretchiest on the true bias. The easiest way of finding it is to fold the fabric so that the lengthwise and crosswise grain match; the resulting fold is on the true bias.

TUCK-IN

The fabric that will be tucked into the crevices around the seat of a loose cover, to allow movement.

TUCKS

Stitched folds on either the right or wrong side of the fabric.

UNDERSTITCHING

Stitching through a facing and seam allowances to prevent the facing from rolling out to the right side.

VALANCE

On a bed, a valance is a skirt that conceals the bed base and space underneath. On a window, this is an unstiffened strip of fabric that covers the top of the window. An attached valance (also known as an integral valance or a self pelmet), is a valance that is attached to the top of a curtain.

WADDING

Thick cotton or polyester padding, used in cushions, tiebacks and quilting.

WARP

Lengthwise threads in a woven fabric, over and under which the weft threads are interlaced.

WEAVE STRUCTURE

The formation of the warp and weft threads of a woven fabric in the arrangement that determines the characteristics of the fabric.

WEFT

Crosswise threads in a woven fabric, which are interlaced over and under the warp threads. Also known as woof.

INDEX

CREDITS

Quarto would like to acknowledge and thank the following for providing pictures used in this book.
While every effort has been made to acknowledge copyright holders we
would like to apologize should there have been any omissions.
Key: t=top b=bottom r=right l=left c=centre

Ametex (U.K) Ltd p.36; Anna French p.55, p.81, p.128(BL), p.172;
Art Park Design Pty Ltd p.5 (CL), p.10; Calico Corners p.9; Country
Curtains p.46, p.75, p.93, p.95 (T & B), p.97, p.105, p.107, p.109 (TL),
p.129, p.135; Crowson Fabrics Ltd p.5 (BCR), p.124, p.131, p.132,
p.170, p.177, Dorma p.73, p.77, p.108, p.134; E.W. A p.2, p.6, p.58,
p.79, p.87, p.102, p.109(BR), p.120; Firifiss p.171; Habitat U.K Ltd
p.139, p.161; Harrison Drape p.5(BL), p.5(BCL), p.5(BR), p.41, p.43,
p.69, p.83, p.112; Hillarys p.5(TCR), p.40, p.125, p.126, p.128(TR);
ICI/Dulux p.45, p.86(BC), p.117, p.122, p.127, p.143, p.182, p.184;
Ikea Ltd p.94(BR); Integra Products p.3(C), p.66, p.111, p.119; Malabar
p.3(R), p.5(TCL), p.5(TR), p.64, p.156, p.158(BL), p.159, p.165(BL);
Monkwell Ltd p.5(TL), p.169(T); Next PLC p.94(TL); Neisha
Crossland p.158(T); Nimbus bed linen supplied by Delbanco Meyer &
Co Ltd p.5(CCL), p.53, p.130, p.137, p.138, p.141; Pret A Vivre p.49,
p.136, p.152, p.155; Romo Fabrics p.7(BR), p.80, p.162, p.180; Rufflette
Ltd p.5(CCL), p.35, p.68, p.85(BL), p.85(TR), p.86(TL), p.96, p.100,
p.104; Today Interiors Ltd p.7(TL), p.8, p.39, p.92, p.114, p.142, p.147,
p.148, p.165(TL), p.165(BR), p.167, p.169(B), p.174; Thomas Dare
p.3(L), p.165(TR); Wendy Cushing p.5(CR).

All other photographs are the copyright of Quarto Publishing plc

Particular thanks are due to Codicote House Interiors, 106 High Street,
Codicote, Herts, for the loan of the hand-pleated curtains shown on
page 90; Hilary Mackin for designing and embroidering the bed linen
on page 61; Sally MacEachern, for managing always to be so consider-
ate while firmly guiding the book through the production process, and
Kate Simunek, for the painstaking care she took with the illustrations.